Vāstu

Breathing Life

Into

Space

BOOKS BY DR. ROBERT E. SVOBODA

The Hidden Secret of Ayurveda,
1st Edition Bombay 1980, 2nd Edition The Ayurvedic Press, Albuquerque, 1994
Prakriti: Your Ayurvedic Constitution,
1st Edition Geocom, Albuquerque, 1988, 2nd Edition Sadhana Publications, 1999
Ayurveda: Life, Health and Longevity,
1st Edition Penguin Books, London, 1992; reprinted by The Ayurvedic Press, Albuquerque, 2004.
Tao and Dharma,
(with coauthor Arnie Lade) Lotus Press, 1995
Ayurveda for Women,
David & Charles Publishers, Newton Abbot, 1999
Aghora: At the Left Hand of God,
Brotherhood of Life, Albuquerque, 1986
Aghora II: Kundalini,
Brotherhood of Life, Albuquerque, 1994
Aghora III: The Law of Karma,
Brotherhood of Life, Albuquerque, and Sadhana Publications (a co- production), December 1997
Light on Life: An Introduction to the Astrology of India,
(with coauthor Hart de Fouw) Penguin Books, London, 1996
The Greatness of Saturn: A Therapeutic Myth,
Sadhana Publications, 1997
Light on Relationships: The Synastry of Indian Astrology,
(with coauthor Hart de Fouw) Samuel Weiser Inc., 2000
The Ayurvedic Home Study Course,
The Ayurvedic Institute, Albuquerque, 1985

Advisor *Nāmarūpa, Categories of Indian Thought*

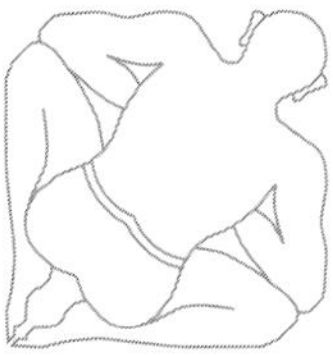

VĀSTU

Breathing Life Into Space

Dr. Robert E. Svoboda

NĀMARŪPA, *Publishers*

Nāmarūpa, Publishers
430 Broome Street
Suite #2
New York City
NY 10011

Designed by
Nāmarūpa, Publishers
P.O. Box 271
Dublin
NH 03444

ISBN 978-0-9889169-0-6

Editor: Jeremy Lehrer
Sanskrit editor: Zoë Slatoff
Proofreader: Meenakshi Moses
Design, illustrations, and production: Robert Moses
Element sketches on the cover and p. 66 by Satya Moses
Photograph research: Elizabeth Blomster
Encouragement and support: Eddie Stern

All quotations from the *Bṛhat Saṁhitā* are from the following edition:
Varahamihira's *Bṛhat Saṁhitā*, tr Prof. M. Ramachandra Bhat,
Motilal Banarsidass, Delhi, 1981

This book is dedicated to my parents,
Laura & Edwin Svoboda,
and to Vimalananda,
my friend, philosopher and guide.

Thanks to Ellen Leary and Maria Rodale,
without whom this volume would never have been completed.

Thanks to those who read and commented:
Samantha Colt, Rosanne Malinowski,
Dr. Fred Smith, Dr. Claudia Welch.

Thanks also to Dr. A. Achyuthan and
Vāstuvidyāpratiṣṭānam,
the Kaimal Family,
the Kanippayur Namboodiri Family,
the Raby Family.

Last, and in no way least,
thanks to the participating spaces:

Ayvali Turkey, Benaras India, Bombay India,
Brattleboro Vermont,
Coimbatore India and its environs,
Floresville Texas, Hallandale Florida,
Holualoa Hawaii, Parowan Utah,
Kanippayur Mana, Kunnamkulam India,
Santa Maria di Lignano & Assisi Italy,
Koottala P.O., Pattikad, Thrissur, Kerala India,
Toronto Canada, The United Kingdom, Tortola BVI.

Preamble

My intention in writing this tome has been to offer readers a more measured, more highly textured exposition of Vāstu than can be found in most other currently available books on the subject, without turning it into an academic, historical study. As it is, only a handful of sources, such as *Bṛhat Saṁhitā*, from which I quote extensively here, are actually ancient; and even had I wished to provide an account of Vāstu as it has been "traditionally" presented, there are no truly traditional presentations, for *Sthāpatya Veda*, from which Vāstu evolved, always existed more as a theoretical construct than a well-laid-out body of architectural knowledge.

Theory can be valuable so long as it is applied intelligently to the specific time and space in which it is employed; the principles of Vāstu emerged, as did the principles of *Āyurveda*, *Jyotiṣa*, and other Indian *vidyās*, slowly over generations as practitioners collected and codified real-world data in their own spaces and times. One can no more master Vāstu by mastering its conjectures than one can get the hang of medicine, music, and other hands-on lores by merely hanging on to their hypotheses. There is no substitute for experimentation, and it is those who accumulate at least some personal experience who will successfully employ the distillation of the accumulated experiences of others.

In this monograph I therefore focus on the concepts and practicalities that individuals who know little or nothing of the system of Vāstu can use to begin to gain the personal experience that they will require to make systematic use of Vāstu's theories. What I present here is not a detailed exposition of the Vāstu Vidyā (however we may conceive of it), but rather a series of musings on Vāstu, through which I seek to sensitize the reader to the nuances of spatial awareness. I have deliberately integrated concepts from Āyurveda, Jyotiṣa, meditation, breathing practices, yoga, and the like into this work to create exercises for readers that may both illustrate Vāstu's principles for them and also assist them to align themselves with *prāṇa* which, as the base of all life and thus all knowledge, is the foundation of those fundamental principles that all Indian vidyās like Vāstu share.

My ruminations have led me to add to and subtract from what has appeared before. I have occasionally extended identifications unconventionally, as when I equate the directions with the *guṇas*; and there is of course much that I have left out, including the Vedic notions of the east-west grid versus the north-south grid, which evolved by some obscure process into the *Vāstu Puruṣa Maṇḍala*. My reluctance to potentially confuse readers with yet another set of direction-deity designations also led me to omit describing how in a Vedic sacrifice offerings to the Vedic gods are made in the east, on the *Āhavanīya* fire; to the domestic deities in the west, on the *Gārhapatya* fire; and to the ancestors in the south, on the *Dakṣiṇāgni* fire (north was the only direction not to enjoy a major Vedic fireplace; it was where offerings were made to demons and spirits). And, I neglected to explicitly explore how Vāstu can be applied to all three realms of human awareness: the *ādhibhautika* (mundane), *ādhyātmika* (spiritual), and *ādhidaivika* (astral).

My aim in being neither too detailed nor too simplistic was to be accessible, to offer readers a taste of what Vāstu has been and is, and what it can offer; to provide them with practical tools for harmonizing the spaces of their lives; and to offer a pathway forward for those few who, after establishing in themselves a genuine sense of spatial alignment and directionality, become so keen that they may choose to try to become vessels for the Vāstu Vidyā. May the Vāstu Vidyā be pleased with what has been wrought!

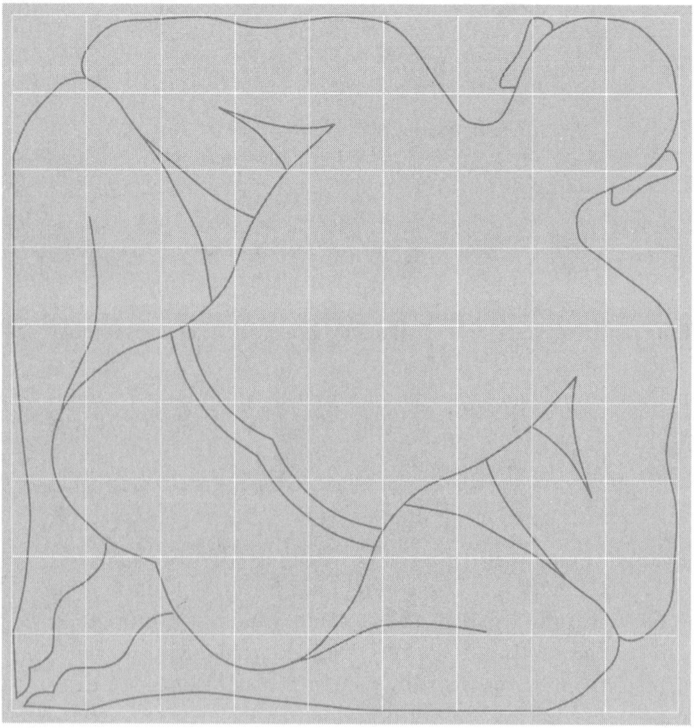

Contents

1 Encouraging Space to Cooperate

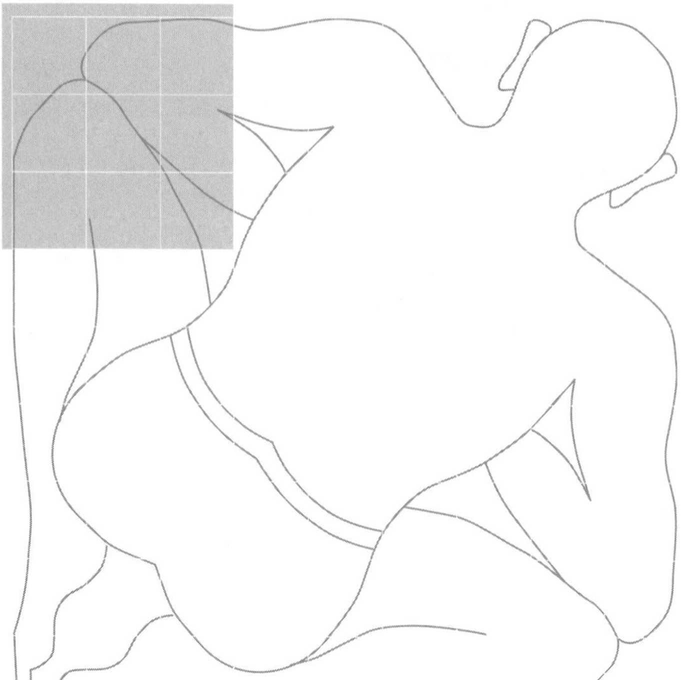

My mentor Vimalananda was the most versatile man I have met in my life thus far. He was introduced to me as an owner of thoroughbred racehorses and a connoisseur of things equine, and he proved to be a talented musician, dancer, cook, therapist, astrologer, linguist, raconteur, and general bon vivant as well. There were many times when I felt that I had finally taken his full measure, only to have him startle me again with his command over yet another idiom of the language of living.

My mentor's spiritual teacher lived for many years on a sacred hill in South India, in an ashram built for him by some of his rich Bombay devotees. On my first visit there, as my teacher and I stood facing the ashram about to knock on its door, Vimalananda suddenly said, "Tell me what you notice about this building and the land around it."

By then I was used to him quizzing me at a moment's notice, but until that time, he had never asked me about architecture. Noticing very little, I eventually stammered out something about the garden. He said, "You're close. Look carefully at the front edge of the property, which extends from this wall here to that wall over there, and then compare it to the parcel's rear edge." After staring carefully at those lines for several moments I finally replied, "Are you talking about how much wider the front of the plot is, compared to the back?"

"That's it!" he beamed. "This is a perfect example of a *Vyāghra-mukhī Bhūmi*, a 'Tiger-mouthed Tract.' A plot with these proportions looks and acts like a tiger. Doesn't a tiger's head look wider than its hips? Like a tiger, which consumes lots of meat from which it produces very little dung, a Tiger-mouthed Tract will eat up all your resources and give you very little in return—which will most likely make you miserable.

"Far better it is," he counseled, "to have a *Go-mukhī Bhūmi*, a 'Cow-mouthed Tract,' whose proportions are just the opposite from the tiger's: narrower in front than at the rear. Think of a cow: narrow face, but wide, roomy hips. All you really have to feed a cow is grass, which is basically free. In return, she will provide you with milk and cream to eat, urine for medicine, dung for fertilizer and fuel. And she will love you like a mother. Will the average tiger ever love you? I think not! A tiger will be waiting instead for the moment when it will finally get a chance to pounce on you, and enjoy you for a snack!

"Invest a little time, money, and effort in a Cow-mouthed Tract, and you will obtain good results of all sorts, just like taking good care of a cow can promote your physical, mental and spiritual well-being."

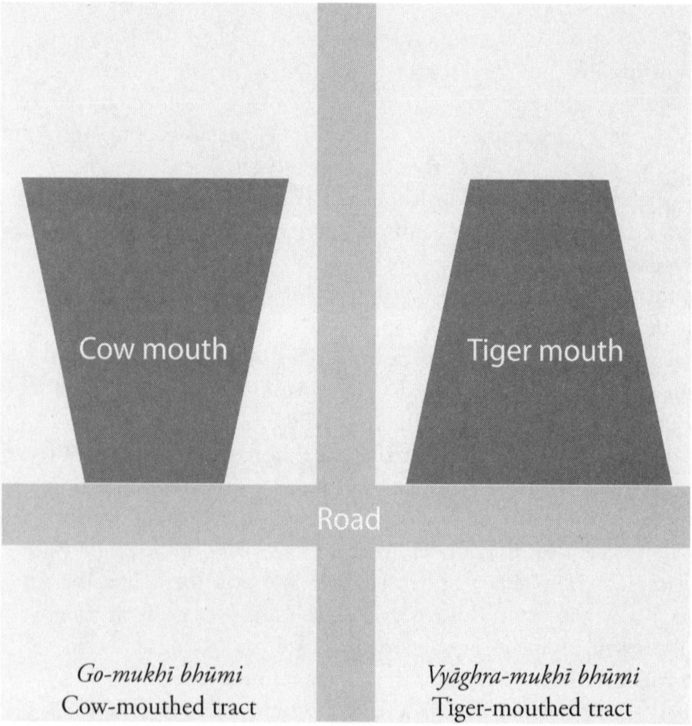

"Is it that simple?" I asked, in some disbelief.

"Well, no, not exactly," he admitted, "this is just one factor among many factors that help to determine whether a particular piece of land will be 'beneficial' for you or not. But it *is* a major factor."

"So even land can be 'beneficial' or 'detrimental' to its owner?"

"*Even* land? My God, what are you *thinking*? *Especially* land! How your land and house are configured makes a tremendous difference to your happiness in life, my boy."

"Are there ways of compensating for poor land placements?"

"Naturally. There is always some sort of answer for any such problem. In this case, one answer would be to shift the entrance to the property from the long side of the trapezoid to the short side. Then this Tiger-mouthed lot would automatically become a Cow-mouthed lot, and everything would be different."

"Just changing how people enter and leave the property would make that much difference?"

"At least in this case, yes, it would. Unfortunately, there is no way for that to happen here, because the people who live behind the ashram won't give up any of their own land.

"Another approach would be to turn the plot into a rectangle by partitioning off two small triangles of land on both sides. And there are other possibilities too, but none of them have been tried out because of the pigheadedness of the devotees, who refuse to believe that a piece of land can gobble them up like a tiger. They pooh-poohed this idea, called it 'superstition,' and had the ashram built to suit their own idiosyncrasies. The result has been that the ashram is eternally penniless, because any funds that get donated to it are immediately spent. What should be a place of meditation and peace is now a site where people squabble over how to raise money."

"Looks like the ashram is in danger of being eaten by the tiger."

"I can't guarantee," Vimalananda carefully countered, "that this land is the only cause of the trouble here. But it is certainly contributing to it. You know, Indians pay lots of attention to time, they pester astrologers to give them good times for doing all sorts of things. But too few people in India, and almost none in the West, think about space, and the best ways to make space work for you."

Prāṇa

This initial expedition into the mouths of cows and tigers introduced me to the idea of a space's "positive resonance." Everyone has had some experience of spaces that feel "just right," in the Goldilocksian sense; we've visited countries, cities, neighborhoods, and houses where things feel more agreeable than elsewhere, places in which one can breathe more easily. Sometimes we get this sense of well-being and benevolence because we're familiar with the location, or have dear friends or relatives living there, or find ourselves bathed in benign breezes. At other times, though, this feeling appears to emerge from nowhere, or from all directions at once, with no apparent cause.

Many of us also know places where we feel naturally uptight, where we sense something off-kilter as soon as we arrive. This impression of menace often has no apparent reason behind it either, just the palpable awareness that all is not well. "Sick building syndrome" (caused by elevated levels of radon, the presence of power lines, chemicals, metals, particulates, fungi/mold, etc.) might be to blame, or a hot wind like the mistral or the Santa Ana, or something else altogether, but the result is the same: discomfort, distress, disorder.

Some spaces produce a positive "feel" in most everyone, and other spaces feel "off" to nearly everybody. Another category of places agree wonderfully with a few people, drive a small group of others to complete distraction, and have little or no effect on the rest of humanity. A space as small as a room can attract or repel a visitor, and even a room that finds favor with most people may still be intolerable to somebody. Rooms themselves have "sweet spots," places where people automatically position themselves because they feel best there; conversely, there are other areas that everyone will try to avoid because something feels amiss in them.

Live long enough in conditions that agree with you, and you can expect those conditions to support your quest to enjoy an ample share of the good things in life: good humor, good health, prosperity, a happy family, harmonious relationships with friends and neighbors, a flourishing career, and, ultimately, enhanced longevity. Spend too much time in disagreeable places, and disagreeable events—disease, poverty, conflict, annoying neighbors, obstacles to progress in life—become more likely, unless you've developed a talent for transforming negativity into positivity.

The force that produces these feelings of ease or dis-ease within us is the life force, which in Sanskrit is termed *prāṇa* (in Chinese, *qi*). Prāṇa is the life essence, the vitality of all living beings, the power that propels us on our path through life, the energy that, by pervading an organism, enables its body, mind, and spirit to function efficiently as a unified being.

Our world is such that, of the infinite ways we could arrange a space, only a small selection of arrangements exist that can nurture its full potential; many more actually impede its energy. As I have tested techniques of making time and space work for me, however, I have found again and again that in any situation there is usually at least one "ease-promoting" spatial arrangement, a configuration that invariably promotes the healthy circulation of prāṇa in that setting.

Achieving accord in all things was the aim of ancient India's savants, those wise men and women who developed methods for producing and promoting harmony in every avenue of human endeavor. Their experiments engendered the several sciences that describe pathways to equilibrium and serenity in almost every walk of life. For the arrangement of space, the sages created *Vāstu Śāstra*, India's science of form.

Vāstu vs Vastu

The word vāstu *comes from the word* vastu, *which derives from the Sanskrit root* vas *meaning "to dwell, exist." A* vastu *(with a short "a") is a material reality, a "really existing thing," the matter from which other things are made.* Vāstu, *with the long "a," means "a building site, an abode or dwelling place, a home."* Vāstu *is thus manufactured out of* vastu. *Vastu is the potential, and vāstu its realization; vastu is the raw material, vāstu the finished product. Vastu is (relatively) subtle and vāstu, dense; vastu is (relatively) unmanifest, vāstu manifest.*

In its most basic sense, vāstu denotes a dwelling place, but its meaning has been extended to include the earth one inhabits (bhūmi), *the buildings on that earth* (harmya), *and those moveable artifacts of our lives* (paryaṅka), *including furniture* (śayana) *and conveyances* (yāna), *that act as our "temporary dwellings" while we use them.*

Vāstu is a philosophy of living that specializes in determining the "aptness" of site and situation, particularly in architectural contexts. Vāstu recommends that we enrich our lives by arranging the spaces we create for ourselves so that those spaces may align us and our individual dwellings with our larger communal spaces of town, state, planet, and universe. "Good" Vāstu appears when we create spaces that promote equilibrium, prosperity, and health in our lives, and when we act appropriately within them. "Bad" Vāstu results from spaces and alignments that, by impeding the circulation of prāṇa, prevent us from enjoying "ease" in our lives. Beneficial Vāstu exists in configurations that promote concord; arrangements that bring about discord, within us or outside of us, display inimical Vāstu.

Vāstu guides us to inspect every space that we shape and that shapes us, from the most miniscule to the most mammoth. Like it or not, we are connected to everything and everything is connected to us. Each of us is a small but key territory in the enormously intricate domain that is our universe, and each of us who wishes to pursue happiness must investigate the relationship between microcosm and macrocosm. One cannot understand the whole without examining the part and cannot align with other parts (or with the self) until one can at least appreciate and be open to the reality of the whole. No individual's well-being is ever independent of the well-being of the land, the community, or the cosmos.

Right relationship requires an individual to strike a wholesome balance between respect for self and respect for "other," weighing individual needs and wants against the requirements of family, society, and ecosystem. We relate well when we revere self and other equally in our every interaction, and when enough of our relationships become healthy, we become truly happy—we enjoy *sukha*.

Sukha

When we pursue happiness, what we really seek is *sukha*, a state of general well-being that develops when our internal contentment blends with external abundance. *Sukha*—which, like most Sanskrit words, has many related meanings, including "happiness," "health," and "ease"—literally means "good space" (*kha* = space). The related word *duḥkha* indicates the polar opposite of sukha: misery, misalignment, difficulty, disease. In Sanskrit the prefix *su* denotes excellence, rightness, beauty, ease, swiftness, willingness, lack of obstruction; it adds a general flavor of harmony to any other word. We know it in English as the prefix *eu*, as in the word *euphoria*.

Sukha represents a "wholistic" condition in which the many "spaces" of life are in good order: the body's physical space, the family's living spaces and economic spaces, the mind's psychological and emotive spaces, the soul's moral and spiritual spaces, even society's communal spaces. Every one of us craves happiness, but far too few of us seek sukha. The many of us who imagine that we can consume our way into contentment forget that true satisfaction comes only from within. Sukha, the "good space" of body, mind, and spirit, requires that all the spaces of our lives be well-aligned and harmoniously interacting. The cultural commentator Alain de Botton muses that from an architectural viewpoint, "the buildings we admire are ultimately those which, in a variety of ways, extol virtues we think worthwhile—which refer, that is, whether through their materials, shapes or colors, to such legendarily positive qualities as friendliness, kindness, subtlety, strength and intelligence. Our sense of beauty and our understanding of the nature of a good life are intertwined."*

Stendhal maintained that "Beauty is the promise of happiness," and suggested that "There are as many styles of beauty as there are visions of happiness." Environments and spaces that promote sukha need not, however, always be beautiful in the terms that most of us use to define beauty; simply because one moves into an ostensibly beautiful house or surrounds oneself with beauty does not ensure that sukha will follow. Few of the great despots who stocked their palaces and castles with gorgeous art permitted the art to actually speak to them and so failed to be affected by it. Many hermits dwelling in ruins create within themselves a heaven of bliss.

Sukha dictates that houses should be cozy and secure, workplaces efficient and agreeable, community spaces healthy and inviting, but it also compels us to recognize that corporeal pleasure must ever be secondary to mental and spiritual fulfillment. There was a time when we in the West could feel the immanence of the unseen world in our daily lives, when we would never have dreamed of divorcing the material realm from that of the spirit. We constructed grand spaces in those days, buildings like the great cathedrals of Europe that cast in stone our ascendant quest toward the spiritual that is the human birthright. After we chose the primacy of matter over spirit, though, we dissected the spiritual out of our daily lives as we focused on wallowing in the mundane. For generations now, a substantial proportion of us have lived and died as materialists, denouncing the immaterial as being "immaterial," irrelevant to our lives. We have as a consequence permitted our vistas to become blighted with buildings of the coarsest, most uncouth variety—structures that pander to our basest drives and instincts.

Vāstu and Feng Shui

"Live like a pig and you learn to grunt," said my wise Texan mother; the fact that we live surrounded by the bleakness of our decayed aesthetic cannot help but contribute to the general decay of civility and tolerance in our society. Health, of an individual or a culture, requires dynamic balance, a homeostatic poise as active as that of a ballerina on point. We who wish to be happy and healthy need to look past our personal concerns to also consider nature's well-being.

The ancient civilizations of India and China founded enduring traditions of "spatial science" to promote wholesome alliances

* Alain de Botton, *The Architecture of Happiness,* p. 98

between land and people. Vāstu and Feng Shui diverge in their many details, but their fundamental similarities far outnumber the differences. Both assert that the chief prerequisite for learning how to create "good" living and working spaces is a basic understanding of balance and alignment. Both are spiritual approaches to architecture that teach us that there is more to life than its merely material dimension. Both focus their evaluations on the condition of the life force (prāṇa or qi) in a space: how fluidly that force circulates, where it's obstructed or stagnant, and what can be done to enliven it.

Both Vāstu and Feng Shui find similarities between our outer and inner worlds. Following India's ancient *Law of Microcosm and Macrocosm*, a general rule of metaphysics developed by the sages, Vāstu teaches that each human being is a living microcosm of the universe, a tiny self-enclosed cosmos that mirrors the giant cosmos without.

Every human life entails a web of relationships, a summation of a multitude of temporal, spatial, and causal interactions between the smaller cosmos and the larger. If we take nature as a resource to be exploited, then nature will respond by exploiting us in return. Align yourself with nature, and your own personal "lesser universe" will start to function as a harmonious, sukha-filled component of the greater.

When the denizens of India and China have followed their own traditional advice in these matters and worked with nature, they have prospered; when they've neglected good alignment in their spaces, public or private, the resulting disarray has been plain to see. India's Mughal empire, for example, found its architectural zenith in the transcendent Taj Mahal; succeeding generations have permitted the city of Agra that surrounds it to sink to an urban nadir.

Current conditions in both nations testify eloquently to what can happen when the principles of good Vāstu are ignored, or when Feng Shui is used for personal benefit alone, rather than for the benefit of self and society alike. The result has been the haphazard growth of giant, highly polluted cities, often thrown up in the hastiest fashion, chockablock with high-rises ringed with slums. Once India's and China's citizens elect to return to their traditions, and devote themselves again to nurturing their spaces, they will find nature as ready as ever to align with them.

Inspiration caught in stone

Tawdriness frozen in concrete

Alignment

A human being consists of a range of amazingly specialized, multi-surfaced, intersecting spaces, each housing a unique "attribute profile," a defining slate of characteristics. Some of our innate personal traits may be effectively unchangeable; traits that we have adopted can often be discarded; the influence of other traits will rise and fall with changes of season or climate. The sum of these qualities determines who we are and how, with whom, and with what we can reasonably expect to align.

Every substance and every action in our world, including space, has its own "attribute profile." When the qualities of any two spaces complement one another, those qualities will resonate with each other and thus induce alignment. Simple spaces—those with regular dimensions, primary colors, and straightforward textures—align more readily than do intricate spaces. Think of your average wardrobe, which contains some garments that are, in terms of hue and cut, neutral enough to wear with a wide range of accompaniments. Other shirts or skirts, though, are so bright, gaudy, inimitably surfaced, or uniquely styled that they can be worn with but one pairing. The more specialized an item is, the more restricted are its potential matches.

Most of us make it a point to select attire that reflects, through agreement of form and color, who we are and what we aspire to. Most of us do something similar with the space around us as well, choosing furniture, upholstery fabric, wall coverings, and plants that reflect how we exteriorize our internal tastes and desires, how we materialize our internal personalities. But we cannot healthily reflect "who we are" without also addressing "where we are." Space "clothes" us, and we need to apply the same care to aligning the attributes of the inner and outer spaces of our lives—our houses, gardens, public venues—that we use to match our clothes.

When the attributes within us resonate with the attributes of the spaces that we inhabit, those inner and outer worlds will resonate with each other, which nurtures and propagates resonance in all areas of our lives. When we are cheerful, our spaces become cheerier; thankful people encourage their very dwellings to promote gratitude; cooperative attitudes make space itself "cooperative." In this context we can translate *sukha* as cooperative (*su*) space (*kha*), and *duḥkha* as uncooperative space.

A well-perched palace

A pond-poised pagoda

Buildings are brought to life by the currents of prāṇa that spring up within them, desirable or undesirable. Sometimes these currents manifest as obvious airflows, as has been the case with the new Yankee Stadium, the most expensive baseball field ever built; the structure's roof has shifted wind patterns in such a way as to dramatically increase the number of homeruns hit there. Most of the time, however, a structure's prāṇa flows without such glaringly visible physical effects. But the impact is palpable nonetheless, and a well-designed building generates self-perpetuating currents of healthy prāṇa that will actively facilitate the beneficial circulation of prāṇa in whoever inhabits the structure. Simply walking into such a well-structured, prāṇa-resonant, cooperative space can cause one to feel an unprompted uplift, a spontaneous feeling of benevolence and beatitude that conjures a spontaneous smile.

Most of us also know what it feels like to be stifled or suffocated by a space, to walk into a room and immediately feel oppressed by it. Attribute "disagreements" can jar us in spaces that are personally uncooperative just as surely as a harmony of qualities can generate spaces that will perceptibly cooperate with us. Sometimes this feeling of uneasiness arises from a simple sense of dislocation when a space is too big or too small, or poorly proportioned, or has doors or windows laid out improperly, or when the ceiling has a bizarre shape. Sometimes the oppression may be due to a physical factor: stuffy air, draftiness, fusty odors, colors that clash, outlandish furniture unwisely arranged, acoustics that have a peculiar reverberation. Even rooms that are structurally sound and adequately proportioned may still host some disparity that will prevent the prāṇa in that space from circulating satisfactorily, which can also discourage the prāṇa of the house's residents from circulating well.

Often the abnormality is even subtler, such as an intense pattern of thought or behavior from some previous inhabitant whose residual vibration directly affects the way we think. A top-quality concert hall can seem to sing with music even when empty; some abandoned churches can still inspire one to prayer. More malevolently, violence can remain palpable for years in houses where murders have taken place.

The potential resonances or dissonances, subtle and gross, that just one person can create in a singular space are nearly innumerable. This complexity compels us to learn how to determine, at any one moment

Relentless spikiness

Eye-splitting cacophony

and for any one context, which factors deserve greater consideration. For each situation, there is a unique set of solutions, some requiring alignment chiefly of external physical space, others demanding largely inner work.

Vāstu generously offers us tools to deal with each of these puzzles. Vāstu's Five Element and Ten Direction analyses, for example, summarize how external space will attempt to compel us to align with it, and how we can respond optimally to these demands. Ayadi calculations, a specific set of mathematical equations in Vāstu, determine apt proportions for our structures, enabling us to align them precisely with the directions and (if we like) with our own bodies.

In all its methods, however complex, Vāstu strives to make friendly and sweeten the spaces that surround us, to encourage these spaces to nourish, support, and defend us, so that we can enhance happiness and prosperity in our lives. As we use Vāstu to help us attain comfort and contentment in our spaces, to make our spaces our own, we learn how to enlist those spaces to work with us in our quest for real, lasting sukha.

Skins

Good space develops as we learn to "grow" our structures. Any kind of growth, of roses or homes, gardens or businesses, requires an adequate supply of healthy prāṇa, the vital force that drives all life of any sort. Prāṇa is ubiquitous in the universe. Even seemingly empty space is actually packed with prāṇa, which accumulates wherever awareness concentrates. When space is defined by walls, whether cell walls or the walls of a house, the energy closes in on itself, producing in that limited field of energy a rudimentary awareness of its own limitations. The awareness born of restriction makes the prāṇa in that space behave in a life-like way.

Breath is one of prāṇa's vehicles. Every living being breathes, and though the physical mechanics of the process of respiration differ from species to species, the ultimate result of respiration is the inflow and outflow of prāṇa. You can cultivate your personal prāṇa by breathing well, and you can cultivate the prāṇa in a space by encouraging that space to "breathe" well:

All those objects in which Vāstu gets itself established are obviously animated objects, are 'breathing' substances. — eminent architect and Vāstu scholar Dr. V. Ganapati Sthapati, in *Temples of Space-Science,* p. 52.

The world lives and breathes, and we can draw its spirit into us. — Marsilio Ficino, in *The Book of Life*, p. 134.

Like space, Earth, and human lungs and skin, buildings also respire, drawing air, light, water, and prāṇa into their inner spaces, and releasing them thence. Houses that breathe well encourage their residents to breathe vigorously, for our dwelling spaces form one portion of our "supplementary skin."

For as long as a being lives, it maintains a physical separation from every other living being. Single-celled organisms have cell walls; multi-celled organisms use cell membranes to keep cells distinct, and more complex creatures have shells, exoskeletons, or skins to sequester and protect themselves from other organisms. Humans, like other higher animals, live in bodies defined by our external skins and the internal skins of our digestive tracts. Unlike our fellow creatures, we humans can use our faculties of self-perception and craftmaking to generate additional skins for improved self-protection. In many regions, the earliest clothes consisted of animal skins; today we still wear leather, though our "wearable skins" are mostly made of other fabrics.

Shelter is another variety of "secondary skin" that many species have adopted. For us, shelter now includes houses, offices, churches, shopping malls, vehicles, furniture, and other modern "skins" that assist our own skins in regulating temperature, providing protection, and keeping our nervous systems calm. Even our sheltering structural skins have developed skins: lawns and gardens act as go-betweens between houses and streets, fences demarcate boundaries between houses and their surrounding neighborhoods, neighborhood boundaries form the cellular structures of the city, cities mediate between neighborhood and state. From the state to the nation, then to the continent, the planet, the solar system, the galaxy—to infinity, and beyond!

Within your flesh lurk other skins, other natural boundaries: between lymph and blood, blood and flesh, flesh and fat, and bone and marrow. Your central nervous system shelters your prāṇa, safeguards your senses, and, when working properly, stabilizes your mind. Deep within the mind is the locus of pure awareness, which adorns itself in all these "skins."

Being thus layered, like onions, we, like onions, need careful cultivation for our several layers to flourish. Some of these inner sheathes fit together hand in glove, while others are not quite as snug, mainly because of differences in the materials that make them up. One sizable discontinuity that we must pay close attention to, if our lives are to go well, is that disconnect between our birth skins and the skins of our structures, that border zone between our protoplasm and the architectural structures we live (or work) in. A well-designed, well-constructed residence can bridge the gap between human protoplasm and the environment in which it exists, promoting a natural, easy transition that encourages breath, prāṇa, and awareness to flow with vitality, grace, and nourishment into all dimensions of our being and those of our surroundings.

Mind, Prāṇa, Breath

In the interaction with our living spaces, we develop a three-layered relationship with the large, earthy organism we call "house":

- our breathing bodies relate most readily to the house's "body," its physical contents and functions
- our personal prāṇa tallies with the residence's prāṇa flows
- our dwelling's subtle sediments and vibrations affect most powerfully the mental partitions that we construct within ourselves, composed of habits and idiosyncrasies

Good Vāstu structures create a resonance between you and your space; as you breathe, so will your dwelling. You both need to be able to enjoy unencumbered respiration. Breath, prāṇa, and awareness work together in constructed "skins" very much as they do within the human skin; they work together the same way in a house as in a human being. Breath, prāṇa, and mind are similar expressions of manifested consciousness on different levels of existence. Control one leg of this life-supporting tripod, and you control the other two, which is why control of prāṇa (*prāṇāyāma*) via breath control is a cornerstone of Haṭha Yoga practice.

Here is an important classical principle, employed by Āyurveda, Yoga, Tantra, and Vāstu alike, applicable equally to microcosm and macrocosm: Whenever one structure or function interacts with another, there will be a reciprocal influence between them; ordinarily, that structure or function that is subtler will have a greater influence on its counterpart.

For instance, prāṇa flow characteristically has a greater influence on breathing than the other way around, which is why regulation of the breath can control prāṇa only when those breath exercises are carefully repeated over time. Prāṇa flow provides a conduit for attention, but attention guides prāṇa. Since attention is subtler than prāṇa, its impact on prāṇa is greater than prāṇa's impact on attention. Generally, in fact, attention directs prāṇa; wherever our attention goes, so goes our prāṇa—and so go we, impelled to move in the direction followed by our awareness and life force.

Living beings obtain prāṇa via food, water, air, and (to some extent) light and sound. After taking in these nutrients, we release their prāṇa by utilizing our internal digestive fires. A subtle form of "cooked" prāṇa "rises" within the space of the physical body just as savory steam rises from a pot that is boiling on the stove; in fact, the Chinese characters for qi represent the vapor that arises from cooking rice.

Just as prāṇa has to circulate well within us if we are to be healthy, prāṇa must circulate well within our buildings. The energetic vapors within us require just the right amount of space for their circulation: if the space available is insufficient (and how much is sufficient will depend on the individual), impediments and eruptions follow; too much space, and the prāṇa-vapor gets lost within some internal void, just as cooking fragrances get lost when a kitchen is too cavernous.

At least three separate sets of "vapors" need to circulate freely within us, inside three distinct but related spaces:

- nerve impulses, flowing within the physical nervous system
- prāṇa, flowing in the *nāḍīs*, the ethereal vessels in which prāṇa moves (the rough equivalent of the meridians of acupuncture)
- thoughts and emotions, flowing in the mind

Spaces are good when the prāṇa within them moves fluidly, without impediment. When you're able to induce one of the spaces in your life to become cooperative, other spaces will spontaneously seek to cooperate. The more harmonious your inner spaces, the more nourishing your dwelling will be; energetically blocked spaces will result in dwellings that impede the flow of prāṇa. Those who aspire to health need to breathe well, circulate prāṇa well, and think well.

Prayer and meditation can improve your thinking, and "energy cultivation" (via methods like yoga, tai qi, qi gong, or martial arts) can train you to circulate your prāṇa effectively. Breathing correctly can improve both prāṇa and mind. A good way to begin your study of Vāstu is to train yourself to pay continuous attention to your breathing:

Exercise One: Breath Awareness

Sit with your back comfortably straight in a position of ease, cross-legged on the floor if your body feels contented in that arrangement, sitting in a chair if not. Place the hands on the knees with the palms upwards, close your eyes, and begin to pay attention to your breathing. Breathe in and out without pause, permitting your breath to carry your mind along with it, from outside your body to the inside as you inhale, and from the inside to the outside as you exhale.

After several breaths, you should notice that this simple attentiveness to your breathing is causing you to breathe more slowly and more deeply than before. Now, without applying any force other than the focus of your relaxed intention, permit the point from which you're breathing to descend yet deeper into your abdomen, and let the breath flow lengthen further, gradually and effortlessly, until you're taking only a few breaths each minute. Once you reach the point when you feel you've reached the greatest depth and the slowest rate of respiration—as well as the most profound state of relaxation that you are likely to attain during that sitting—take a few more breaths to "bookmark" this state within your body, to make it easier to return to the next time you do the exercise. Then arise, very slowly; try to retain that awareness of deep, slow, relaxed abdominal breathing as you return to your daily activities.

Make it a point, from then on, to concentrate on your breathing for at least a few minutes each day, sitting with your back straight and breathing with your abdomen instead of your chest. Once this becomes a habit, start to pay attention to how your breathing shifts with changes in your activities. Notice how your breathing feels when you're calm and when you're agitated; on awaking from sleep and just before you go to bed; before you begin a meal, and then afterwards; before, during, and after exercise; before, during, and after lovemaking. When you notice your breathing becoming shallow, rapid, and strained, try to return to your space of calm, and note the effect that this intentional, calm breathing has on your body, your prāṇa, your thoughts and emotions.

After you've become familiar with your breathing patterns, spend a little time in each of the rooms of your home, paying careful attention to how each change of space changes the way you breathe. Later, move on to explore other houses, and different kinds of buildings, noting breathing shifts as they occur, correlating them with shifts in your awareness, your life force, and your limbs as your body aligns with each space.

Sometimes it's easier, when initially exploring this experience, to sense bad Vāstu than to be aware of good Vāstu in different spaces. For example, if you know of a house that has an upper story whose ceiling follows the angle of the roof, or that has a room beneath a staircase, go sit or lie in the space within the acute angle formed by the slanting ceiling and the level floor. It shouldn't take long before a sense of oppression arises within you, as the room's angle cramps the movement of your prāṇa.

In any observation, a relationship is established between the observer and the observed, a relationship that shifts along with the observer's shifting attention. The equilibrium established is the total of:

- the human awareness of the object
- the object's awareness (innate, if the object is a living being; projected onto it by living beings, if not alive itself)

- the awareness accumulated in the space where the observation takes place

When human attention is strongly directed onto one feature of a particular setting, the prāṇa that the attention carries will strongly reinforce the significance of that feature—for good or ill. A sacred object in a room will become more potent as respectful attention falls upon it, the prāṇa that it carries being fortified by the pranic content of the admiration; this will improve the quality of that room's space. Prominent angles in a room disturb the qualities of the room's space by generating eddies in that room's pranic circulation. The more often these angles are noticed, the more the prāṇa of observation will expand the eddies, and their effects.

To get a sense for rightness in a good space, you may first want to visit a temple, church, mosque, or other space where people go to focus their prāṇa and align themselves with Reality. If that space of worship is truly good—if it has been created with care and fortified by praise and adoration over years, decades, or centuries (the longer, the better), it will align you perceptibly, making your prāṇa circulate properly, putting you into a better spiritual and mental (and, ultimately, physical) state.

Initially, it will probably take some minutes for you to get onto a building's "wavelength," and get a sense for that space's harmonious flow or energetic imbalance. Some ancient worship spaces, however, will work on you almost instantly; you'll feel your awareness extending upwards toward Spirit as soon as you enter into them. These are good spaces!

When the Vāstu is right, God's house becomes God's own skin, within which the Ultimate Reality loves to dwell. Early Vāstu texts mainly concerned themselves, in fact, with how to construct temples in such a way that the prāṇa of the Divine could easily invigorate them, a task in which many of India's ancient temple architects clearly succeeded.

The perpetually falling wall

Visitors to the minsters at Durham, York, Chartres, Mont St. Michel, and other similarly glorious spaces of prayer and rejoicing will find that their architects succeeded as well, despite knowing nothing of Vāstu or Feng Shui. Instead, they followed their own traditions of sacred architecture, and felt out rightness in their own bodies and minds as they went along.

Go into a place of worship and your breathing will quiet to stillness as awe takes root within your soul. Go into a slaughterhouse, and you'll find your breathing becoming shallow and panicked, like that of the frightened animals around you who are about to die. Visit a battlefield, and you may experience a similar effect from the lingering anguish of those who were killed there. The fields around Ypres, in Belgium, where about a million men died during World War I, affected me strongly; so did Antietam, in Maryland, the site of the largest one-day loss of life during the American Civil War.

Go into a crack house, and you may well be able to sense the misery that has seeped into its walls, one pipe-full at a time. Visit instead a house that has been well-tended, a home that has been cultivated carefully into a personal cathedral, and you'll find your mind, prāṇa, and breath slipping into alignment there.

A house with good Vāstu is much like a tabernacle, its very arrangement and orientation promoting cooperation, serenity, productivity, and joy amongst its denizens. Building good Vāstu into a dwelling right from its architectural genesis is ideal, but arrangements in space come to life only when prāṇa is breathed into them. Good Vāstu involves good planning, true, but it also requires a worshipful cultivation of pranic flow at every stage of construction, beginning right from the moment that you actually select a site on which to build, or—if you are moving into a structure you did not build yourself—when you take possession of a new residence or office.

Even if your house is not as perfectly planned and constructed as a temple, it remains your personal temple, and can still host the Divine if you create the appropriate conditions. The best way to do that is for you to worship Reality within it, in your own chosen way, each day. Just as you found your breath becoming calmer as you encouraged it to be calm, you can make your own space calmer simply by willing it so. Painting, rearranging, and redecorating can help substantially, but there is no substitute for intention.

Nor is there a substitute for breathing. As with the body, so with the home; the organism, both biological and spatial, requires just the right amount of unoccupied space if it is to breathe properly. When I visit New York, Bombay, or some similar megalopolis, all too frequently I find people living there in the middle of a mountain of possessions. Acquisitiveness often reflects an inner emptiness: de Botton observes, "What we seek, at the deepest level, is inwardly to resemble, rather than to physically possess, the objects and places that touch us through their beauty."* But even people who are psychologically well-adjusted find that as their eventful lives progress, they become confined by their possessions. As a pack rat myself, I know how tempting it is to hang onto meaningful objects and mementoes, but when your space is small, you have to acknowledge its diminutive reality. Clutter obstructs the free movement of prāṇa, in room and human alike, and obstructed prāṇa hampers health and prosperity.

Excesses of empty space are also unhealthy. Remember the old horror movies in which the evil monster in human form entertains the unwary guest who's been forced to take shelter in the wraith's lonely castle? A stiff, formal dinner is invariably served in a cavernous dining hall; the guest and his host sit at a long dining table that, though enormous, is too small for the room. Part of the sense of foreboding in this scenario

*de Botton, op. cit. p. 98

The relentless refectory

Chaos in clutter

comes, of course, from the portraits glaring down from the walls, the rusty suits of armor standing at attention, the musty moth-eaten tapestries inadequately covering the depressing stone walls, and the sinister gait of the hunchbacked butler. But a good part of this feeling of unease comes from finding yourself in a place that you know in your bones to be drafty and cold, both literally and figuratively. Where prāṇa has nothing to relate to, it will wander aimlessly, a condition that promotes excess nervous energy in the body as well as anxiety and fear in the mind—all of which hinder health and prosperity.

Free-flowing prosperity requires free-flowing prāṇa, within yourself and around you. This prāṇa must simultaneously be stable, lest things come into your life but then depart before you can grasp them firmly. Healthy prāṇa is well-rooted, in body and in living space. In a well-rooted body, the head is correctly aligned on the spine, which should itself be firmly set in the pelvis. A well-rooted living space needs a stable, ordinarily unoccupied center. An area of open space at the center of a room, home, office, or temple offers the structure's prāṇa the "breathing room" it needs to take root, and nourishes that prāṇa by drawing to it the attention of that space's occupants and visitors. Obstruct the center, and prāṇa is obstructed; lose "sight" of the center, and your attention, and prāṇa, will diffuse toward its periphery.

Exercise Two: The Gut Feeling

Select an appropriate room for this experiment. You may want to try out a room in someone else's home first, as it's often easier to be objective about someone else's situation than about your own.

Obtain a baseline for your evaluation by sitting quietly in the room, facing east if possible, and noting the effect that the room has on your prāṇa. Sit as long as you need to, until you're sure you know what you're feeling.

Next, move any piece of furniture or other item sitting against a wall away from that wall, and remove anything that might be occupying the middle of the room. Sit again and, using your breath to get a feel for the room, note how it feels different. It should feel lighter, airier, roomier, or changed for the better in some other way. If indeed the change is a positive one, see if you can identify the process that allowed you to become conscious of it.

Now fill the room with "stuff" until it is full to bursting, and sit again. Subsequently empty everything out of the room, and sit yet again. Compare the feeling you get from a room that's bursting at the seams, in which there is nowhere for prāṇa to circulate, with the feeling you have in a room that is wholly bare, where there is nothing for prāṇa to hold onto. Neither is likely to feel "right," even when the room itself does not feel "wrong."

Concinnity and Confluence

For all its calculations and configurations, Vāstu is based firmly in perception: the awareness of "rightness" or "wrongness" in space, understood primarily in the context of prāṇa, the life force. Vāstu speaks in the lingo of the life force, in messages you can feel through your breath, or in your gut, just below your navel, at the place that the Japanese call the *hara*. The body's prāṇa centers itself there, which is roughly your bodily center of gravity. It's usually simple enough to get a "gut feeling" of what's wrong in a room or building that is pranically "off-center," or to use your hara to sense when a structure is pranically on target.

Your home being an extension of your body, Vāstu language fundamentally speaks to us at the level of our bodies, our senses, our prāṇa. Your first impression of a house—as being welcoming or threatening, cold or warm, inviting or off-putting—is often your most accurate insight into its overall condition. That house is speaking to you, making a statement that elicits an insightful response from you.

First impressions, sadly, cannot always be trusted; nor, given the inherent imperfections of the human organism, can we rely on our bodies and minds to clearly and precisely provide us all the information we require to understand spaces through direct perception. Ancient India's Vāstu experts therefore developed principles and theories from their collected experiences and those of their predecessors, so that we who followed might use those principles to help guide and inspire our own perceptions. We will study many of these principles and experiment with them to see how they can help us comprehend the dynamics of the spaces we seek to know.

Still, it's wise to get into the habit of first "feeling" your way through a space before you begin to apply Vāstu principles of rightness or wrongness to it. Analysis should build on the firm foundation of an accurate first impression, not begin abstractly on the basis of someone else's theory of how things should be. Principles are useful, but they must always take a back seat to direct personal experience. If you find good Vāstu in a place where theory predicts you should be miserable, tear up the theory and start over, at least in your personal analysis of that space!

Ideally, in a place that is pranically cooperative, you'll sense cooperation in all parts of your being: it should feel right to your gut, should equalize your breathing, attract your mind, and warm your heart. We can call this "rightness" *concinnity*, a word that means both "internal harmony or fitness of parts to a whole or to each other," and "studied elegance of design or arrangement." Concinnity can happen spontaneously, but it often requires planning, aligning, and tweaking in order to manifest that convergence of well-aligned perceptions and pranic flows that we can call *confluence*. When a confluence of indications points toward concinnity, you can be fairly confident that your perception is accurate.

Tiger and Cow, Again

When you do learn some new and useful Vāstu principle, try always to understand its source. More often than not, it has developed from some very basic understanding of human nature and interaction. Take, for example, the Tiger-mouthed Tracts (*Vyāghra-mukhī Bhūmi*) and Cow-mouthed Tracts (*Go-mukhī Bhūmi*) that Vimalananda used as my introduction to Vāstu. Let us now add to this notion the detail that Tiger-mouthed properties (whose fronts are significantly wider than their backs) are said to benefit commercial endeavors, while Cow-mouthed lands (whose backs are significantly wider than their fronts), which are supposed to be good for dwellings, are reported to be inauspicious for businesses.

We cannot be absolutely certain of what the seers who compiled Vāstu's texts were thinking when they proposed this principle, but we can certainly postulate that at least one reason why they would think of Tiger-mouthed Tracts as being good for business is that they lend themselves to being entered. The wider threshold of a Tiger-mouthed Tract is more likely to encourage people to cross it than is the narrower threshold of a Cow-mouthed Tract. A broader threshold provides a longer storefront, which can be used to attract more people to come in.

The average home is meant to provide privacy and protection to its residents rather than to attract the attention of others to it. Usually, in fact, there is benefit to be had in making it less noticeable to certain people (like burglars). Access to a narrow-mouthed property being more easily regulated than to one whose mouth is wider, the former is more easily made secure.

We may add to this commonsensical explanation of this principle a more subtle interpretation as well, one that involves the inherent nature of "prosperity prāṇa." Material prosperity is said in Indian tradition to be very "fickle." The energy of money apparently doesn't enjoy staying with any individual or any family for very long, preferring instead to zip around according to its whim. Money that has been obtained by means such as gambling is said to be particularly unstable, very difficult to successfully "digest."

If you're running a business, you hope for plenty of monetary inflow, for which a wide-mouthed lot is admirably fit. For your home finances, however, you'll most likely prefer to have as much as possible of what flows in to stay put, rather than flowing out again. Narrowing the "neck" of your territorial "moneybag" makes it more difficult for your assets to slink away unnoticed.

Should you happen to be running a home business, your situation's complexity will probably best be handled by searching for a square or rectangular plot of land; i.e., one that is more regular than either a Cow- or Tiger-mouthed Tract. Regularity in design and construction promotes a regularity of prāṇa flow when other factors are present that might confuse prāṇa, or somehow knot it up. You probably would not be willing to invest in a super-sophisticated plumbing system that was so convoluted that it required continual maintenance. Neither would you want to create for yourself a space in which prāṇa is continually getting kinked—unless you enjoy the idea of being continually called upon to unkink it.

2 The Vāstu Vidyā

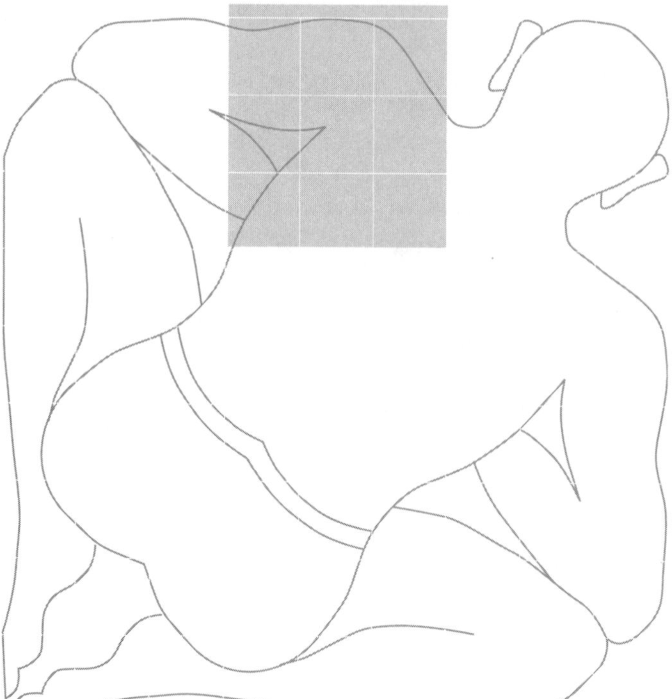

Vāstu, the Yoga of Space

One of the definitions of *yoga* contained in the *Bhagavad-Gītā** is "skill in action" (*yogaḥ karmasu kauśalam*). The word *kauśalam* connotes easy grace, natural proficiency, the attainment of flow with minimal effort; performed with panache, yoga is that which unknots kinked prāṇa and furthers prāṇa's circulation.

We can call Vāstu the "yoga of space," for it is the study of how to skillfully align ourselves with our spaces. Most varieties of yoga focus on cultivating and channeling prāṇa by focusing attention on the inner spaces of body and mind, while Vāstu focuses instead on the external spaces that the body-mind occupies. Vāstu, Haṭha Yoga, Āyurveda (classical Indian medicine), and Jyotiṣa (India's astrology) use differing means toward the same end: to align individuals more perfectly with their own prāṇa and the prāṇa of their environments.

Vāstu, Āyurveda, Jyotiṣa, Haṭha Yoga, and related alignment practices are traditions that have evolved via the expression of *vidyās* through human awareness. A *vidyā* is a subtle all-powerful energetic intelligence, a dynamically active consciousness that is known in Sanskrit as *śakti*. When, by dint of persistent veneration, an individual succeeds at developing a personal relationship with a vidyā, that impersonal vidyā is transformed into a personalized deity, a goddess who, expressing herself through that devotee, can promote concord.

A vidyā is, fundamentally, an extension of the natural human talent for feeling the rightness and wrongness of things. The basic principles of Vāstu are, like the basic principles of healing or of any other vidyā, expressions of fundamental powers inherent in our world's configuration. Where there is disease, nature creates a remedy; where space swerves from cooperation into imbalance, an antidote spontaneously arises that, when well applied, guides us instinctively toward harmony.

Every human enjoys an intuitive feel for the balance or imbalance of arrangements in space. Each of us can at every moment access the basic principles of the *Vāstu Vidyā*, principles which can (much of the time) be used to create "good space." You can be a competent architect if you follow Vāstu's prescriptions of form to the letter, but you become a master builder (*sthapati*) only once you have become a vehicle for the Vāstu Vidyā, by means of spiritual practices that can awaken, enhance,

---

**Bhagavad-Gītā 2.50:*
buddhi-yukto jahātīha ubhe sukṛta-duṣkṛte |
tasmād yogāya yujyasva yogaḥ karmasu kauśalam ||

focus, and refine your innate but sleeping Vāstu talent. "Architecture is frozen music," the solidification of harmony into matter, said the Egyptian architect Hassan Fathy, and those who can successfully marry architectural insight and precept will gain access into boundless realms of melodic design, spatial symmetries, and structural poise.

Vedas and Vidyās

Vāstu, Āyurveda, Jyotiṣa, Yoga, and similar Indian sciences originated with the *Vedas*, India's age-old compendia of sacred wisdom that taught Vedic practitioners how to establish and promote order on earth and in the heavens by means of performing elaborate sacrificial rituals. The numerous vidyās are simultaneously many and one. In their manifested forms, they are varied paths that lead ultimately to a personal realization of the Unity of all existence; in non-manifested form, they directly express that Unity. Each focuses on one aspect of the sukha equation; together, they aid us to identify, shed light on, and pave our path to sukha by addressing life in its every aspect.

Āyurveda advises you what and how to cook, and Vāstu suggests where you might situate your kitchen. The *Nāṭya Vidyā* supplies the drama to be performed on the stage, which itself is constructed according to Vāstu principles. In questions of politics (*Nīti Vidyā*), Jyotiṣa provides advice on when to time events within the political assembly spaces that Vāstu defines. The beauty of each system becomes even richer as its connections to the other vidyās are elaborated within the individual practitioner; sometimes the many expressions of divine wisdom will vie to express themselves through a particularly adept agent. Ultimately, sincere cultivation of a vidyā will direct the aspirant toward the Supreme Reality.

Learning any vidyā requires both careful study of its texts and traditions and firsthand experience of its practices. A veritable authority in any vidyā will know the elements of every other vidyā, and will be fully conversant in the few vidyās that are most germane to his or her specialty. According to the eminent Vāstu exponent Dr. V. Ganapati Sthapati, any "master of establishment" (*sthapati*) worth the name should be acquainted with at least these four vidyās: *Śabda* (rhythm, chanting), *Nāṭya* (dance and drama), *Gandharva* (music), and *Sthāpatya* (architecture and sculpture).*

---

* Dr. V. Ganapati Sthapati, *Some Glimpses of Science and Technology of Vāstu Śāstra*, p. 30

Wisdom,
aspiration,
action.

We may consider the vidyās as muses, divine personifications of inspiration and understanding relating to a particular subject. Āyurveda is the *Āyur Vidyā*, the muse of life; Jyotiṣa is the *Jyotir Vidyā*, the muse of light. Vāstu is the *Vāstu Vidyā*, the muse of objects and spaces. Viewed this way, the vidyās are articulations of the Universal Reality as forms of "living wisdom"; they embody themselves within those human beings who serve as their vessels, gaining richness and fluency with each successful transfer from one generation to the next.

When an individual becomes "inspired" by a vidyā-muse—as when her "breath of inspiration" enters an artist—that vidyā extends her own life force through the artist into the creation, the artist serving as her earthly vehicle. Vidyās live in symbiotic interplay with their human conduits, feeding on our powers of attention as they nourish our imaginations and our spiritual marrow. The effortlessness that an expert brings to his craft is the creative fluidity of his muse acting through him.

A lore, a muse, a path, an exploration: A vidyā is all this, and more. By careful nourishment and cultivation, a vidyā and her human vehicle can succeed at achieving a state of true symbiosis with one another. The vidyā's principles and traditions blossom and flourish as practitioner and vidyā—disciple and teacher—nurture one another in the exchange of life and inspiration.

Vidyās are eternal, in the sense that they express tendencies that are innate to nature. But they are equally as ever-changing as the substances and actions that make up our lives. The ultimate, timeless essence of a vidyā is perpetually available to whoever can locate and please her, as the Vedic seers did. The rest of us can take advantage of what the seers codified, and what their disciples and descendants elaborated upon, to cultivate our own native Vāstu natures slowly, surely.

Vāstu History

Astute Vāstu practitioners develop a feel for patterns. Arrangements and relationships leap out at them, demanding attention; objects call out to them for positioning. Each vidyā produces its own unique patterns, but once you can discern patterns in one vidyā, you'll find patterns from the others revealing themselves to you.

For a successful interplay, every vidyā requires healthy practitioners, cooperative clients, and sound practitioner-client relationships. The vidyā remains in the realm of potential, quiescent, until a practitioner

A worthy muse mouthpiece

emerges to function as a focal point around which the muse's patterns and wisdom can coalesce. The practitioner enlivens the vidyā in the way that zero enlivens the integers one through nine. The practitioner acts as the chairman of the vidyā's board of directors, the nucleus around which the vidyā-pearl constellates, the midwife who directs the vidyā's successful rebirth on Earth.

The Vāstu muse has been guiding architects and builders in India for many thousands of years, since the heyday of the Vedas or even earlier. Of the four Vedas, the *Yajur Veda* is the text that focuses on the details relating to sacrifices, and *Sthāpatya Veda* is its *upaveda* (auxiliary body of knowledge). *Sthāpatya Veda*, which facilitates the performance of sacrifices by detailing sizes and proportions for fire altars, ritual implements, and the like, is often considered to be Vāstu's progenitor.

Life in Vedic times was simpler and more straightforward than it is now, for individual personalities were far less individuated. The people of that archaic era lived in such close contact with nature that their profound interrelationship with the natural world permitted them to sense directly the rightness and wrongness of spatial configurations:

> *They were whole and one with cosmic forces. They felt themselves as integrated parts of the universe, of one and the same substance. Their vision therefore was not blocked up within the narrow limits of their own individuality and their own small ambiance, but transcending them went to explore the tremendous mystery of creation. … [Man at that time] drew all his inspiration and his strength from the contemplation of the divine powers, by which he himself and the whole cosmos were created and sustained.*
> Vāstusūtra Upaniṣad, *p. 8*

As the simplicity of their early, nomadic lifestyle gradually yielded to the convolutions of urbanization, the wise among the Vedic peoples systematized what had once been applied via spontaneous inspiration in their various fields of endeavor. Shamanistic medicine developed into the empirical medical system known now as Āyurveda; observational astronomy expanded into the representational astrology that is Jyotiṣa; instinctive grammar was codified into the orderly rules of *Vyākaraṇa*. Vāstu also changed, from intuitive observations of space and spatial arrangements into a set of standardized principles, a "grammar for visual forms," the better to address the intricacies of life in densely packed environments.

Perfect proportions

From hill to temple

We know little about how long it took for these changes to transpire, though we do know that urbanization had reached at least the northern and western portions of the Indian subcontinent as early as the Harappan civilization, which was probably founded sometime during the fourth millennium B.C., and which persisted for a couple of millennia. The many Harappan cities that have been found thus far were well-planned, usually on a grid system, with main streets and individual houses alike oriented north-south and east-west. Harappan citizens enjoyed many civic conveniences, including efficient sewage systems. The relationship that the Harappans had with the Vedas is unclear, but their extensive mud-brick constructions speak volumes for their state of urban sophistication and their awareness of Vāstu principles.

By the time of Gautama Buddha, during the 6th century B.C., towns and cities had sprouted across India. Construction was at first mainly in wood, and initial experiments in stone imitated wooden structures. Rock-cut temples in places like Ajanta and Ellora, or Karla and Bhaja, show the same sort of ribbed and vaulted ceilings that carpenters use to create wooden roofs. As stone structures gradually replaced wooden ones, architects and masons developed more appropriate construction techniques, and brick and stone remained India's primary building material until the recent advent of cement and concrete.

Sthāpatya Veda is focused almost exclusively on sacred architecture built from brick. The application of Vāstu principles to secular construction probably didn't become widely popular until shortly before Buddha's appearance. Vāstu and its sister vidyās achieved their fullest flowering during the period of India's classical civilization, between roughly 1000 B.C. and 1000 A.D. After that time, repeated invasions frayed the fabric of India's culture, and practitioners of the various vidyās found it difficult, during the centuries of political turmoil that followed these upheavals, to refine and expand their arts. The Turk, Persian, and other dynasties that ruled India during this period were sometimes benign and sometimes repressive; a few of them—the Mughals in particular—contributed significantly to India's architecture, in buildings like the Taj Mahal and cities like Fatehpur Sikri.

When the British took control of India, they decided, as part of their plan to enforce political unity, to discourage the teaching of all traditional lores. As a result, much of the substance of these traditions was lost, and many of the traditions unraveled. Several generations of Indians were educated to value Western aesthetics alone and to be embarrassed of their indigenous arts. This compulsory disdain for the past persisted almost unchallenged until India began its independence struggle at the onset of the 20th century, and has ebbed but slowly since then. Only in the past few decades have Vāstu and her sister vidyās begun to regain real vigor in their homeland.

Vāstu Texts

Today, most Vāstu specialists agree that Vāstu's purpose is to create sacred, convivial spaces for body, mind, and spirit. Substantial disagreement persists, however, on precisely what philosophy and practices constitute Vāstu, and in what manner they should be implemented. Impending catastrophe is predicted for the slightest deviation from some rigidly formulated Vāstu spatial or structural plan; debates rage over how to interpret a certain Vāstu principle.

A temporary stiffness of opinion is natural in a vidyā-body that, after long lying near-dormant, is now awakening, stretching its limbs again into life. Tenaciously asserting the incontrovertible validity of one opinion and the utter invalidity of every other outlook is, however, unnatural and unhealthy, both for Vāstu herself and for those who serve her.

Vāstu's entirety is too vast for any individual to ever wholly embody her full complexity. One can at best hope to develop a personal system that elaborates her with some relative degree of accuracy, while acknowledging the limitation of one's chosen perspective. To insist stubbornly that one's own vision is the only way to see the world is to fall into the error of the blind men who, each comprehending only a portion of the elusive totality that is an elephant, wrangled bitterly over whose perception was correct.

The *Vedas* embrace a more pluralistic viewpoint on reality. "Truth is Singular," states a Vedic proverb, "the wise speak of it in various ways." Each Vedic seer glimpsed Reality from a different perspective, then collected and collated his perceptions and transmitted his own life force into them to create a living text that was activated again and again by initiates into his lineage. As the Creator set in motion the cosmic spheres, so each sage created and brought to life the cosmos of living knowledge embodied in his text.

Each seer's perspective gradually ripened into its own system. There is more than one tradition of Āyurveda, many differing styles of Jyotiṣa, and multiple varieties of Indian music, dance, and cuisine. The several (sometimes competing) schools of Vāstu (a subject traditionally taught during the curriculum for the study of ritual and of Jyotiṣa) are a legacy of this propensity for diversity.

Each traditional Vāstu text presents a unique "take" on the Vāstu Vidyā, the reality of space and form, as this wisdom is expressed through a human conduit. Among the many Vāstu texts, Indian art and architecture's conceptual basis is expounded most clearly, meticulously, and succinctly in the aphorisms of the *Vāstusūtra Upaniṣad*, which explains how to use sacred geometry to infuse inner meaning into sacred art. In the classical literature, one of the earliest passages describing the details of Vāstu is found in the *Bṛhat Saṁhitā* ("Big Compendium") of Varahamihira (5th or 6th century A.D.), which addresses the system in a succinct chapter of 125 verses. The majority of subsequent texts, including the prominent *Mayamata*, *Mānasāra*, and *Samarāṅgaṇa Sūtradhāra*, elaborate on the principles introduced in the *Bṛhat Saṁhitā*.

Vāstu principles, like those of music, dance, astrology, yoga, and medicine, govern a language whose basic vocabulary and grammar we must digest before we can read, speak, or understand it. The contemporary practice of Vāstu need not confine itself to ancient modes of expression, but we can't really appreciate its present-day seedlings until we've inspected its old-growth roots.

Vāstu's major expositions appear in several Indian languages, with Sanskrit the most significant of the various tongues. Acquaintance with Sanskrit is especially useful for Vāstu study, for Sanskrit is integral to the Vedic experience and to every Veda-engendered vidyā. Sanskrit (more precisely transliterated as *saṁskṛta*, which means "well-constructed") is an engineered language, systematized by the Vedic seers and the ensuing grammarians to pack many meanings into each of its words. Sanskrit's grammar enables the language to express complex, multi-layered meanings in pithy sentences, and its sounds and their arrangements convey the gist of its words energetically and directly to its speakers and listeners.

Most classical vidyā texts are composed in Sanskrit poetry, the better for students to recite and commit to memory, since, until recently, all vidyās were passed down orally. Those who memorize several thousand verses on a subject create within the ephemeral mind and the physical brain a *saṁskāra*, a "thing done well." Well-done saṁskāras—those that have been thoroughly cooked in the fire of cognition and conveyed with the blessings of a master—enhance desirable qualities and diminish negative attributes. Just so, Vāstu is the study of "space saṁskāras," of methods for turning ordinary or "aggrieved" spaces into "good spaces" by tweaking their dimensions, shapes, arrangements, and other characteristics. Every space you interact with, constructed house and natural setting alike, is a field in flux with which you form a (hopefully nourishing) relationship. "Good space" in the outer world results from the creation of orderly and healthy spatial relationships.

A text is a "knowledge-space," a conceptual structuring of thought, and the saṁskāra of learning a text actually reorders the learner's thought faculties and rearranges synaptic connections. "Mind-space" and "brain-space" reorganization enable the student to access a level of consciousness that ordinary education cannot impart. Studying Vāstu in this way creates a literal "good space" within the student, a space that encourages the kind of profound, "beyond rational" modes of thinking and perception that, by allowing access to the Vāstu Vidyā, enable the learner to develop a true feel for Vāstu.

Studying from books alone can never groom anyone into a true Vāstu practitioner, but bound volumes can offer a good introduction to the subject, information that when enlivened by a teacher can blossom into real wisdom. This book was written with the intention that it serve as an introduction for the general reader, and a text for those fortunate enough to have an instructor available to clarify and explain difficult concepts. As such, you will get better results if you read and digest it slowly, to avoid mental indigestion.

Sampling the Vāstu Language

Studying Vāstu in English is rather more difficult than in Sanskrit, for in the act of reworking Sanskrit poetry into English prose, the original flavor is damaged, its essence partly perverted. The "saṁskāra-promoting" Sanskrit delivers a taste of the direct experience of the seers who cognized it, and permits easier access to the other vidyās that complement this philosophy. Studying Vāstu in poetry better transmits its curved lines, hints, and innuendoes than does the direct, workmanlike communication of prose. A talented poet is an architect of sound; an architect should be a poet of form.

Even if you don't know Sanskrit, you can still enjoy some of its savor simply by sounding out the words in a verse, and enjoying their rhythm and tune. You will find within these pages a few Sanskrit phrases and stanzas to permit you to do just this. As you chant the verse in Sanskrit, you welcome the breath of the vidyā into you, to enthuse and enliven your awareness as you continue on to the English translation and the explanation of the principle in question.

Here's an example, from the *Bṛhat Saṁhitā*:

Tat tasya bhavati śubhadaṁ yasya ca yasmin mano ramate.

Any site becomes auspicious for a person, provided that it gladdens his heart.

Bṛhat Saṁhitā 53:95b, p. 486

In the verses that come before this one, Varahamihira, the *Bṛhat Saṁhitā*'s author, provides many details on the subject of how to select the ideal building site. Yet he concludes his discussion by essentially stating that you should opt for a site that speaks to your heart. While acknowledging the utility of the principles he has just enunciated, Varahamihira reiterates that your instinctive, intuitive impressions of a site count for more than merely rational calculations do. When a piece of land speaks to your heart, you should listen to this sacred intuition, even if your Vāstu analysis detects problems there. Having your heart set on a site doesn't make the issues disappear, but it does suggest that you are likely to summon up the energy, enthusiasm, and focus to deal with its obstacles and generate amity there.

Problems may also arise for you as you open yourself to some of Vāstu's more complicated concepts, a predicament that also can be resolved by relying on your sacred insight. Should you find it difficult to comprehend precisely what you're reading in this book, try to listen to the words with your heart instead of with your mind. As you read, let the words speak to you of more than their mere definitions. Let nuance and image wash over you until you go beyond intellectual understanding into *feeling* what is true, and right, for you. Once your head and heart are working together, each in service to the other, both cooperating with your prāṇa, sukha will begin to flow into you and revitalize you of its own accord, like the bracing waters of a pristine hillside spring, or like a fortifying, unbidden zephyr.

3 Elemental Space

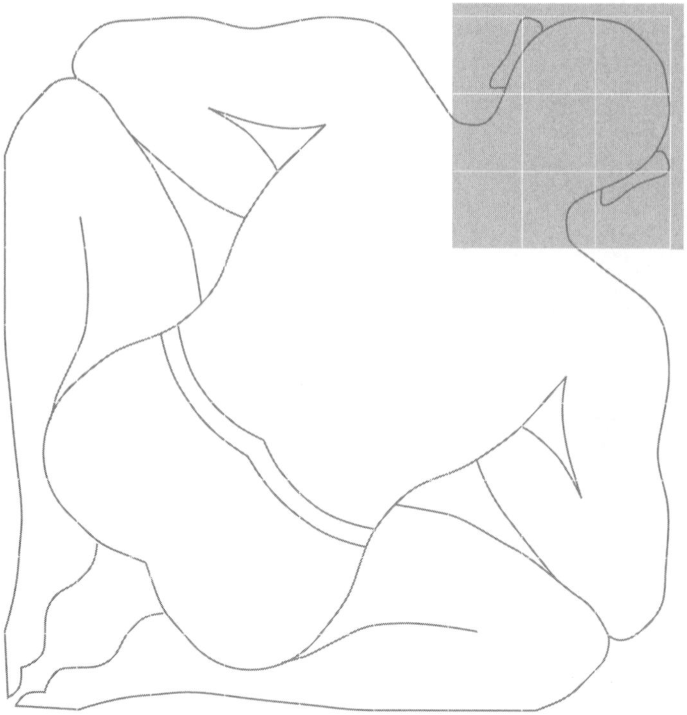

Vāstu Training

No treatise on any vidyā was ever intended to be used autodidactically. Each text was written with the assumption that it would be read and studied under the guidance of a guru who would explain it to the student. The Sanskrit word *guru* means "heavy," and real gurus are true "heavyweights." Vāstu gurus are men and women who have actualized the vidyā within themselves, and the vidyā herself speaks through them. Books may transmit facts relating to Vāstu, but only a *sthapati*, a "master builder" who has received the needed energetic transmission from his or her own mentor, can transmit the Vāstu system to a student.

The principles presented in this book are time-tested and reliable. Like any set of overarching guidelines, the "rules of thumb" explained here will work much—but not all—of the time. To succeed at making your every pronouncement on a subject come true requires a *siddhi*, an extraordinary level of achievement that can ordinarily be obtained only by carefully following specific, stringent spiritual practices (*sādhanas*) supervised by an expert teacher who lives and breathes that vidyā. Only very rarely can one become a "master builder" without the personal guidance of such an adept.

Few of us are ever likely to be so aligned with the Vāstu Vidyā that we could make a prognostication like that given by an elderly farmer from the Nilgiri Hills of South India when he was brought into a certain Indian metropolis. One day, he was sitting inside, casually surveying the landscape visible through the window. A building caught his eye, and he asked, "Who owns that building?" Then, with pithy candor, he commented further, "I don't like the looks of it." When the farmer's companions told him that they didn't know the owner, the old man responded, "Whoever owns it is going to be in big trouble very soon." As it turns out, the building was owned by a prominent politician, who was arrested the very next day on charges of corruption.

Exceptionally precise assessments like this are, alas, the exception rather than the rule, for Vāstu can't explain every problem or failure in life, though this has not stopped people from trying to force it to do so. A friend of mine writes, "I still remember the incident 50 years ago when my father invited the then-doyen of Vāstu in [the South Indian state of] Kerala to our house. His visit came after calamities like the deaths of two of my brothers occurred, and the great expert advised my father that it was all because the portico in the house was 18 inches longer than what Vāstu Śāstra would approve! What an absurd misuse of Vāstu! Yet I think such superstitions were fostered by our ancients to instill the fear of God into the professionals so that they took the utmost care not to make any mistake in their work."

There is much more to Vāstu than mere superstition, of course, but to lay the blame of tragedy on a minor architectural detail is a perversion of Vāstu's wisdom. Even when a Vāstu principle seems to foretell calamity, we shouldn't put too much stock in that prophecy unless other principles reinforce it with a clear indication of confluence. You can usually trust the pronouncements of a "master builder," should you be fortunate enough to locate one, but it's wise to evaluate even that advice through the reactions of your own breathing, heart, common sense, gut, and rational mind.

Expert practitioners of Vāstu are few in number, and fewer still are the world's true Vāstu gurus. Until one comes your way, you will need to learn how to access your own Vāstu intelligence if you want to make good use of Vāstu's principles to define and arrange your spaces. Once you've gained a basic introduction to Vāstu, you'll have sufficient guidance for your personal experience as you experiment with arranging and defining space on your own. The knowledge and practical experience you gain from this book should at least assist you in creating your own "good spaces," and should enable you to gauge the skill of potential Vāstu consultants, and to assess the advice they offer.

Cleaning House

You'll get better results at connecting with the Vāstu Vidyā if you first invest a little time putting your physical "home" in order. Most of us, when we expect guests, will tidy up before they arrive, so that we can welcome them into a clean house. When you invite the Vāstu Vidyā into your bodily abode, you ought to do some cleansing as well. An unpolluted physiological space makes your senses more balanced, acute, and subtle, and causes your breathing, gut, heart, and mind to become more reliable as indicators of Vāstu aplomb.

You need not be fanatical in your pursuit of purity; a little wholesomeness goes a long way. If you eat modestly, exercise regularly, eliminate addictions, and get the right amount of good, sound sleep—

all at the right time—the effects of your space on your physical and mental condition are likely to become more palpable. Cleansing yourself of accumulated toxins in your body that make you more prone to illness can improve your ability to think clearly. Breathing exercises and yoga postures (preferably learned from a capable local instructor rather than from a book) help to remove grime from the ethereal inner vessels in which your prāṇa moves. Your every prayer and meditation further helps to purify your mind.

A good way to keep your mental house neat and tidy is to adhere to the yogic principles of life known as the *yamas* and *niyamas*. The *yamas* prescribe restraint from detrimental actions; the *niyamas* stipulate the performance of meritorious acts. The sage Patanjali, in his *Yoga Sūtras*, listed five of each.

The *yamas* are:
Nonviolence (*ahiṁsā*)
Honesty, Truthfulness (*satya*)
Non-stealing (*asteya*)
Control of the senses (*brahmacarya*)
Non-covetousness (*aparigraha*)

The *niyamas* are:
Purity (*śauca*)
Contentment (*santoṣa*)
Austerity (*tapas*)
Study of the Self (*svādhyāya*)
Surrender to the Supreme (*īśvara praṇidhāna*)

You may not be able to perfectly follow the behaviors mandated by these precepts, which are elucidated in commentaries on the *Yoga Sūtras of Patanjali* and the *Haṭha Yoga Pradīpikā*, but if you accept these as goals and try sincerely to adhere to them with as much integrity and devotion as possible, you'll find it progressively easier to open yourself to the Vāstu Vidyā.

Exercise Three: The Body Container

Yoga is all about "skill in action," about ensuring prāṇa's healthy circulation and bringing intelligence into space. Bring more consciousness into the world inside your skin, and you automatically promote both prāṇa's flow and the mind's calm.

One way to develop inner awareness is to lie on the floor on your side—your right side, if possible. Lie there comfortably, breathing as deeply, slowly, and regularly as you can; then, slowly, with movements as minimal as you can manage, turn onto your back. It should take you several minutes to do so. As you change positions, bring your attention to bear on the movements of the fluids within the many compartments of your organism, focusing in particular on the abdomen, the thorax, and the head. Feel the sensations generated by the motion of the musculoskeletal system, the bodily framework that creates the wall of your "container"; notice the shifts caused by the movement of the prāṇa that energizes you; and by the various liquids and solids moving within you as your compartments "roll." Try to develop a sensitivity to the differences in each of these movements.

Once you're on your back, continue onward until you've switched positions to rest on your left side. Remain there for a few moments, to allow your fluids to come to rest, and your prāṇa to become calm, then repeat the whole process in the opposite direction. Does the left-to-right transition differ from that of right-to-left? If so, how?

Āyurveda

Understanding a bit about Āyurveda will make it easier for you to get a feel for your internal spaces, and how they can be affected by the spaces of the external world. Take for example the Ayurvedic precept that "like increases like." Lie in warm sunlight and you become warm; go out coatless on a winter's night and you'll get cold. Eat fatty foods, and your body will tend to accumulate fat; follow a fasting regimen, and you'll tend to lose weight.

There are, of course, always exceptions. Go too far in the direction of one polarity, and you'll find its opposite waiting for you at the other end. Sunbathe too long and you'll burn, which will make you feel cold as your skin temporarily loses its ability to regulate temperature. Jump into an icy pond, and when you promptly jump back out again, you'll quickly warm up, as your body reacts to the extremity of the cold. Fast too often, and too frequently, while binging in between, and you'll gain weight that will be very difficult to remove.

Most of the time, though, the qualities of your environment will stimulate similar qualities within you. Living in an arid climate, or in a house whose heating system dries out the air, will cause your body to dry out. Torrid locales and houses where the thermostats are kept too high will heat up the body. Humid climes and damp houses will enhance the body's sogginess.

Ordinarily, stimulating one quality will stimulate other qualities that are linked to it. The number of potential linkages is theoretically limitless, but practically speaking, three patterns of qualities serve to describe most any bodily physiological situation. These three patterns and their salient attributes are:

The Dry Pattern — dry, cold, light, unstable, clear, rough, subtle

The Hot Pattern — oily, hot, intense, light, fluid, liquid

The Heavy Pattern — oily, cold, heavy, stable, viscid, smooth, soft

These three patterns encompass the world of possibilities contained within Āyurveda's Three Pairs of Opposites: Dry-Wet, Hot-Cold, Heavy-Light. Living organisms are perpetually obliged to modify themselves in response to variations in their environments, and these modifications only rarely stimulate homeostasis. More commonly, organisms react to their environments by leaning in the direction of a selected few attributes with which they are familiar. Any substance or action will tend to resonate with, and so enhance, the qualities of the pattern to which its own qualities are most similar, while decreasing those that are dissimilar.

These three patterns exist within the inner spaces of our bodies as three physiological tendencies, three predispositions of protoplasm that are known in Sanskrit as the *Tridoṣa*, or *Three Doṣas*. *Vāta* engenders the Dry Pattern, *pitta* the Hot Pattern, and *kapha* the Heavy Pattern. When empowered by diet and activities that strengthen their qualities, these patterns of attributes often behave as if they can act autonomously within the organism, directing the actions of our bodily processes, and ignoring our preferences.

Vāta, which is mainly related to the nervous system, controls all body movements. Kapha, which is concentrated in the musculoskeletal system, regulates body stability and all the sorts of lubrication that are needed to permit that system to function smoothly. Pitta, which appears primarily in the body's endocrine and enzymatic systems, determines the balance between anabolism and catabolism, dilation and contraction, action and inaction, movement and stability. Vāta, pitta, and kapha preserve physical and mental health when they exist in equilibrium, and when that equilibrium is lost, disease becomes likely.

Āyurveda: Constitution & Condition

*Your constitution (*prakṛti*) is your inborn pattern of doṣa predominance, fixed in your metabolism at the time of your conception. Your constitution strongly influences your condition (*vikṛti*), which is determined by all the factors that affect your doṣas.*

While knowing your constitution is very important in Āyurveda, in Vāstu it is often most important to know your current condition.

You can be sure that you have a substantial amount of vāta in you if you:

are quick to act, and expend your energies impulsively • are prone to varying levels of stamina, with your energy coming in spurts or bursts • enjoy intensity, and tend to seek out opportunities to over-stimulate yourself • have good short-term memory, but tend to forget things quickly • often prefer theory to practice • often have trouble falling asleep or staying asleep, but sometimes become so exhausted that you sleep as if dead • tend to feel both cold and pain more intensely than other people do • find it very difficult to tolerate loud noise • tend to feel fear or anxiety when first confronted with stressful situations • live an erratic life, finding it difficult to create a routine.

A substantial amount of pitta is evident if you:
are intense and hot, and tend to irritability • anger easily, but don't always lose your temper outwardly • carefully calculate each expenditure of your life energy (except when acting recklessly) • love both food and confrontation • can be unforgiving to those with whom you compete • have a sharp memory, particularly for insults and slights • have an acutely logical, intelligent mind • tend to become impatient with people who are slower or less focused than you • usually sleep well, except when you become obsessed with something • have strong willpower • are competitive in most everything you do.

A significant quantity of kapha is characterized if you:
enjoy excitement and stimulation, but don't crave them like your vāta and pitta friends do • are physically or intellectually slower than some other people, but are more resolute and regularly paced • are generally consistent and efficient, and naturally kind and considerate • are averse to needless change • tend to become complacent when all is going well, or stubborn when challenged • are prone to sentimentality • are heavy-boned • tend to use food as a means of emotional fulfillment • sleep soundly, and really enjoy sleeping • need time to consider things before deciding on a course of action, but once decided you stick with your decision.

Multiple factors—including climate, season, age, personal strength, mental state, and personal habits—influence how the power of the Three Doṣas waxes and wanes within us. Often, the greatest influence comes from the qualities of the substances we consume and the actions we perform, which enhance or attenuate the natural attributes of the doṣas. Everything you experience—a particular setting, the apparent movement of time, the foods you eat, your own actions and thoughts—increase the qualities of your being that are "like" them, that resemble them by trait, while they decrease "unlike" qualities. Live in a dry space long enough and the Dry Pattern of vāta will eventually increase sufficiently to throw the body out of balance. Become sufficiently hot, and the Hot Pattern of pitta will go ballistic. Wallow in humidity, and kapha's Heavy Pattern will swamp the others.

In the Ayurvedic context, *sukha* means good health, and *duḥkha*, ill health (its literal translation is "bad space"). No matter how attentive you may be, some portion of your space, internal or external, will occasionally "go bad," and when this happens, your doṣas, and then you, will go out of balance. You'll have to discover the cause of your imbalance—since all results have one or more causes—and attempt to find a remedy. If the remedy is appropriate, and appropriately applied, good space, and sukha, will soon be yours again.

Balance is health. Understanding how to apply different substances and actions to adjust our inner patterns is the recipe for balance. When performed judiciously, any interaction with any substance, or any activity, can be included in the recipe. Should you desire to use yoga as a remedy, you'll want to select a practice that will control vāta by grounding the body and consolidating prāṇa, or that will calm pitta by circulating and equalizing the pranic current, or that will activate kapha by lifting it in the body and separating it from the tissues.

Even space is a substance. Every space you move through, visit, or inhabit will influence your internal patterns, and your own physical and mental condition will tend to stamp itself on your surrounding space. Many people orient themselves and their possessions in ways that reflect what is going on inside them, which makes it sometimes possible to "read" the doṣas of the people in a household just by noting how they arrange their living areas.

You may find it difficult at first to discern these attributes, but as your senses become more sensitive, and as you become more familiar with your body and its responses to stimuli, you'll find your body informing you of how particular shapes, directions, and patterns—in addition to food and activities—are likely to affect your doṣas.

Most texts on Āyurveda (a few are listed in the bibliography) describe the Three Doṣas in greater detail, and provide details of which foods tend to enhance or reduce them. Even if you prefer not to change your diet initially, you can nurture your perceptivity substantially by reducing the load of toxins in your system. Fasting is one way to accomplish this; regularly consuming the Ayurvedic preparation known as *Triphala* is another. These two practices can be performed separately, or, for synergistic effect, in combination. (As with any food and dietary regimen, it is necessary to implement such procedures carefully, preferably under the supervision of a knowledgeable Ayurvedic practitioner or guide.)

Triphala

Triphala (literally, "three fruits") is a mixture of three unique Indian fruits. The preparation gradually and gently purifies and rejuvenates as it scrapes toxins from the body's tissues.

Often described as Āyurveda's panacea, Triphala can be used to wash hair and body in addition to its uses as a laxative, purgative, and emetic, as well as in enemata. Its decoction is useful as eye, nose, or ear drops, or for gargling.

Triphala is harmless, but it can sometimes mobilize stored toxins faster than a weakened system can process them. This may lead to a transient rash, as the body tries to expel toxins through the skin. If such a rash develops when you begin using Triphala, stop the Triphala immediately, let the rash disappear, then begin Triphala again, taking half the dose you had taken previously.

Triphala can be found in many herb or natural-food stores and is easily available by mail order.

The Five Elements

As your senses awaken and become keener, you will find yourself becoming yet more productively aligned with the unseen world, the interior world of spirit. This realignment develops in part from your awareness that your every thought alters your physiology, making you become precisely what you believe yourself to be. Beneficial habits encourage you to resonate with and nurture the "good," harmoniously altruistic aspects of your being, which will nourish your highest possibilities; bad habits feed the unhealthily contracted, selfish parts of you. You are what you eat, what you think, what you do; repetition and resonance create your reality for you. Knowing what's good and what's not so good for your own body, mind, and spirit enables you to make informed choices in all walks of your life, particularly with regard to how you arrange space.

The practice of Vāstu no longer demands complicated religious rituals, but it does continue to follow the Vedas in recommending simple acts of veneration to focus prāṇa and intention. When you can get your own prāṇa to focus and circulate well within you, you'll soon find a similar flow manifesting in your environs. If you keep up your practices long enough, they'll even start to perk up your neighbors.

As your prāṇa starts to align and resonate with the prāṇa of your environs, you'll find the world beginning to cooperate with you. Things will come to you just at the moment when you most require them; plans will automatically fall into place when planning is required; obstacles that arise will resolve themselves, or will submit to resolution with minimal serious effort. Interact mindfully, gently, and reverentially with the world, and watch the world become well-disposed toward you; try instead to tell the world what to do, and see it become ill-disposed and unfavorable in response to you.

Right thoughts and attitudes literally induce sukha, for "good space" is attracted to that person who approaches space with respect for the way it holds and directs prāṇa. One popular, nonsectarian approach toward encouraging space to foster sukha involves making offerings to the Five Great Elements (*pañca mahābhūta*)—Space, Air, Fire, Water, and Earth—which are the building blocks for everything that exists in the manifested universe, including the physical bodies of living beings.

The Five Great Elements express for us the basic states of material existence, for they are the most solid of the forms of matter that we humans can directly perceive (thoughts and emotions also possess a material reality, but the stuff of which they are made is too refined to be experienced as matter by our senses). These Elements are better termed the Five Great States of Material Existence, for Earth represents everything that is solid under normal conditions, Water represents the liquid state of all matter, and Air represents the gaseous state. Fire, the transformational principle, converts solids to liquids and liquids to gases—and vice versa. Space is the field from which matter manifests, the arena in which events occur.

The tradition of the science of breath evaluation known as *Svarodaya* assigns each of the Elements a shape, based on the shape of the vapor that one's breath leaves on a mirror when that Element is predominating within one's body. For example, Earth is said to be square, because your breath tends to cover the whole of the "flat ground" of the mirror when the Earth Element is most pronounced within you.

Water's shape is that of a crescent moon that is concave side up. Fire is triangular, the shape of flame; Air is oval. It's difficult to display Space, something that has no form, so a pattern of small dots, which conveys presence with negligible actual form, is regarded as reflecting Space.

The human body is made up of all Five Elements: The bones are basically Earthy, the blood, lymph, and other fluids Watery, the digestive juices Fiery, the nervous system Airy, and the vacant spaces in the body (e.g., the interiors of the lungs, heart, and intestines, and the ventricles of the brain) are composed chiefly of Space.

The Three Doṣas of Āyurveda themselves condense from the Five Great Elements. Vāta arises from Air and Space, pitta from Fire and Water, and kapha from Water and Earth. The doṣas, which are more substantial than prāṇa (they are denser, composed of matter that is thicker and heavier than prāṇa) but less substantial than the Five Elements, gravitate to the parts of the organism where their originating elements concentrate. The condition of the doṣas in a living organism

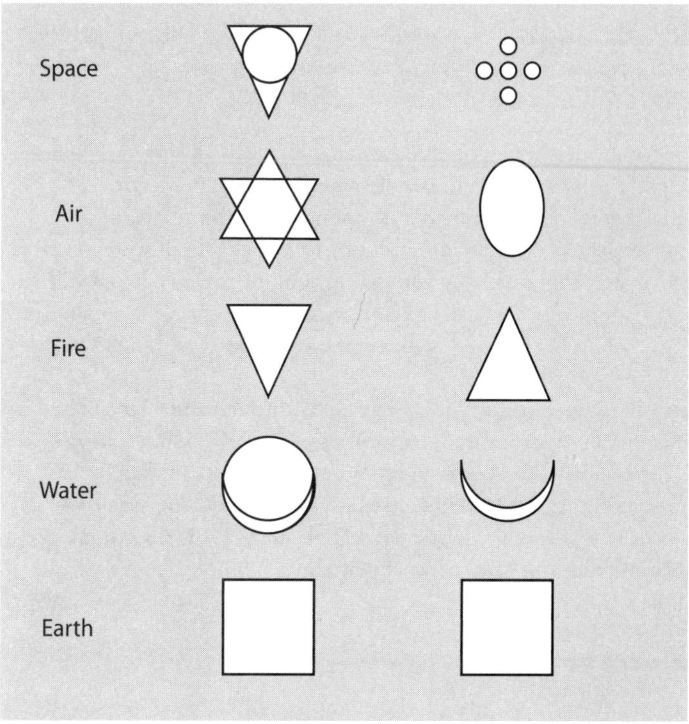

Symbols for the Five Great Elements

thus directly reflects the condition of the Elements in that body. Though it might seem counter intuitive that the doṣas, themselves made from the Elements, are nevertheless less substantial than them, this fact is precisely why the doṣas can move the Elements around—each doṣa is in a way a "joint" generated at the point where two of the Five Elements meet and must interact.

An amplified doṣa amplifies its parent elements in body and mind, and each of the Five Elements can nourish, balance, or disturb their doṣa progeny. Earth can provide physical and mental firmness and stability in life, or it can hinder and petrify. Water makes your life "juicy" or "gummy" depending upon whether your body and mind are filled with well-digested food or with toxins. Fire gives you clarity—a sharpness of mind and body that can be used to benefit the world or to manipulate it selfishly. Air may provide either vigor and exaltation, or exhaustion and emaciation, according to how it flows in your system. Space gives you either the bliss of an unobstructed body and the illumination of a silent mind, or it can generate the ache of hollowness, depending on your condition.

Worship Ritual

Eating well, detoxifying, and practicing yoga will all improve your inner space; as will creating a wholesome relationship with the Five Elements. Even the densest matter is to some degree sentient and open to some variety of sentient interaction. Develop a healthy rapport with the matter that makes up your world, and the material world will begin to respond automatically to your wants and needs, without your needing to actively petition for them. The world itself will then work to facilitate your sukha!

One way to develop such a relationship is through ritual reverence, which is known generically in Sanskrit as *pūjā*. Pūjā, which can also help us open our Vāstu eyes, is an important facet of traditional Indian culture; but the Five Elements are nonsectarian, and the ritual you create need not follow any particular sect, so long as it is sincere. Your personal invocation should fit your personal philosophy, your way of seeing the world (*darśana*).

One simple personal ritual that focuses on the Five Great Elements is known in Sanskrit as Pañcopacāra Pūjā, "the five-offering ritual." Before you begin this pūjā, clean the area where you plan to perform the rite, then purify your own body (and with it, your mind) by bathing. Next, put up a small altar in your chosen sacred spot. The altar need be nothing fancy, just a place to hold the implements you'll use in your rite. If possible, establish your altar where it can remain intact, and need not be taken down after each sitting.

For your sacraments, you'll require pure water, incense, some liquid or solid fragrance, a bell, a lamp or candle, one or more flowers, and a small amount of some sweet food. Other than the lamp, the offerings must always be fresh, never reused. Never smell or taste any offering before you offer it; to do so is as impolite as to take a bite from your guest's plate before serving it.

Remove your shoes, and sit facing east or northeast, if possible. If you can sit cross-legged on the floor, with or without a cushion, good; if not, then sit in a chair, or stand before your altar. Using your mind's eye, draw a circle around you, and visualize that circle getting filled with golden light. This act isolates you from the outside world, putting you into "worship space" and "worship time" for the duration of your ceremony. If you find this visualization difficult, use some more physical means, like a golden ribbon, to draw the circle.

Next, light some incense and offer some of its fragrance to each of the ten directions beginning with the direction that you're facing and continuing in a clockwise pattern through the points of the compass (in the sense of moving from east through southeast, south, southwest, west, northwest, north, and northeast) and then up and down, requesting as you do this that the directions be supportive to you.

Now, using your right hand, offer sandalwood paste or oil, or some other naturally fragrant paste or oil, to the Earth Element, requesting that it be pleased with you, within you, and around you, in your every action. Visualize as you do this some scene that symbolizes to you the ultimate nature of Earth, and salute that scene respectfully.

Many people performing this ritual wave each offering clockwise three or more times around some focus, like an image of a deity, saint, or other spiritually significant figure whom you are asking for help; similarly, you can make such movements in relation to a rock or crystal or other object that's meaningful to you. Some people ring the bell in their left hand to coincide with each offering, while others consider this to be optional.

After you've finished your homage to the Earth Element, offer the food, which stands for the Water Element, with the same ritual as you did Earth, visualizing something that (to you) stands for Water. Do the same with the lamp or candle, for Fire, and the incense, for Air. The flower is for Space.

Some aspirants make offerings in precisely the reverse order, beginning with the flower and ending with the sandalwood paste. Follow the method that works best for you; you may want to try out both before you decide on one, and you may even want to change from one direction to another from time to time (but not too often). Whichever progression you select, envision with each offering a current of purification entering your body, cleansing that element and its manifestations everywhere in your organism.

When you've completed your five offerings, offer a prayer that all will be well for all sentient beings and bow to nature and her amazing bounty. Then consume a little of the food and water, sniff the incense and the flower, apply some of the paste or oil, and stare for a few moments at the tip of the flame or lamp. Your body and mind thereby imbibe purified versions of the Five Elements that will help purify protoplasm and philosophy alike.

Bow to the Five Great Elements, arise from your seat, then leave your circle. With this, your ritual is complete.

Getting to Know the Five Elements

The Five Elements described within Vāstu, Āyurveda, and Jyotiṣa are not elements in the periodic table sense (like lithium, beryllium, or boron), nor do they correlate perfectly with the Five Elements of Chinese medicine—though correlations can be drawn. Rather, they provide one system of correspondences through which the many vidyās can communicate with one another. Fire is Fire, wherever it appears; it is the architect, and archetype, of transformation in any vidyā. What is Fire in Jyotiṣa (Mars) is also Fire in Āyurveda (pitta and tejas) and in Vāstu (the southeast direction). To work with any one of these Fiery correlates is to influence them all, and we can use the forms of the Five Elements from one vidyā in the context of another vidyā, if need be.

As embodied beings, we cannot ever entirely escape the Five Elements; we are born from them and live within them; they act on us come what may, even if we refuse to acknowledge and relate to them openly. By "seeing" the Five Elements, bringing them into our personal states of awareness and encouraging them to orient themselves pleasingly to the boundaries we establish, we make explicit their implicit impact on us, which permits us to evaluate and regulate that impact, and encourage the Elements to cooperate with us.

To "see" the Five Elements, you'll need to get to know them, to get a feel for their energies. You can get a feel for Earth by going rock climbing, or walking barefoot on the grass in the park. Aligning your awareness with that of Earth will allow the stability and weightiness of the terrain to "ground" you, to make you more stable and substantial.

You can get to know Water better by permitting its energy to flow through you when you visit a waterfall, "moon bathe" under the full moon, or meditate on a river current. Good ways to expose yourself to Air include wind-bathing in a gentle breeze, enjoying a massage, and traveling skyward in a plane or balloon. Gazing at the stars in the sky, chanting, singing, and listening to uplifting music are all ways to access Space.

India's seers of old worshipped Fire, the transformational element, in order to gain access to its power to transmute. You can do something similar by staring at the rising sun or the flame of a candle or oil lamp, by building fires and meditating on them, or by performing yogic Sun Salutations.

A fine way to get to know all Five Elements is to treat yourself to a massage with warm fragrant oil. The fragrance and heaviness of the oil are Earthy, the liquid fluidity of the oil is Watery, the warmth is Fiery, and the gentle movements are Airy. And, by exalting your

Earth

Water

Fire

Air

Space

tissues, a well-rendered massage enhances the beneficial qualities of the Space that you occupy, inner and outer.

Gaining a feel for the Five Great Elements makes it easier for you to open your "Vāstu eyes," to see how best to organize your life spaces in concinnity-enhancing ways. Vāstu eyes are akin to a gardener's eyes: They see life and its potential for growth. Not that long ago, when the average person lived on a farm, surrounded by open space, plants, and animals, it was much easier to develop this Vāstu sight. It's far more difficult to get a feel for the flow of prāṇa when our exposure to nature is limited to specimen animals held in detention in zoos and specimen plants on exhibit in zoo-like parks.

As you get more comfortable in your relationship with the Five Elements, you'll find it easier to "see" how the principles of Vāstu relate to those elements, and to the world they create. You'll also find it easier to see the Elements when you look out on the world.

Exercise Four: Messages from the Elements

Each morning, when you first leave your residence, note the first thing you see that reminds you most viscerally of one of the Five Elements. The street in front of you is Earthy, for example, but it probably doesn't change its features very often. Should you find that a great heap of sand has been dumped in it one morning, however, that would be a noteworthily Earthy kind of sight.

Or take Air: It's everywhere, but if a

gale is blowing when you walk outside, or a runaway kite happens to pass right in front of your nose, or a histrionic cloud scuds low along the horizon, then Air is speaking to you that morning.

Once you have your "vision" for the morning, be on the lookout for further demonstrations of that Element during the day. On a Fire day, you may find yourself noticing Fire pretty much everywhere you look: Someone burning leaves in one yard, brilliant sunlight flashing off a burnished copper panel on a downtown building, bright red speedsters passing you on the road.

Your Vāstu study is your Rosetta Stone to help you interpret the messages that the Five Elements are continually strewing in your path. As your rapport with the Elements grows, you should find yourself in some interesting conversations with them.

Become comfortable with the Five Great Elements, and they will make you comfortable with them, willingly arranging themselves into "good" spaces. Align your home and office well, and the Five Elements will be able to cooperate with you more easily. Well-organized spaces generate harmonious states around themselves, benefiting those who live in them, and those who live nearby. Build a Vāstu-friendly building, and you encourage a balanced body to develop within it, and a healthy neighborhood to develop around this locus of harmony.

Remain relaxed while alert if you want the world to become your sukha-facilitator. Never let anyone convince you that your life is in danger if you do not immediately close that southern-facing entrance to your house (as some Vāstu "experts" sometimes recommend), or fail to meticulously readjust each dimension of each room according to some Vāstu calculation. Transform your environment as you are able to do so, as your range of constraints permits, and be assured that each judicious transformation will augment your sukha. As sukha amasses, so will a momentum in your life that will promote the healthy flow of prāṇa, encourage cooperation with your environment, and further enhance your sukha.

Vāstu is all about the quest for "good space" in life, and sukha is all about ease. Every time that we acknowledge the divinity and influence of the natural world, salute the vibrancy of our connections with nature, and celebrate our uniqueness—by using beloved possessions selected and placed with a judicious eye to define that external space—we are living the Vāstu life. As we study Vāstu's details, we are wise to continually keep the bigger picture solidly in mind: the well-decorated rooms, the benign lines of the facades, the judiciously proportioned edifices of architectural music embodied in stone, brick, and wood—graceful structures that please inhabitants and onlookers alike, harmonized spaces that proffer sukha to all comers.

Conscious Space

Vāstu encourages us to view nature from the perspective of Space, the field from which everything arises, within which everything interacts, and into which everything dissolves. All too often our lives pass at a speed that promotes an awareness of time, yet a neglect of space; when giving directions, for instance, how often do we mention how far a destination is in terms of how long it will take to reach, rather than how distant it is in space? Space is easy to ignore, for it seems "empty." Like each atom, our universe is itself mainly "empty" space, a vast vista of apparent barrenness punctuated sporadically by matter. Quantum mechanics has taught us, though, that "empty" space is really permeated by a "vacuum energy" that whelps numberless virtual particles each second. We call them "virtual" because most of these dance into and out of existence in a blink, but some linger long enough to gain residence in our world: jots of real matter materializing in endless imitation of that original genesis that brought about the cosmos.

Space (in Sanskrit, *ākāśa*) both hosts and gives birth to particles, and to the structures made from them. Space-time gets "bent" by gravity, but responds in kind by serving as a matrix that prevents gravity from collapsing the universe entirely. Some researchers term Space, *quintessence* (Greek for "fifth element"). The ancient Greeks believed the universe to be built out of earth, water, air, and fire, plus quintessence, an ephemeral stuff that kept the heavenly bodies from tumbling towards the center of what they envisioned as a celestial sphere. Quintessence is regarded today as a "dynamic quantum field, not unlike an electrical or magnetic field, that gravitationally repels. … Quintessence interacts with matter and evolves with time."*

* Jeremiah P. Ostriker & Paul J. Steinhardt, *The Quintessential Universe*, p. 47

Science and the Akashic Field, Professor Ervin Laszlo's thought-provoking book on the subject of the relationship between *ākāśa* and the quantum field, details these concepts of how Space "interacts with matter and evolves with time." Neither empty nor inert, Space is itself a form of matter, albeit matter that is rather too subtle for most of us protoplasmic beings to perceive or interact with palpably. This modern concept of Space as an interacting and evolving field that can "learn," structured by what occupies it as it simultaneously structures its inhabiting objects, forces, and beings, does in fact closely resemble India's ancient concept of ākāśa. Ākāśa, though, is a richer concept, for it proposes that Reality shines through Space's gossamer fabric—the word *ākāśa* comes from a Sanskrit root meaning "to shine"—in the form of awareness.

In a very fundamental sense, ākāśa *is* Vāstu; or, more precisely, Vāstu *is* ākāśa. Vāstu is nothing more and nothing less than the evaluation of the attributes of a particular location, and the adding or subtracting of characteristics to create desired attributes in that location. What we must always remember is that Space is *alive*. Like the other four Elements, it carries prāṇa, and responds to prāṇa; and where there is prāṇa, there is awareness. The awareness that belongs to ākāśa, the awareness that has been added to and resides within ākāśa, and the awareness that we contribute (consciously or otherwise) to ākāśa is far more subtle than is day-to-day human waking consciousness—which means that this awareness can affect us far more easily, and pervasively, than we can easily imagine.

Akashic Confoundment

A little familiarity with Sanskrit can be a dangerous thing, as I found to my dismay one afternoon a few years ago as I flew from the U.K. to the U.S. As I leafed through a copy of the usually reliable International Herald Tribune, an article about Akashic Books, a new publisher in New York City, caught my eye. The writer was kind enough to explain parenthetically that "akashic" means "giant library"—a definition that caused me to choke on my in-flight snack.

The origin of this particular (faux) meaning is clear. The nature of ākāśa is such that every event that happens in a particular location leaves its traces on the ākāśa of that location.

Anyone whose perception is adequately subtle can, by scanning these traces, identify any salient events that have occurred there. Some decades ago, the theosophists got the bright idea of referring to these informative traces collectively as the "akashic records"—and, given the modern concept that all decent records will be kept in a suitable building erected just for that purpose, someone then got the idea that the "place" where these records were stored must be some sort of library—instead of in their real location: the fabric of Space itself. "Akashic" thus became equated with "giant library," and one ought not be surprised if all manner of "cognoscenti" have begun to use that word in just this—exceedingly wrong—way...

Vāstu Awareness

Our contemporary scientific paradigm recognizes as "existing" only the world of matter. The traditional Indian paradigm instead sees the grossly material sphere as merely the densest among a broad range of perpetually interacting domains of existence, at the core of which sits pure, unalloyed consciousness, free of material substance, untainted by any qualification.

The most fundamental difference between the sciences of East and West is this: Modern science avers that consciousness somehow arose spontaneously from matter, and ancient science asserts that consciousness pre-existed matter, that matter in all its forms derives from consciousness. In this view, consciousness is a singular, unqualified Reality that creates matter, underlies it, weaves it together. Matter cannot exert any influence on this One Reality, for there is nothing material to it that can be manipulated. According to this paradigm, everything that exists other than Unqualified Consciousness, including even the most abstruse thought of the finest mind, is material, and can be influenced, maneuvered, controlled.

All matter thus possesses a certain sort of life, and life thus extends from the infinitesimal units that make up individual atoms to the colossal galactic clusters located in the distant reaches of the cosmos. Consciousness drives stellar and terrestrial evolution alike, striving ever to project itself more effectively through material vehicles. Plants express life and consciousness more effectively than do minerals, and animals are in this regard superior to plants, but the human being houses and channels consciousness more effectively than any other material platform evolved thus far. Generations of Vāstu experts have taught that even the most miniscule among material particles enjoys at least a tiny dollop of consciousness.

The Five Elements can learn to respond to you because they are themselves faintly conscious, and display a small sliver of the universal drive to express awareness. As progressively denser embodiments of the Ultimate Reality of Absolute Awareness, the Five Elements represent the extension of the light of consciousness into the shadowy corners of the ponderously heavy, slow-to-change physical world. On our Earth, the awareness that the Elements harbor within themselves remains mostly dormant until protoplasmic beings extend their consciousness into those Elements, to "awaken" them.

Vāstu is a way of awakening the awareness possessed by the Five Elements within a well-defined region, to create a healthy, cooperative relationship with them on the basis of this Unitary Consciousness that all energy and matter share. When we look at a space, we need to look right down its core, to its animating Indwelling Spirit. It is this Spirit—pervasive in all the spaces we inhabit and experience—that mediates both your relationship with the world and the world's responses to you. The Five Elements, the Three Doṣas, prāṇa—everything in the cosmos—is as alive as we are, thanks to this Underlying Oneness. We humans may be "differently skilled" than other beings in our enhanced abilities to express ourselves, and to externalize our awareness, but at base, we, like every other created structure in our universe, arise from, exist in, and return to Pure Awareness.

The Three Guṇas

Like every other vidyā, Vāstu studies what is called *guṇa dharma* ("innate characteristics"); it presents an evaluation of the *guṇas* (characteristics) of the varied substances and actions in the world, and the infinity of effects that these qualities instigate when they interact with one another and with the internal worlds of living organisms. Pure consciousness may be free of all attributes, but in our world, awareness is conditioned by a host of traits. The most fundamental of the many qualities that individualized consciousness displays are the Three Guṇas: *sattva* (equilibrium), *rajas* (activity), and *tamas* (inertia).

Sattva is the subjective consciousness that we use to model, illuminate, and ponder over our environments. Sattva is said to be the progenitor of the thinking mind and the ten senses—the five of perception and the five of action. We take in from the world information and nourishment through the senses of perception (hearing, touch, sight, taste, and smell), and use the senses of action (symbolized by tongue, hands, feet, genital organ, and anus) for communication, manipulation, locomotion, creation, and elimination (respectively).

Rajas is active consciousness, awareness that is always on the move, searching for something—a body, a mind, a unit of existence—with which to associate itself. *Tamas* is the expression of consciousness veiled in materiality that evolves into the five subtle objects that our senses can detect: sound, touch, form, taste, and smell. These subtle sense objects then evolve directly into the Five Elements themselves.

The Three Guṇas act, as do the Three Doṣas, by mutual suppression: When one becomes particularly prominent, it temporarily suppresses the functioning of the others, driven as it is to express itself more substantially. When sattva is working well within you, your mind perceives situations accurately, and responds to them appropriately without the overreaction of rajas or the confusion of tamas. A rajas-dominated mind eternally craves new and different relationships, and is ever ready to make changes even when change is inappropriate. A tamas-blanketed mind sees the world in terms of objects to be doggedly gripped, and resists change even when change is essential.

Every substance and each action promotes one or more of these Three Guṇas. To take television as a "for instance," a documentary on lotus flowers is likely to promote sattva in the awareness of its watcher due to a clear confluence of sattvic factors, since, among flowers—which are substantially sattvic to begin with—lotuses are particularly so. To view lotuses, in a pond or on screen, is to take some of their sattva into your consciousness. Documentaries are characteristically informative (a sattva trait), and a lotus biopic is likely to echo the serenity of its subject in sattvic form, with thoughtful editing and a quietly informative tone.

If, instead of lotuses, you elect to watch loud, quick-moving, stimulating music videos, they will deliver some of their rajas to you. Watch them long enough, and that rajas will have you bouncing around the house, screaming their songs at your family members. Reruns of tired, formulaic old sitcoms will ratchet up your tamas, making you want to do no more than lie inertly on the sofa watching the tube and drinking beer until you fall asleep (sleep being a very tamas-instigated and tamas-promoting activity).

The Three Guṇas apply to everything in your space. Any person, place, thing, or activity that interacts with your sense organs will increase some combination of sattva, rajas, or tamas within you. We need all of the Three Guṇas to manifest in the proper quantity at the proper moment, which means that each space in your house, and everything in it, should promote the guṇa that belongs there. For example, your bedroom should modestly encourage tamas, because tamas makes sleep possible. Not enough tamas, and you won't be able to get to sleep; too much tamas, and you'll never get out of bed.

Your game room should support rajas, to encourage activity; let rajas get out of hand, though, and your game-playing will develop its own momentum. It will become an end in itself, and you'll wind up spending hours maniacally trying to master the latest video game.

Every space should ultimately promote sattva, because sattva harmonizes, and harmony points us in the direction of sukha. In your house, your meditation space should be the most sattvic space of all. It should be your "sattva storehouse," the space you can return to whenever you need a quick sattva "hit."

As we will see in a later section, certain regions of your space will show a predilection to enhance one or another of the guṇas—relatively speaking, of course, because everything about the Three Guṇas is qualified, relative, relational. Relative to sattva, all of the Five Great Elements are tamasic, full of ignorance, opaque to awareness. And compared to the others, Earth's stability gives it the greatest measure of tamas among the quintet. Water, Fire, and Air, in that order, display decreasing tamas and increasing rajas. Space is the most sattvic element, the most conducive for equilibrium.

But all is relative, and some principles of Vāstu are paradoxical. From one Vāstu perspective, Space, though sattvic, also promotes tamas substantially, by being less receptive to our efforts to change it than are the other Five Elements. Air is rajasic, while Fire is sattvic and rajasic. Water and Earth, though they foster tamas by their density and heaviness, are easier than the other Elements for us to control, shape, direct, and stabilize; and so, when harmoniously arrayed, these two Elements encourage that harmony to persist, thus promoting sattva.

Ahaṁkāra

The perspective from which you view your situation, at any one moment, is governed by your innate "I-creating" power, which is known in Sanskrit as *ahaṁkāra*. From its genesis out of prakṛti, ahaṁkāra develops into the Three Guṇas, the mind and senses, and finally into the Five Great Elements. Ahaṁkāra generates "I-ness," the sense of the individual, separate self in all created things, particularly in living organisms. By aggregating all the building blocks that form you, including the Five Great Elements, the sense organs, and the mind, ahaṁkāra gives birth to the "you" that you know as you. It preserves your life by ceaselessly identifying, as long as you live, with each of the trillions of cells in your body, reminding them incessantly of their status as sub-units of the great confederacy that is you. When ahaṁkāra fails to perform her task properly, your immunity plummets in tandem with your self-confidence, and you fall prey to disease or decline. When finally ahaṁkāra loses the plot entirely, you die.

Ahaṁkāra also brings perception, and thus experience of the world, into being. Every created thing, from atom to galaxy, has its own ahaṁkāra, its own "force of cohesion" that causes it to stick together. Relationships between things, including especially the relationship between items in a space, are basically relationships between the ahaṁkāras of those things.

Exercise Five: Prāṇa, Tejas, Ojas

Your vision provides you a useful tool with which to promote the functioning of your personal ahaṁkāra, which will enhance your health and sharpen your Vāstu eyes. Begin by performing *trāṭaka*: Put a candle or a lamp burning *ghee* (clarified butter) or oil at the height of your head and at arm's length. Pay attention to your breathing as you sit with your eyes closed, keeping your back comfortably straight and your body at rest. When you open your eyes, focus your gaze on the tip of the flame, the point where it loses its color and form. Stare steadily at that point as long as it's comfortable to do so, or until tears come to your eyes. As thoughts arise to interrupt your concentration, sweep them gently but firmly from your field of awareness (any thoughts that are important will return, later).

After you close your eyes, return your attention to your breathing, and visualize yourself breathing out all your physical, mental, and emotional tightness and anxiety as you breathe in the gentle golden light of the flame you have just been observing. Let that light permeate every part of you. Let your awareness follow your in-breath as you focus your mind to distinguish between the current of your breath and the current of the energy that it brings into you. The energy that breath carries (which is distinct from the breath itself) is prāṇa.

Where prāṇa moves smoothly in your body and mind, encourage it to move with greater vigor. Using the force of your awareness—and the power created by the current of your calm, slow, deep breathing—redirect extra prāṇa to those areas within you where the energy feels obstructed. Those are the areas that need prāṇa most, at that moment. Tend your prāṇa well, and you will nurture the healthy functioning of the power of self-identification within you.

Next, follow your prāṇa down into your cells. Prāṇa is the breath of life, the body's most refined representative of the Air Element. One of prāṇa's chief tasks is to enkindle the body's *tejas* (or *agni*), the flame of life, the body's most esteemed and subtlest representative of the Fire Element. The health-giving flame of tejas transforms everything we consume, transmuting it into our physical, mental, and spiritual selves.

Like prāṇa, tejas exists in each cell, and when you follow prāṇa down to the level of your cells, you can use it to breathe life into the fire manifested within you. As you do this, you'll find your life fire cooking along well in some tissues, and not at all well in others. Gently rebuild those of your fires that have died down, and as you do, watch each of your cells begin to glow, to radiate subtle warmth into your consciousness. Well-enkindled tejas enhances the ability of your force of "I-ness" to "see" what is right, and what wrong, within you.

As your tejas gets well-kindled, use it to cook up some *ojas*. Ojas, the body's superlative and most intelligent form of the Water Element, is the subtle glue that integrates body, mind, and spirit into a living individual. Ojas is a quasi-physical material that produces your aura, and governs the functioning of the immune system.

You can create ojas by envisioning your every cell being thinly coated with warm, liquid ghee (this should feel deeply satisfying in itself). Then, continue the visualization by layering a film of pure honey atop the ghee. The flame of your tejas will use these substances as fuel to generate a golden-yellow radiance that will suffuse your whole body as it emanates out into your surrounding space. Well-nourished ojas enables ahaṁkāra to glue you together well.

Remain in this state of well-integrated luminosity as long as you feel led to do so, then slowly open your eyes. Try, as you return to your everyday life, to extend the newly-enhanced sensitivity to prāṇa, tejas, and ojas into your awareness of the world.

Filling Space

Ahaṁkāra plays a defining role in space, time, and energy as well, and in Vāstu, these are as much substances as brick, balconies, and fabric are. Boundaries and contents "educate into I-ness" the space of a plot of land, a building, or a room by confining, defining, and filling it. Properly boundaried and furnished, a space begins to participate in, and ultimately to direct, its interactions and evolution.

Any space can be predominantly "filled" or predominantly "empty." "Filled" spaces characteristically reflect the attributes of the objects that occupy them, while "empty" spaces are defined more by the substances and shapes that enclose them. A filled space thus mainly reflects the self-identity coalesced by its contents, while an empty space reflects more of the self-identity created by its margins and partitions. Almost always, well-designed filled spaces emerge from well-demarcated empty spaces.

At any particular moment, for any particular configuration of energy, there is for every space an apt amount of detail, an appropriate set of attributes that make that space feel "right" for that time and place. Concinnity usually comes more readily to simple spaces structured into regular shapes and filled with simple objects, than to irregular spaces that are chock-a-block with bric-a-brac. Every space usually has at least a few "equations of suitability" that suit it and our sensibilities at the moment that we evaluate its possibilities.

Two questions you'll want to ask yourself when you have a space to design and adorn are:

What items should fill this space, and how should they be arranged?

What qualities should these items possess, to achieve the results desired?

Your answers to these two queries will commonly depend on your answer to this one:

How full should this space be, and how empty?

Develop a feel for a space's ideal extent of fullness or emptiness, and the items and qualities that might best fill it will readily make themselves known.

Exercise Six: Addition and Subtraction

Return to the room you used for your experiments in Exercise One, "Breath Awareness" (carrying with you a chocolate cake or other suitable bribe if that room happens to be in a friend's house).

Again obtain a base line for your evaluation by sitting quietly in the room, facing east if possible, and noting the effect that the room has on your prāṇa. Sit as long as you need to, until you're sure that you know what you're feeling.

Next, move any one piece of furniture out of the room. Sit again and, using your breath to get a feel for the room, note how it feels different. Is it a positive difference, or a negative one? If positive, remove another piece. Keep removing furniture, plants, and pets (if they are hanging about) until you can't remove anything more without the room feeling too "empty" to be comfortable.

As soon as you reach that point, start returning furniture to the room, one piece at a time, assessing the impact of each piece that you add, until the room is clearly too full to accommodate additional items comfortably. Note the difference between the minimum amount and the maximum amount of "fullness" that feels comfortable. This differential will vary from room to room; the better shaped the room, the bigger the differential, and the more liberty you'll have in your plans to adorn the room.

Try this experiment in several rooms—in your own home or in that of some generous friend—and note how different room shapes, sizes, and proportions influence this "differential fill potential."

Each article of furniture that you repositioned in this exercise has its own ahaṁkāra. Despite the fact that the ahaṁkāra of an "inanimate" object is only rarely as strong as that of a human (magical objects like genie-containing lamps and curse-toting monkey's paws excepted), items of furniture often share with humans, animals, and plants very specific preferences for rooms and neighbors. Rocking chairs, for example, are generally supremely adaptable; they enjoy a broad self-definition, and can fit in most anywhere. Recliners, however, are beasts with greater limitations, tamasic thrones that belong in front of home entertainment centers and similar omphali of leisure-time diversions. No recliner would be likely to feel at home in a workshop, a place of rajas, where it would loll like a beached whale, forcing all to detour around it. Put the right rocking chair in a workshop, though, and you have a powerful statement of how even the most diligent of us must take a break from time to time, or of how some tasks are best accomplished while gently rocking.

A thing's ahaṁkāra defines its personality by identifying with and collating its distinguishing characteristics. We gain perspective on the many ahaṁkāras (human and otherwise) in a room by invoking our faculty of discernment. The ability to discriminate, to judge, to perceive "rightness" and "wrongness," is an innate property of the cosmos that devolves, in appropriate conditions, into the little bundles of discriminating force that are ahaṁkāras. In Sanskrit, the term *mahat* describes the overarching power to discern that gives rise to ahaṁkāra. *Mahat* means "gigantic," which it is, indeed.

Mahat asks the fullness-emptiness question and also poses queries like, "What should be the proportion of detail to bareness in this space? How should what is present connect with non-presence? How should our space be filled, and with what?"

Using reasoning to move backwards from these concerns of fullness and emptiness, we discover a yet more fundamental inquiry:

What can materialize in this space, and how can it do so?

Some home spaces (like laundry rooms) are so specialized that they define and create themselves. Many other spaces in the home are, however, malleable enough to serve in more than one capacity. You, as overall creator of your home, bear the ultimate responsibility of discerning which of your available spaces are best for bedroom, library, study, playroom, or meditation room, according to the criteria you most want to satisfy.

As creator, your creative process is steered by the *Law of Karma* (the Law of Cause and Effect), which most of us know as Newton's Third Law of Motion: *For every action there is an equal and opposite reaction.* This principle of "as you sow, so shall you reap" ensures that the reaction produced by each creative act will limit every creative act that follows it by adding to the "relationship web" that binds all sentient beings together as co-creators of our reality. About the Law of Cause and Effect, Vimalananda liked to say, "Cause is effect concealed, and effect is cause revealed." Cause is in no way separate from effect; they are two time-divergent states of the same thing. Cause-seeds sprout and blossom into effect-flowers, which produce the fruits whose seeds will blossom into future effects.

Each space that is new for you is a singularity, a unique and (relatively speaking) blank tablet on which you can record personal statements. Each creative act is a limiting karma: Select one color, and additional hues are constrained by the necessity of complementing the first; invoke one shape, and future shapes are compelled to conform to your initial choice. Each of your subsequent actions as creator of your space will be governed, directly or indirectly, by reactions flowing from your initial creative impulse. So let that first impulse be a good one!

Before you build or move into a residence, your home is just a dream; as soon as you take control of it, your every subsequent act sets into motion consequences that limit and guide its developmental future, that concretize and finitize your dream. If you want your creation to proceed smoothly, you must have a clear idea of what you want to create well before you begin to create it. Keep your goal in sight, and your chances for actually reaching the objective improve dramatically. Even if you're speaking only with yourself, always express your intentions clearly, particularly when you initiate a new project. Your every thought, word, and deed is an action whose consequences will eventually reach you, according to the dictates of the Law of Karma.

Symphony in stone.

4 Expansion and Contraction

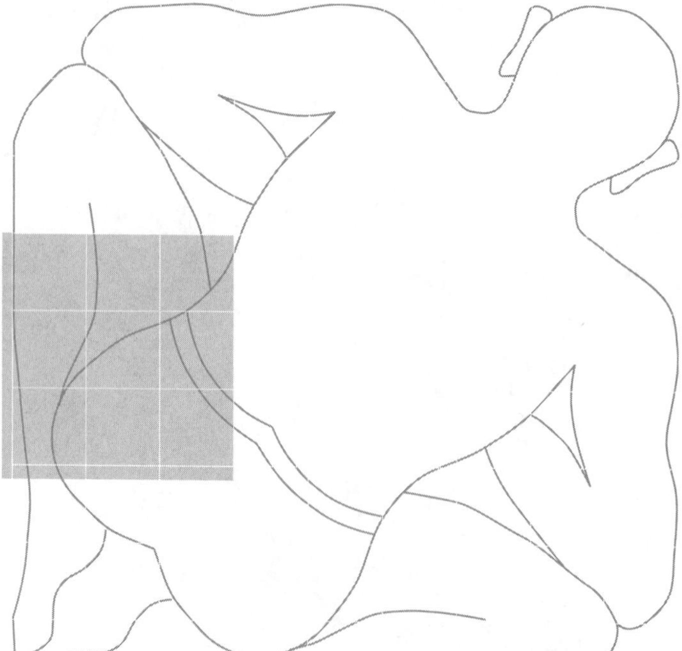

Sāṁkhya

Almost every Indian thinker has accepted the reality of the Law of Karma, but how precisely that Law should be interpreted has been a matter of great debate. Like Āyurveda, Jyotiṣa, and most other Vidyās, Vāstu considers the Law of Karma from the perspective of the *Sāṁkhya Darśana*. *Sāṁkhya* means "number," and the Sāṁkhya philosophy is composed of a number of *tattvas* (principles; literally, "thatnesses") which evolve from one another. The first and foremost tattva is the Total "Thatness" that is the Supreme Singularity, the One, transcendent consciousness beyond time, space, and causation; all other tattvas are mere permutations of this One Reality that remains even when the universe ceases to exist. *Darśana*, the Sanskrit word for "philosophy," literally means "seeing," and seeing is for humans a creative act of mutual interconnection: The way we see the world generates our world view, and our world view generates the way we see the world. The Vāstu system mostly adheres to the way that the Sāṁkhya philosophy sees the world, suggesting that students of Vāstu use the Sāṁkhya perspective to open our Vāstu eyes.

From Sāṁkhya's perspective, the universe is eternal and without beginning—it is changing continually, manifesting periodically and also periodically disappearing into unmanifestation, waxing and waning like the moon. While unmanifest, the universe exists as an indescribable Singularity, a single point without dimension, bereft of any type of trait, expressing nothing other than the One Reality of consciousness. The progressive evolution of the light of consciousness into the density of matter that is the process of cosmic creation begins with a sudden, unimaginably furious, initiating expansion that brings space, time, and causation (*karma*) into existence.

This "Big Bang" of the Sāṁkhya philosophy is remarkably similar to the "Big Bang" that modern physicists envision in their own cosmologies—to a point. Though modern physics assures us that the Singularity was obliterated in the creative expansion, Sāṁkhya assures us that the Absolute never ceases to exist. The created universe arises from the Absolute and dissolves into It again without disturbing It, in the same way that ocean waves swell and break without a lasting reminder in the underlying water that they were ever there. The Absolute, though, can only enjoy the play of manifested existence when It expresses itself through matter; the Absolute's craving to perceive Itself thus initiates Its expansion into being.

This yearning of the Absolute to experience Itself, the desire that initiated the outward projection, was our universe's founding karma; likewise, the desire to create something is the first step in any creative process, the act that guides all that follows as development unfolds. Desire is the foundation of both macrocosm and microcosm; it appears in every atom of creation and every cell of every living being—in each reflection in matter and form of the One that desired to experience Itself, and so brought *prakṛti* (nature) into being.

This desire is expressed in humans as the drive to create, and to procreate. When sexual yearning reaches its fruition in a human couple, they unite to conceive a child, an embodiment of their creativity, a microcosm that will (at least while still young) look up at them in awe and wonder, just as men and women of faith look up to the heavens that birthed them. When that primal desire is channeled into inventive vision, a person's primary motivation becomes the longing to create artifacts, and from his or her hands emerge works of art, the created forms that populate the territory of Vāstu's jurisdiction.

Life and Limitation

The creative explosion that created our "multiverse" was the first-ever Vāstu event, for it generated an apparent partition within a portion of what had been a Singularity of consciousness. The outward emanation was followed immediately by a desire of that which emerged to return to the source at the center. Each atom contains within it both a fragment of that Singular consciousness and a portion of that original emanation. Sāṁkhya uses the term *prakṛti* ("nature") to indicate that portion of the One Consciousness that comes to see itself as separate, and refers to the originating awareness which remembers that All is One, as *puruṣa*.

Prakṛti's intrinsic nature is to limit, finitize*. Until the moment of the "Big Bang," any cosmic configuration is conceivable; after that moment, limitations arise and become immutably fixed. Each individual human

*When we introduced these concepts above, we proceeded from Earth, the densest form of manifested prakṛti, to puruṣa, the most rarefied. They are, however, normally studied in the reverse sequence, corresponding to how they emerged and differentiated.

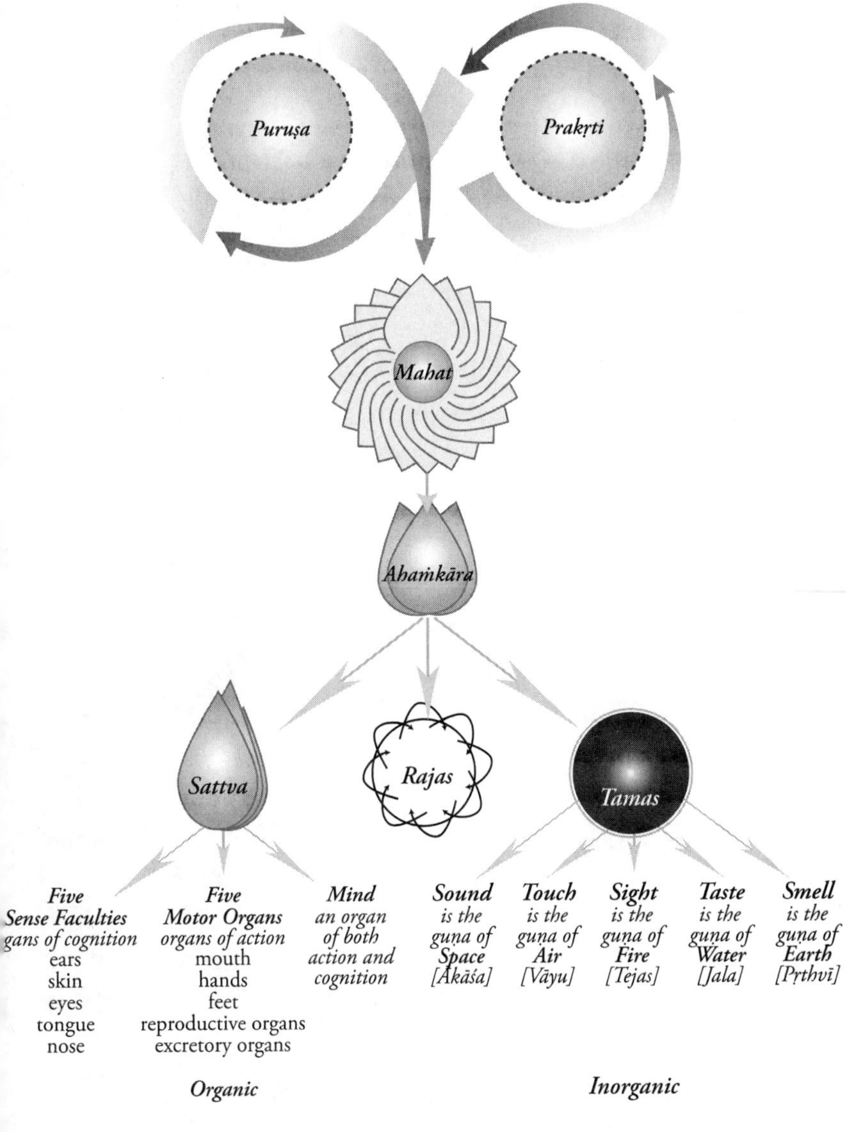
Puruṣa
Prakṛti
Mahat
Ahaṁkāra
Sattva
Rajas
Tamas
Five
Sense Faculties
gans of cognition
ears
skin
eyes
tongue
nose
Five
Motor Organs
organs of action
mouth
hands
feet
reproductive organs
excretory organs
Mind
an organ
of both
action and
cognition
Sound
is the
guṇa of
Space
[Ākāśa]
Touch
is the
guṇa of
Air
[Vāyu]
Sight
is the
guṇa of
Fire
[Tejas]
Taste
is the
guṇa of
Water
[Jala]
Smell
is the
guṇa of
Earth
[Pṛthvī]
Organic
Inorganic

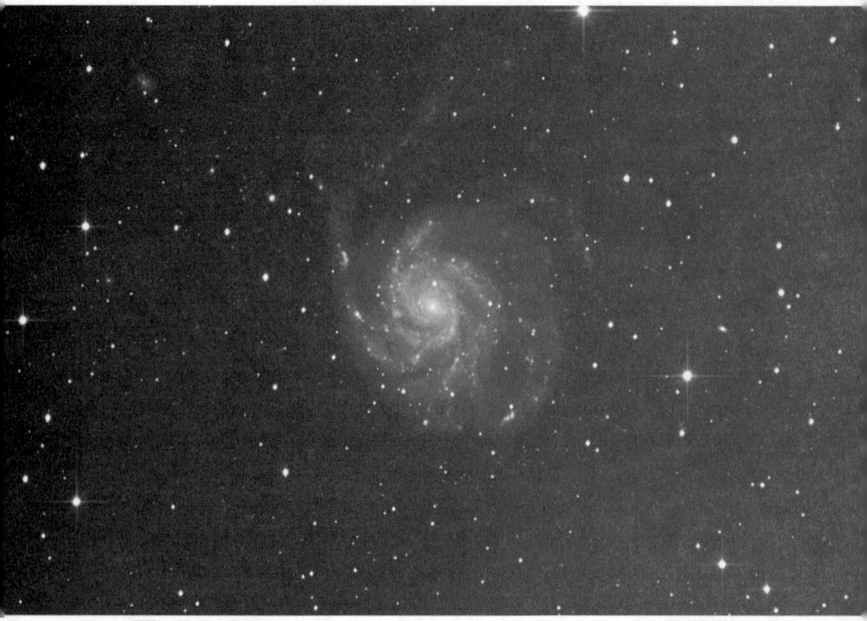

Waxing macrocosm

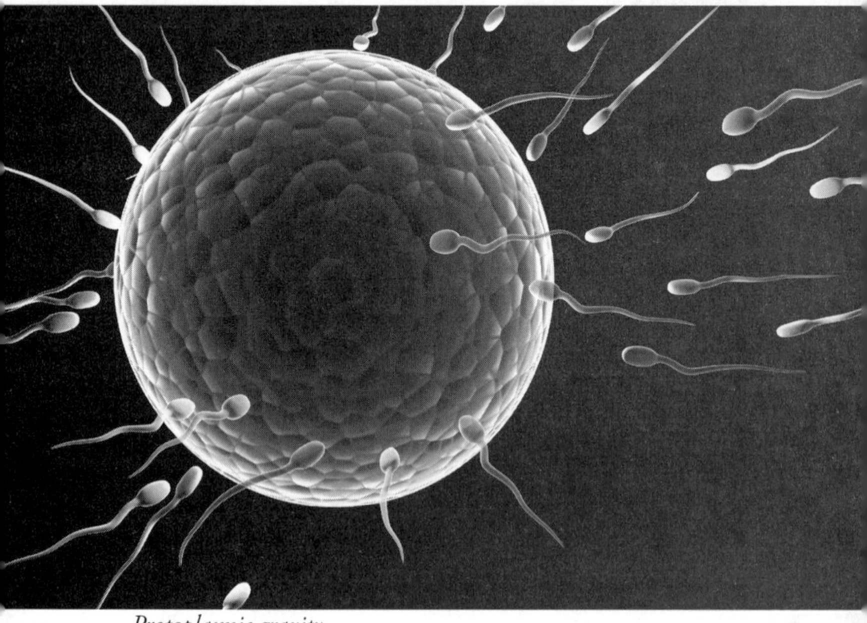

Protoplasmic gravity

begins as well from a singularity, from a zygote, a single cell that contains every potentiality of the emerging human. The Law of Microcosm and Macrocosm, which tells us that whatever appears in the external cosmos, in heaven and earth, appears as well in the internal human cosmos, assures us that creation unfolds for the human as it does for the universe. Like the outer universe, the zygote explosively expands into a physical form that grows and develops, then reaches a relatively stable plateau, and subsequently degenerates and dies.

Evolution is thus a paradoxical process: Even as the macrocosm projects outward to develop its billions of galaxies, limitations accumulate within it, circumscribing its potential for future development. Similarly, a baby's range of developmental possibilities contracts with each additional cell that the nascent form creates. The instant that sperm meets egg, the embryonic child gets dunked into the stream of time, space, and causation, a torrent of progressive differentiation that shapes its progress from then on. A mother can sense distinctiveness developing in her child's burgeoning personality even when the baby is still in the womb. After birth, this differentiation accelerates, with each influence on the child, and the child's own actions, creating equal and opposite reactions that combine to limit the individual's future options in life (at least until a being becomes sufficiently enlightened to be able to relate differently to the laws of karma and limitation).

As with the microcosm, so with its surrounding environment, for churches, houses, and parks develop just like children and cosmoses. An open space enjoys freedom of development until boundaries get applied to it and constraints appear within it. Each constraint contributes attributes to the space that it impounds, and these qualities help to define that space. By limiting certain characteristics of space, we develop form; circumscribe other attributes, and we determine color. In the macrocosm, prakṛti is the developing "child" that undergoes ever-increasing restriction as it develops. In Vāstu terms, we can think of prakṛti as the "residence" that the universe is creating for puruṣa.

Evolution

When we wish to use Vāstu to evaluate a space, we should begin at the beginning, at the great divide between being and nothingness, the point where limitlessness and limitation meet. The noted French playwright Alfred Jarry once defined God as "the tangential point between zero and infinity," a statement that evocatively conjures the relationship between puruṣa and prakṛti. We need to explore this relationship in all our spaces, trying always to ensure that we have established the right balance between the zero and infinity of color, of form and texture, of density and detail, thus allowing the tangential point of the Divine to exist happily within those spaces.

This ever-changing "right balance" between zero and infinity is as mutable as water, fire, or wind. None of life's puzzles have perfect solutions; all are conundrums that must be repeatedly re-calibrated into steadiness, coaxed back into cooperation each time the perpetual flux of our existence causes them to go awry. We have to be able to identify *duḥkha*, bad space; discover the causes of that duḥkha; determine a remedy for those causes; and be able to discern when that space has become good, and sukha has returned.

Too often people presume that they can live their lives only according to set formulas and can, through this boilerplate regimen, find happiness in any circumstance. Yet in fact all is negotiable, all relative. Our lives unfold with ease and grace when we commit to an ongoing realignment of self and space, preserving poise between unity and diversity, between profusion and absence, as they relate to the quality, substance, and action of both the inner and the outer world. We who seek sukha need to mirror the shifting balance between the emptiness of puruṣa and the fullness of prakṛti in our own lives by tailoring our spaces to who and what we are, and are becoming.

The *Vāstu Vidyā* requires that any "residence" (house or office, church or public place) always be regarded both from its own perspective and from the perspective of its "residue" (everything in its surroundings that it is not). When we begin our Vāstu analysis, we're interested in learning what sort of residence can emerge from the environment, the area that will act as its residue. Our first Vāstu question thus asks:

What can materialize in this space, and how can it do so?

What is it that can emerge from the nothing in this space, and how? Are we building a mansion or a mortuary? Do we want a home or a henhouse? Will this room become a bedroom, a study, or a playroom? What sort of mood shall the garden express? How you answer the initial question of intention will guide everything that happens after, just as the primary impact of the Big Bang was to serve as a cause for the next effect, creating an unending chain. Your response to the preliminary question will determine whether that maroon couch will continue to be welcome where it is now, or if it will have to find itself a new address.

Once you have yielded to the desire to create something, you'll need to grasp what it is that you've conceived, and what is to be left out of your conception—what is your *residence*, and what is its *residue*. If you've ever taken a drawing class, your instructor may have told you to draw an object not by focusing on the space it contains—its "positive" space—but rather by drawing the "negative" space around it, the space that envelops and encloses it. "Negative" here does not mean harmful; it's simply a technical word used to indicate what is left over—the *residue*—after lines have been used to enclose the "positive" space of the desired image—the *residence*.

After emerging from Oneness, prakṛti yearns to reunite with It. Prakṛti craves for reunion with the Ultimate, and that craving underpins everything that manifests from prakṛti—indeed, it spurs the self-awareness of those manifestations. Prakṛti's self-awareness permits her to view herself and to view the One as if they were discontinuous; Sāṁkhya calls this self-reflective (and Self-reflective) transcendent intelligence *mahat*.

Mahat, which is general and undifferentiated, evolves into the individualized self-awareness of *ahaṁkāra*. Ahaṁkāra (as explained in greater detail in Chapter Three) permits us self-definition, lets us demarcate ourselves as carpenters, soccer moms, Floridians, Zoroastrians, tennis players. Ahaṁkāra's self-identifying power permits us each to believe in our individuality.

In the Vāstu context, ahaṁkāra takes the mass that we put into a space and turns it into discrete objects. Ahaṁkāra directs us to ask, "What items should fill this space, and how should they be arranged?" Once we determine to build a family home instead of a bachelor pad, how do we position its rooms? Should our space encourage gregariousness or introspection? Shall we embrace rococo, or pursue a Zen-like austerity? Should the bedroom say, "Martha Stewart!" or "Mary Kay!" or "Madonna!"? Will it be a rock garden or a flower garden, overgrown or closely trimmed, wet or dry, light-filled or luxuriously shady?

Embodied life, says Sāṁkhya, is the functioning together as one unit, in one place at one time, of the Five Great Elements, the five subtle sense objects, the ten senses, the thinking mind, ahaṁkāra, and mahat (see Chapter Three for a more detailed explanation of these subjects). These are all galvanized into life by the action in the individual of cosmic consciousness (puruṣa) as it manifests within the field of matter (prakṛti).

Of the collection of "thatnesses" that Sāṁkhya identifies as necessary for embodied life, the five that stand out to our Vāstu eyes are the Five Great Elements, from which are generated the objects experienced by our five senses of perception. Any space that we take responsibility for cultivating should be enclosed in such a way that it becomes pleasant to all the senses, so that our very sense perceptions will promote healthy relationships between ourselves and these elements.

Though all five of these elements are essential to Vāstu analysis, Vāstu focuses most intently on the elements of Earth, which forms the material, tactile realm of our experience, and Space, the (to us) seemingly limitless three-dimensional field surrounding and underlying all material existence. Only Earth can partition Space into "residence" and "residue." The Earth Element, matter in its most solid form, is the ultimate outcome of prakṛti's initial movement away from puruṣa; Space, "matter" in its most rarefied form, offers prakṛti a path through which it can move in the direction of reuniting with puruṣa.

Earth and Space can only be understood by being "felt," which is why gardeners will probably pick up on Vāstu more readily than will the rest of the population. Astute gardeners nurture plants to thrive by positioning them in the best combination of shade and sunlight, at the right distance from one another, in the right company for maximum fruitfulness, and thereby show some "feel" for both Earth and Space. If you can cultivate a carrot, you can cultivate a cosmos, or a cottage.

Cottages being less sure of themselves, less self-actualizing than carrots (the ahaṁkāra of constructed entities being less strong than that of biological ones), you as Home Creator may occasionally lose track of what you are doing with the space you're trying to define. If you do, return to those key questions that Sāṁkhya taught us to ask, and your path will again become clear:

What can materialize in this space, and how can it do so?
How full should this space be, and how empty?
What items should fill this space, and how should they be arranged?
What qualities should these items possess, to achieve the results desired?

Marie

As I let facts and ideas sluice over me while writing this book, the Vāstu Vidyā gave me an excellent opportunity to ask and respond to these very questions one afternoon in South Florida, during a sojourn with my hostess there—let's call her Marie. Marie and I were discussing the effects of one's surroundings on one's well-being; she had asked me to tell her about my new book, and I was explaining to her, as we sat on her back porch not far from a stand of bamboo, about the nature of space.

A light rain began to fall as I explained to Marie that how we regulate and decorate our spaces can have a direct effect on our physical health: "There's a 'passive' effect, from the qualities of the space you create for yourself, and an 'active' effect, from the relationship you create with that space," I told her. "It has a lot to do with your own 'personal myth.' You're a nurse—have you ever asked patients to tell you their life stories?"

"All the time," replied Marie forcefully, warming to the subject, "and I've seen how the people who describe themselves and their conditions in terms of doom and gloom—'Oh, woe is me, how miserable I am'—are usually the people who don't heal. The people who can remember all the blessings they've had in their lives are more often the ones who get well. Not all of them, of course, but lots of them, and those of them who don't recover at least die in peace."

"So you would agree that being able to tell a fundamentally positive life story is a sign of—vitality, at the least. Changing your belief system changes your condition; improving your life story improves your life. An invalid has an 'in-valid' self-image, one that has lost its 'validity' and resulted in illness or infirmity. Ayurvedic doctors, Jyotiṣa astrologers, and Vāstu practitioners do their jobs properly when they 're-validate' life stories for their clients, to give them a clearer picture of where they are now, and where they can realistically expect to arrive in the future. Āyurveda does this in therapeutic terms; Jyotiṣa uses astrological lingo. Vāstu 'revalidates' an individual by using the language of space, form, color, and texture to revise personal myths."

Personal Myths

The rain had let up, and the clouds parted to reveal a sun preparing to sink beneath the horizon. Lucy the dog came over to wag her tail in anticipation of being petted. "We all construct personal myths," I told Marie, "stories of ourselves that have some ring of truth to them, however 'true' they actually are. These narratives pilot us through the seas of our worldly existence. They take on a life of their own, and as they express themselves, they alter the spaces in your body and mind, mapping out the paths your prāṇa will follow, organizing your brain, re-engineering your body structure. Everyone's living space tells their story; I know you've seen this."

"Of course I have. My mom kept her house much differently from the way I keep my house, and both of us keep house differently from my sister. We don't really have all that much in common. So we each have our own personal myths?"

"You do. Vāstu can help you change your personal myth, by suggesting how to change the organization of your house. Instead of using words to alter your individual storyline, Vāstu, which is a language of shapes and forms, uses patterns of arrangement and alignment.

"And just look at your kids." I've known Marie's son, James, now in his twenties, and her teenage daughter, Sarah, since their births. "Look at how James organizes his room, and then look what Sarah does with hers. You can tell so much about their personalities just from how they use their space! And if they are influencing their space so much, doesn't it stand to reason that their space is influencing them in return?"

After a pause, Marie responded, "Yes, I guess it does."

"Your space tells your story, visually and energetically," I continued. "If you want to be healthy and happy, if you want 'good space' to come into your life, then you're going to need to make sure that your story is a good one—which is where Vāstu comes in."

"Okay!" said Marie, grabbing hold of my shoulders. "I'm sold on Vāstu! In fact, I'm so completely sold on it that I want you to drop everything you're doing, and help me rearrange my house, my yard, and my life, right now!"

Vāstu Reality

I laughed as Marie tugged on my arm, trying to drag me back into the house for an immediate makeover. There's a lot to be said for Vāstu enthusiasm, except when it starts to demand instantaneous fruition from just-planted seeds. "Whoa! Let's take things one step at a time," I pleaded. "You'll need a good foundation on which to rearrange your whole life, and good foundations don't grow on trees; they have to be built up from the ground of your current reality. Do you remember what Vimalananda used to say about living with reality?"

Marie met my mentor when he came with me to Florida in 1981, the year after I had met her, and she took to him like a duck to water.

"Remember it? How could I forget? He told me, 'It's always better to live with reality, because if you don't, you can be sure that at some point, reality will come to live with you!'"

"Exactly! Let's make sure you are truly living with reality so that it won't show up pounding on your door one day, demanding to be let in." We smiled as we remembered my mentor, and I continued: "A good place for us to begin is with your 'house reality.' Any house, even one with four walls and no roof—or with just a roof, and no walls—creates a Vāstu statement, a relative reality that you'll have to cooperate with as long as you live within it. While you're there, you'll be subject to the Law of Karma as it applies to that space of yours, the space that you've demarcated for yourself, to the extent that you have constructed and interact with it.

"Obviously, you need to have an idea of what you plan to create before you set about creating it, but you also need to think through the implications of your creation. Vāstu suggests that first we perform the *karma*—the action—of visualizing, in detail, whatever it is we want materialize. Only after visualizing should we perform the karma of trying to materialize it. If you strategize carefully, you'll make your critical changes of plan during the visualization and blueprint stages instead of during the actual construction."

Marie's Living Room, in Theory

"Great!" Marie responded. "Let's start with the living room."

"Fine," I said as the three of us (including Lucy) reentered the house and proceeded into a room whose furniture had been rearranged more than once, not always for the best, since I had first been a guest here. "To begin, ask yourself, '*What can materialize in this space, and how can it do so?*' Then tell me what you come up with."

"Okay. Well, what I *want* to materialize here is the center for *living*, for the whole house."

"And is this possible? Can it happen? Is this room big enough for the whole family to congregate in? Is it located centrally enough for this purpose? A living room should be fairly central, shouldn't it?"

"Yes, it should be, and yes, it is. And I think it's big enough."

"Good." I had paced through the room, offering her a human angle on its size, and then sat with a discreet flourish on the piano stool. "Next question: '*How full should this space be, and how empty?*' I'll answer this one: it should be just full enough to promote *living*. Pretend for a moment that the room is empty, that you've moved out the sofa, the piano, the cactus, the rug, and the dog. Start from there, and think about how full the space really *should* be, in order to be the best living room that it can be. Don't think about what to put in it yet; just think of how much space it encloses, and how much of that space should remain empty. Can you get a feel for that? For now, just give me a rough estimate—you can refine it later."

"Thirty percent."

"Now think about what you want to include in your thirty percent. This is the next question: '*What items should fill this space, and how should they be arranged?*' Will everything that is there at the moment fit into 30 percent of its space?"

"I think so."

"How you arrange those things will of course make a big difference as to how the room feels. If you put all of them in the middle of the room, it would feel like a lot more than 30 percent, wouldn't it? And if everything was against the wall, it might feel like less than 30 percent."

"Right."

"Now for the last question: '*What qualities should these items possess, to achieve the results desired?*' Is the sofa comfortable? Do you want it to be comfortable? Do you want people to sit on it, or to keep off it? Does the piano get played enough to justify it sitting there? Would you be better off with a hibiscus in your planter, instead of a cactus? Do you need a different rug, or no rug at all, or should you carpet the floor?" I paused momentarily to let these questions sink in, and then continued, "Don't try to come up with answers yet. Come up with questions first. Let questions come to you, and much of the time, they'll bring their own answers with them."

As I fell silent, Marie fell silent too. Lucy, never one to enjoy long gaps in the conversation, came over to lick my face.

"Now," I began again as soon as Lucy would permit it, "do we have enough time to rearrange the living room before you have to cook dinner?"

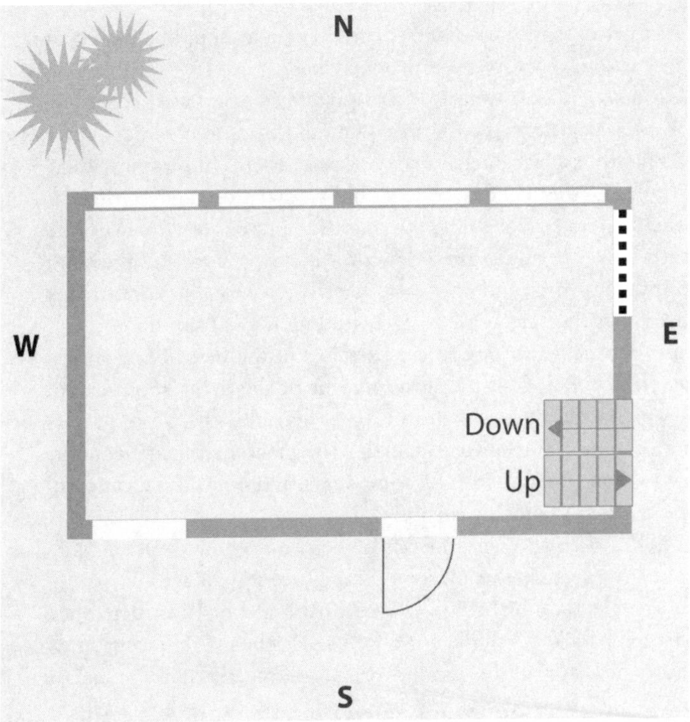

Marie's living room

"We do!" replied Marie with enthusiasm. After we escorted Lucy into the backyard, I walked Marie through Exercise Two, "The Gut Feeling," and Exercise Four, "Messages from the Elements."

Marie's Living Room, in Practice

Marie's living room is a rectangle, 18 feet long by 14½ feet wide, its longer side running roughly east-west. This room occupies a good part of the front of Marie's house, on the second of its three levels. Its western wall is windowless, and its northern wall consists almost entirely of near-floor-length windows. This is good, because the Vāstu system enjoins that light should enter the home chiefly from the north and the east. Outside, there are a couple of royal palms in the front yard, on the northwest side. From the Vāstu perspective, they would be better in the southwest corner of the yard, but the northwest corner is at least better than the northeast corner, which should be free of all large objects, however splendid they may be.

The room's southern wall is interrupted at its southwest corner by a doorless passage into the dining room, and by a door, almost never closed, slightly east of center, into the kitchen. There is no "eastern wall," as such; the southern end of what would be that structural partition is occupied by two sets of stairs, the one to the upper level being more southerly than the one leading down to the lower level and the front door. At the northern end, the "eastern wall" is a wrought-iron banister that overlooks the narrow passageway leading to the front door.

Following the Vāstu assessment exercises to the best of our ability, Marie and I wrestled all the furniture out of the living room except for the piano. Since it was too heavy to move easily, we took it as the jumping-off point for our analysis. The piano had made its home against the solid western wall for some years, and gave no indication of being interested in moving thence.

I considered the presence of this object in the now emptied room and asked Marie, "First of all, should the piano stay in here?"

She thought for a bit, consulted her breath as I had instructed her, and responded, "Yes, I think so. All of us play the piano, except Andy [her husband], so it really is an 'instrument of togetherness' for us."

"Okay, fine. Now, use your Vāstu eyes to try to see how well the piano would fit along the northern wall."

"Well," replied Marie slowly, "it would block some of the light coming in. In the morning there would be too much glare there to be able to read music comfortably. And whoever was practicing would always be looking outside to see what was going on."

"Well said. Let's forget the northern wall. How about in the eastern part of the room?"

"It doesn't really feel right there, though I'm not sure I could tell you why."

"Well, for one thing, if you put it there and faced it east, whenever you sat at it to play you'd be looking over what amounts to a precipice, down into the hallway that connects the front door with the stairs. Your attention-prāṇa would take a dive—not a very good way to promote good concentration. Putting the piano there would act like a sort of energy 'dam,' making it more difficult for the room's energy to cascade through the railings and down to the floor beneath. This would be good for the eastern 'wall,' but not for whoever sat down there to play.

"This would also be true if you put the piano in the east but facing west, except that then you'd have that precipice at your back when you played. Even with the railing there, there's something subconsciously uncomfortable about not having your back 'supported.' Would you agree?"

"Oh, definitely!"

After looking back to the piano, and staring for a moment at the stairs, I carried on: "This is one reason why you wouldn't put the piano on the northern wall with its back to the window either. Also, in both cases, the piano would be jutting out into the room, making it more of an obstacle—both to walking and to the movement of prāṇa, than it would be a valued member of the household."

"So east is definitely out."

"I'd say so, particularly because either way it faced you'd have those staircases right next to it, and staircases are too rajasic, too mobile, too encouraging of the movement of prāṇa, to promote concentration for practice. What about in the south?"

"You mean in this tiny space between the opening into the dining room and the door into the kitchen?"

"Yeah, that's a ridiculous thought, isn't it? There you would be between two 'prāṇa thoroughfares,' no matter whether you face it south or north. Not only will you find concentration impossible when you play, but you'll feel anxiety at being 'boxed in' by the two passageways."

"We're back to west now, where it has been all this time."

"For good reasons, it would appear. But to be thorough, let's also consider the corners. Would it fit in any of them?"

"It would obstruct the stairs in the southeast, and the passage to the dining room in the southwest. In the northeast and northwest? I guess they could work, but they still don't feel quite right."

"Yes, too much like north and east. Of the two, northwest is probably better. But neither is good for the reason that it would create a big triangular piece of wasted space between it and the corner where the walls meet if it were angled as such. If the room was bigger, it might actually be useful to truncate a corner or two that way, to make the space more intimate. But here it's just a bit too much. What about in the center of the room?"

"So that everyone would have to struggle around it? I don't think so! And besides, you've seen how Lucy always tries to hog the center of this room. She would make me feel guilty my every waking moment if I took her central spot away from her."

The Room's Center

As usual, Lucy's instincts were sharp. The center of Marie's living room, like the center of any room, is its real power spot. Each constructed space is a small universe unto itself, with a center that emulates the universe's "center," the point from which existence itself radiated when time and space began. In the macrocosm, that point is the puruṣa; in the developing embryonic microcosm, the zygote; in the developed human, the navel. In temples, homes, images, and furniture, that point is at the entity's energetic center, which is at or near its geometric center.

Energy expands outward from puruṣa to manifest matter, generating an awareness that craves to return again to the Creator. Your soul, which is the Reality of Awareness reflected within the mirror of your being, broadcasts awareness out into you from a central point deep within you, and gathers awareness back to that point. The navel is the omphalos from which the body originates, and the body's prāṇa centers itself at the nearby hara point, which is, roughly, its center of gravity. Prāṇa radiates outwards in all directions from the hara, and prāṇa returns to this hub to refocus.

All your energies—dense and subtle—move from your insides out into the world, then back again. Balance in-breath with out-breath and keep them flowing freely, and health will be your devoted companion. A structure's energies have a parallel respiration: The prāṇa moves from the center out into the structure, then back to the center; from the unity of Space into the multiplicity of Earth, and back again, ideally with a minimum of hindrance. Health, in human or habitat, requires the free flow of prāṇa, and to encourage this, we should keep the space that surrounds a structure's center as free of obstruction as possible.

Rearrangement

Now Marie had established two significant constraints for how she could rearrange her living room: The center needed to remain open, and the piano was already in place. Coupled with the room's structural peculiarities, we had enough information to fill in the rest of its major blanks: the area beneath the windowed expanse of the north wall, from which the sofa had been removed and which now remained open to let in light and energy; the railings of the eastern "wall," which had been the territory of a chair from the sofa set and now hosted a more efficient energy "dam" in the form of the sofa itself; the art on the walls; and the rug on the floor. The sofa's bulk caused the cactus to have to surrender its position in the northeast corner, but it quickly found lodgings more to its liking.

Marie noticed an immediate improvement in the room's energy when we had returned the furniture to it, with the rearrangement designed to make the room feel more "open." As the furniture returned, one item at a time, we gained a feel for the living room's "differential fill potential," which turned out to be not so vast, principally because of its pre-existing irregularities: the two staircases, the "precipice," the kitchen door, and the dining room passageway. Once everything was agreeably arranged, we let the dog in, and Lucy immediately commandeered her central spot once again.

5 Shapes and Arrangements

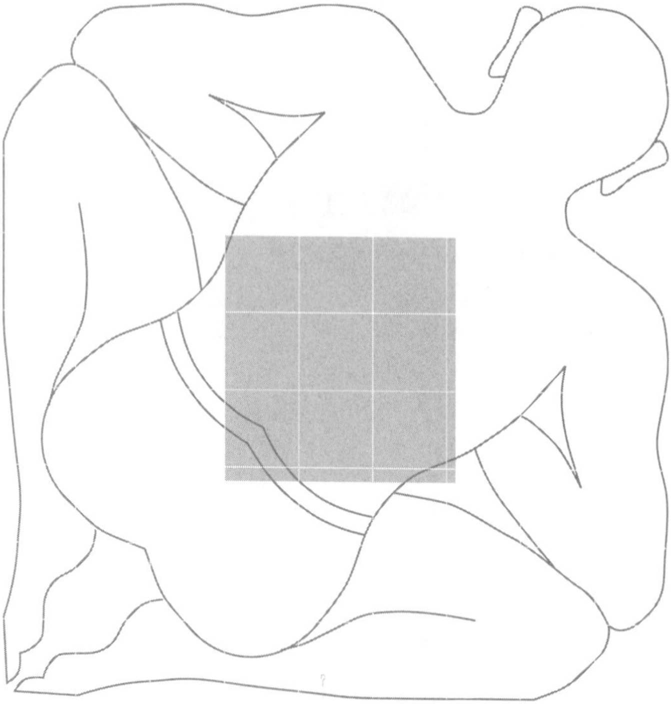

It is not unusual to find, when you analyze one of your rooms, that pretty much everything currently in it actually belongs there. After all, each of us has a natural feel for Vāstu rightness and wrongness, and wrong combinations will often feel so off-balance that they may have already stood out to you, demanding to be addressed.

However, you may find, as Marie and I discovered elsewhere in her house, that in some places, discord has crept in and made itself at home. It may be difficult to sense just how that has arisen, or what to do about it, but a space that feels "wrong" usually does so because of obstructed prāṇa. An area in which prāṇa circulates well is likely to feel right simply because of its strong life force, even if you can't quite put your finger on just why the space has this quality. Often your own prāṇa, working via your innate "Vāstu sense," will eventually figure out a remedy for a room that has energy obstructions. When this intuition isn't sufficient to resolve the problem, Vāstu offers remedies and techniques distilled from centuries of study, experience, and investigation that may be able to help.

Line and Curve

Familiarity with Vāstu's general principles of "right" and "wrong" is a prerequisite for getting the most out of these techniques. It's helpful to begin this exploration by considering Vāstu's two basic forms, the *curve* and the *line*, the geometric building blocks of all other shapes. Circle and line express in visual form the eternal rivalry between the direct and the indirect, the limitless and the constrained, the bound and the free. The noted Egyptian architect Hassan Fathy was fond of saying, "Straight is the line of duty, and curved the path of beauty," which elegantly encapsulates the twinned counterpoints between which the pendulum of human ingenuity everlastingly swings:

Straight	Curved
Duty	Beauty
Tradition	Innovation
Planning	Spontaneity
Restriction	Independence

Though this curve/line continuum covers the wide spectrum from the totally supple to the utterly rigid, people seem to enjoy congregating at its extremities. "Straight arrow" types who conform enthusiastically to society and its mores take positions diametrically opposite from the tribe of convention-flouting, revolution-spouting nonconformists. People who carefully plot their every move take one side; those who refuse under all circumstances to plan their next step adopt the other. "Circle children," who revel in life's unlimited possibilities, and "squares," who dote on convention, rarely see eye-to-eye.

Even the nonconformists, though, tend to conform to the brand of nonconformity that's acceptable to their peers. This yen for community is built into us from birth, for we are as children so dependent for so many years on the kindness of others (and therefore their approval) before we can exist independently. Humans are among the most social of animals; what passes for rebellion among most of us simply involves obeying the rules of a game that is played not by the disapproving majority but by the minority faction that has given us haven. Even our extremism tends to conform to some widely held principle or other.

Extremism is, however, no virtue. In Vāstu, as in life generally, the straight line of duty without the elegance of some beautifying curve is sere, austere, lifeless; and when utterly bereft of the straight and narrow, beauty becomes superficial, frothy, hollow. Most people who finally discover sukha in their spaces and in their lives do so by following a path that leads between the extremes of the wholly linear and the completely curvilinear, embracing now straightness, now curvature, whichever is most appropriate for the situation at hand. Vāstu similarly oscillates between these two poles, veering at one moment toward spontaneity, another moment toward premeditation; expanding today into that infinitude of turning that is the circle, retreating tomorrow into the security of the square, aiming always for the point of balance that lies between.

A Vāstu expert lives on that boundary, at ease in both worlds; in the words of the *Vāstusūtra Upaniṣad*, "Who has the knowledge of circle and line is a *sthāpaka* (master of Vāstu)."* The brain identifies complex visual images by classifying them first into their basic geometrical components. Vāstu masters work hard to see clearly at this more fundamental, more primordial level. They make explicit their implicit human ability to think in these plain shapes, that they may construct new Vāstu phrases and sonatas from these basic Vāstu "parts of speech."

**Vāstusūtra Upaniṣad* I:4, p. 47

Lines, angles, polygons

Exercise Seven: Geometrical Building Blocks

Take a closer look at the contours and outlines in your neighborhood, examining the complex shapes that you normally respond to, and use your Vāstu eyes to try to break them down into their more basic components. Follow lines and curves as they extend and intersect; think of the qualities that line and circle bring to each created shape, and how you respond to different combinations of these two basic forms.

As the example of Marie's living room and her piano made clear, simple, regularly arrayed spaces align more readily than do complex ones with irregular geometries. Boundary and shape are the first "educators" of a space—in terms of defining how prāṇa will flow—and unevenness in layout tends to produce persistent inconsistency in the circulation of prāṇa. Geometrical regularity in design and construction promotes regularity of prāṇa flow even in the presence of other potentially prāṇa-confusing features.

Geometrical symmetry alone is not sufficient, however, for all such symmetries are not created equal. The circle is often considered Vāstu's primary and most perfect shape; since antiquity, it has been the easiest to draw perfectly, for to render a flawless circle on a surface, one needs only a nail or peg, a string or cord, and a steady hand to revolve the twine around its center.

Despite its theoretical perfection, the perpetual motion embodied in the circle's exquisite roundness makes its shape a bit too dynamic as a floor-plan diagram for any but the eternal migrant to inhabit contentedly. The circular Mongolian yurt is admirably adapted to the requirements of its inhabitants, since most yurt dwellers are nomads, wandering eternally from pasture to pasture. Yurts can also be ideal in remote retreat centers, serving as excellent "homes away from home" for retreaters, who move in for a limited period, then move out again.

If curved walls were really such a good idea for general construction, though, shouldn't someone other than the itinerant Mongolians have perfected them before now? Our curvaceously modern geodesic domes are similarly very efficient encapsulations of space, but who wants to live in one?

Even the underground cities in the Cappadocia region of Turkey—comprising centuries-old networks of residences and workrooms dug out of solid rock to a depth of up to eight stories beneath the earth—display a basic squareness in their floors and walls. Cappadocia, which

Ovoid office

Angular sphere

is today still honeycombed with caves, presented builders with the *tabula rasa* of abundant virgin hillsides. They could have carved out structures of any shape, but they liked them linear.

Among curves, an ellipse, with its twin foci, is even less desirable for permanent residence than is the circle with its singular center. The novelty of an oval "whispering gallery" in your home or office would wear off quickly. Aside from the White House's Oval Office, how many other ovals provide real glamour and power to their occupants—and besides, how stable is the energy in the Oval Office, really?

Curves symbolize in Vāstu those aspects of the terrestrial world that are constantly moving, ever-changing—forces that are powerful, but difficult to bring under human control. The square, with its distinct and equidistant sides of equal length, provides a substantially more manageable, if rather less responsive, arrangement of space. Square is the shape of Earth, the most stable and reliable of the Five Elements, while the circle's ever-moving character defines it as a representation of prāṇa, the Air Element, which eternally cycles in and out of bodies and buildings.

If the square represents the fixity of Earth, then the circle is also a good representation of the mutable nature of Water. Yet another perspective sees the circle, being the outline of those illustrious celestial bodies the sun and moon, as representing radiance, and the square as standing for the flat surfaces of pond and lake that were the world's first mirrors. In whatever way we choose to regard curve and line, or circle and square, they mark opposite poles of existence that cannot function without one another. A room filled to the brim with tortuous, unending curves would be as tormenting to reside in as a room harboring an uninterrupted procession of straight lines and knife-edge surfaces.

We need to determine, each one of us for ourselves, to what degree we want to encourage line and curve to cohabit. In the Vāstu system, one preferred method of determining this calls for the dweller or builder to explore the spaces that arise when the initial building plan or existing room diagram is inscribed with a square that is itself circumscribed by a circle; or by drawing on the diagram an arrangement of inscribed circle circumscribed by a square; through these geometrical overlays, the builder can get a feel for how best to balance line and curve within that space.

Another assessment technique involves placing on the diagram shapes that evolve from circle to square via an intermediate stop or

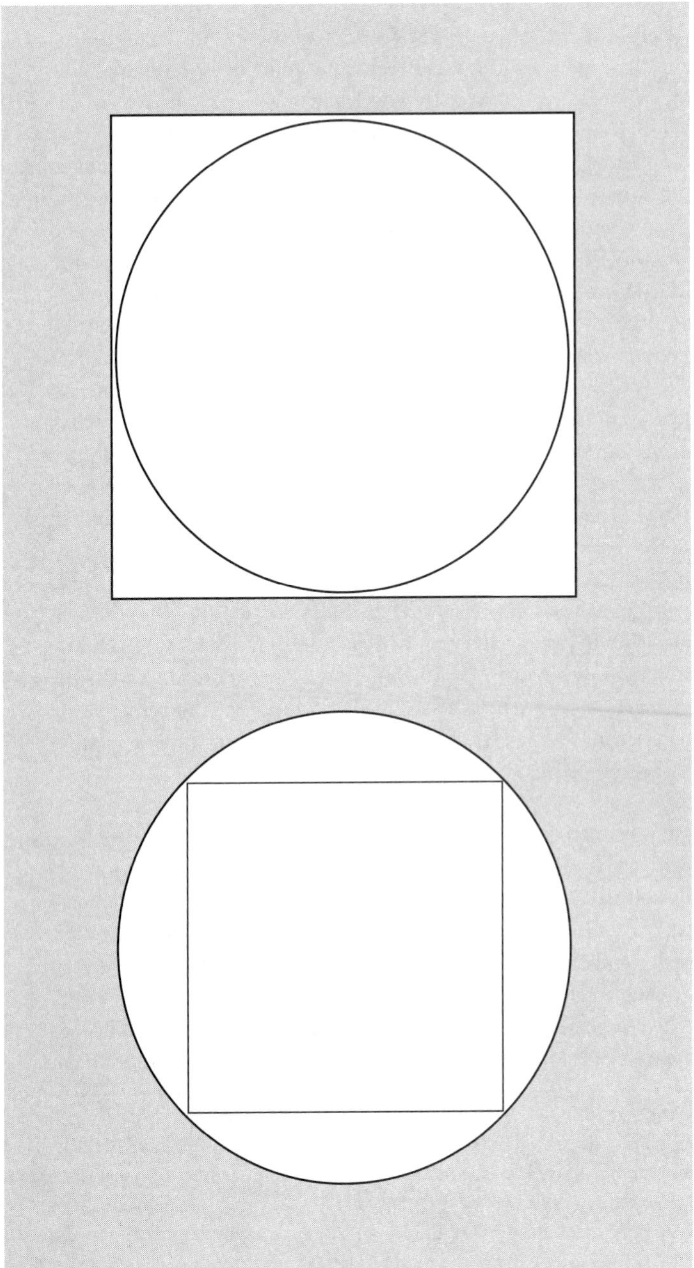

two—polygons are often useful for this purpose. All arrangements in space involve transitions between line and circle, and exploring potential transitions on paper is a good way to gain perspective on how they might look in three-dimensional space. The regular octagon is one such transitional form, made as it is of equilateral lines and equal angles like the square, but tending (because of its multiplicity of lines and angles) in the direction of circularity.* This multiplicity, though, and the difficulties in constructing such a form, make octagonal rooms and buildings no more inherently stable (or popular) than circular ones.

One sacred structure, omnipresent in India, that sometimes incorporates all three of the basic forms of square, octagon, and circle is the *Śiva Liṅgam*, the emblem of the deity of death, transformation, and limitless awareness. In some representations, the Śiva Liṅgam, which may have antedated even the Vedas, extends upward from a square base (Earth) through its octagonal mid-section (the realm between Earth and Heaven) to its circular apex (Heaven), joining the three in immutable harmonic junction.**

Some Indian temples show a similar melding of a square floor plan with octagonal walls and a domed ceiling. More commonly, though, the transition between square and circle is accomplished via geometric multiplicity in the form of furniture, wall decorations, and other such devices, as in St. Peter's Basilica in Rome, the Capitol Building in Washington, D.C., Hagia Sophia in Istanbul, and other structures with large, imposing domes.

A Stable Foundation

Four points, the apexes of its four right angles, along with its four equal sides, define a square. The shape's inherent stability, and its resonance with the Earth element, is evident in numerous manmade creations: Look at an average chair and you'll see four legs, each relating to the earth at one point, all of them together describing a square on the ground beneath. Tripods and three-legged stools also stand upright, but are less stable; they are far

---

*Regular polygons of 16 and 32 sides are occasionally used in India's architecture, mainly for sacred structures. Regular polygons of more than 32 sides were and are rarely used, as they are—for all practical purposes—circular.

**The instinctive rightness of this progression of basic shapes has been recognized in other cultures as well; Hassan Fathy, for example, incorporated a transition from a square to an octagon to a circle in the interior of the dome for the mosque he built in the planned town of New Gourna, Egypt.

Oṁ Namaḥ Śivāya

Squares culminating in circularity

easier to tip over than is a four-legged chair, settee, table, or bedstead.

A square room benefits from the stability of its square, Earthy base. The triangle, the silhouetted shape of Fire, is the smallest-sized polygon that can actually enclose space, but it is no more energetically stable than a tripod or three-legged stool is physically steady. A triangular base has acute angles that are usually too "acute," too sharp to be stable, and triangular rooms usually display the energy of Fire too intensely to promote long-term comfort. Even the *vedi*, the standard Vedic fire altar, is square, so that it can safely contain the transforming fire within.

For certain purposes, Vāstu occasionally espouses octagons and, very occasionally, hexagons. All regular polygons enjoy the benefit of regular geometries, and some, like Washington, D.C.'s Pentagon, consequently succeed as buildings. The Pentagon is home to the (in this sense) aptly-named "Department of Defense," for five is the number of the planet Jupiter, the Protector. The square, however, remains Vāstu's preferred form for structural foundations—square and rectangular are equally preferred, actually, for Vāstu sees rectangles as being essentially equivalent to squares, since every rectangle can be partitioned into two or more squares.

Sacred Centrality

Vedic sacrifices echo the process of cosmic creation by establishing puruṣa, Pure Awareness, at the center of a sacred space. Vāstu recapitulates the Vedic sacrifice by placing puruṣa at the center of the spaces we create for various purposes. Like a Vedic sacrifice, a Vāstu construction seeks to establish a pure center, an unsullied inner space, within protective boundaries. A well-tended Vāstu space, be it walled garden or comforting kindergarten, encloses order, peace and concinnity; this space, insulated from energetic pollution, offers a well-sheltered refuge where life can flourish.

The space contained within a human being should also be well-tended and life-nourishing. The Vedics used a square fire altar in a sacrificial pavilion as their central sacred focus, and Vedic worshippers would commonly employ this external sacrificial panorama as a visualization template for their own human form; by reconstructing it within, they transformed the body into an altar.

In the period following the Vedic era, the altar took shape in the more symbolic form of a sculpture, painting, or other holy images, and

Tending the sacred flames

the pavilion expanded into a temple. Many worshippers continue to internalize such sacred scenes, erecting "protective temples surrounding central altars" within themselves with the help of sacred geometrical designs like *maṇḍalas* and *yantras*.

These numinous diagrams express divinity in a profusion of containing lines and concentrating curves that act as visualization maps for proceeding from a secular "without" to a sacred "within." Mazes that graced the floors of many medieval churches served a similar purpose, as do such consecrating geometries as the path that leads along the slopes of England's Glastonbury Tor, a sacred hill central to several legends.

The Axis Mundi

Just as the maze's center shelters the goal of the pilgrimage, the very center of most maṇḍalas and yantras hosts a point known as the *bindu*, the quintessential essence of the Singularity that represents puruṣa, as does the tip of the Vedic sacred flame. The bindu represents position without magnitude, a timeless, dimension-free existence from which our multi-dimensional space-time arises. In the words of one text, "the central dot is indicative of Time, and the Form emerging at the center is indicative of rhythm."*

The Śrī Yantra, the most widely revered of yantras in India today, displays its bindu proudly within its central triangle.

The central *bindu* ("droplet") also represents the drop of semen that gives rise to and activates the zygote within the mother's protective womb. The bindu's most common three-dimensional Indian incarnation today takes the form of the Śiva Liṅgam, which in addition to embodying the Vāstu progression from square (earth) to circle (heaven), symbolizes the cylindrical penis of the god Śiva resting in a square base formed by the stylized vagina of His wife Pārvatī.

The space contained within a human being should also be well-tended and life-nourishing. The Vedics used a square fire altar in a sacrificial pavilion as their central sacred focus, and Vedic worshippers would commonly employ this external sacrificial panorama as a visualization template for their own human form; by reconstructing it within, they transformed the body into an altar.

While a Śiva Liṅgam looks like a rock to the unschooled eye, in the mind of a sensitive worshipper, it is an endless pillar of blazing

*Mayan's *Aintiram*, p. 469

Cosmic navigational charts

Śrī Yantra (from sriyantraresearch.com)

light (embodying the Fire Element) extending from Earth into the immeasurable expanses of Space. In the Vedic era, this shaft was embodied in the *yūpa*, or sacrificial post, a central component of the *yajña śālā*, the "sacred pavilion." *Atharva Veda* X.7-8 glorifies the yūpa as the *axis mundi*, the Cosmic Pillar that upholds the universe. In its aspect as a pilaster of breath, the yūpa permits Sky and Earth to exchange prāṇa (the life-giving form of the Air Element). As a phallic pillar, the yūpa represents the semen-droplet (*bindu*) of puruṣa, extended into a columnar form that, by intimately joining Earth with Sky, makes life prolific (a quality of the Water Element). As a spiritual emblem, the yūpa testifies to how the "point without dimension" that is the Sacred Center stretches out into the "dimensionless line" that is the Divine Column.

Axiality thus arises from *centrality*, extending into the third dimension the center that we demarcated within our two-dimensional diagram. While the Five Elements can express themselves very well in two dimensions alone—as we shall shortly see—their expression becomes even more effective when they manifest in three dimensions.

Many societies besides India's have worshipped "sky-pillars"; among these worldwide devotees are the pagan Europeans. The Maypole, the tall wooden post once central to nature worship and fertility celebrations, is one such axis. Another representation is the *caduceus*, a winged staff with twin snakes twining around it that is used to symbolize medicine.*

A human being is a "sky-pillar," a reflection of our species' ambition to extend ourselves away from the source of gravity below our feet in the direction of the celestial divinity above our heads. A healthy human being is a life-shielding space constructed around an "inner pillar," the spinal column symbolized by the staff of the caduceus. The coiling serpents signify two great *nāḍīs* (ethereal vessels of prāṇa) that flow along the spinal cord and terminate in the nostrils. The spine is the inward sacrificial post that connects the individual's "earth" polarity, at the perineum, with the "sky" polarity at the crown of the head. That "internal" worshipper able to perceive these inner realities ignites a subtle fire within the central nāḍī that flows along the spinal cord and offers access to the One Essence.

---

*Some authorities maintain that the staff of the once-human, later-deified Aesculapius, which is wingless and has but one serpent, is the symbol of healing, and that the caduceus applies only to Hermes (Mercury), the Greco-Roman trickster who leads souls to the underworld, and rules rebirth. Both, however, are clearly "sky-pillars."

Though we may not notice it continually, the circulation of our internal "atmosphere," our "inner wind," affects and is affected by our every attitude and activity. The science of breath called *Svarodaya* details the proper functioning of the currents of breath and prāṇa, and their use in diagnosis and treatment, applicable both to our inner workings and our external surroundings.

Exercise Eight: Svarodaya

Exercise Two, "The Gut Feeling," in which you monitored your breath to give yourself a feel for the disposition of a room's furnishings, is an example of a very simplified variety of *Svarodaya*. *Svarodaya* (sometimes called *Svara Yoga* or *Svara Vidyā*), not always associated with Vāstu purposes, of course, is a breathing method that typically employs the two nostrils separately. Normally, no one breathes equally out of both nostrils at the same time for very long. Our breathing shifts repeatedly, all day and all night, from one nostril to the other. Follow your own breathing, and you'll notice these transitions. The shift should take place about every hour and a half, though nowadays, in our speedy world, it's often more frequent. Usually, the only times that the two nostrils will spontaneously be open together are at dawn and dusk, the transitions between day and night.

Your left nostril, and the nāḍī associated with it, augments the strength of the Water Element in the body to cool you down. Your right nostril activates the Fire Element in the body, via its corresponding nāḍī, to heat you up. When both work together, they activate the Air Element itself, which promotes alterations in your state of mind and body.

Close off your left nostril with the middle and ring fingers of your right hand (the index finger bent in toward your palm), and take ten deep, slow breaths through the right nostril to activate the Fire Element in your body. After a few subsequent moments of normal breathing, release your left nostril and close off your right nostril with your right thumb. Then take ten slow, deep breaths to activate the Water Element. Notice the difference in how you feel when Water dominates and when Fire is dominant. (Should one or both of your nostrils be significantly blocked, do not try to force the breath; instead, try this exercise after freer flow has returned.)

Svarodaya

Changing the breath pattern influences body chemistry, nervous response, emotional condition, and state of consciousness, judiciously employed, this conscious respiratory control can relieve diseases. It is beneficial to health to actively align your breathing pattern with the "breathing" of the cosmos. To do this, you'll have to start paying attention to which of your nostrils is active at the moment you arise each morning. (This practice traditionally calls for practitioners to pay attention to which nostril is operating at the moment of sunrise, but most people nowadays are either not up before sunrise, or don't have the luxury of sitting quietly before dawn waiting for the sun to rise).

Of the several models of bringing your breath into synchronicity with the cosmos, two are most common: the vāra *(weekday) method and the more complicated* tithi *(lunar day) method. Because tithi is much more complex, we'll confine this discussion to presenting the vāra method. The pattern associated with vāra dictates that your left nostril should always operate when you arise (or just after dawn) on Mondays, Wednesdays, Thursdays, and Fridays, and your right nostril should dominate on Sundays, Tuesdays, and Saturdays.*

To get yourself into this pattern, it will probably be necessary to intentionally change your breathing from one nostril to the other for a few days. You can do this easily, in the space of a few minutes, by lying down on the same side of your body as the nostril that's open, or by plugging the active nostril with cotton. Either of these methods should shift the active nostril to the opposite side. Once you've established the vāra pattern in your breathing, it will tend to persist (with periodic variations, which shouldn't disturb you), and will provide you with a useful diagnostic tool. When your organism is moving in the direction of an imbalance, you'll notice that the same nostril will operate for several days in a row at the time you awaken, and that it will be reluctant to cease dominating when you attempt to switch it over. It's wise to actively rebalance yourself as soon as you notice this trend developing.

An opportune time to change your active nostril is any juncture when you feel the onset of some sort of physical or mental disturbance, like an oncoming headache. Switching your dominant nostril at such moments may prevent the condition from arising, or at least will discourage the worsening of symptoms and will promote rapid recovery.

Some commentators say that the left nostril should, as a general rule, be more active during the day, while the right is more dominant at night (except when performing specific tasks requiring the activity of the other nostril), to promote balance of microcosm with macrocosm; others maintain that aligning with the predominant energies of day and night is more important, and suggest that the right nostril should be generally more active during the day, and the left at night. Typically, the left nostril is more suitable for all routine activities, like sweeping the floor and similar chores, and for "passive" actions, those performed under the control of others (like listening to a lecture). The right nostril is better for dynamic activities, where one is in control oneself (and others). Meditation, chanting, worship, and the like are ideally done when both nostrils are equally open, which occurs normally at dawn and dusk, and (often) briefly during the transition from one nostril to the other.

Examples of activities that are favorable or auspicious during left-nostril breathing include starting a new business, entering a new house, meeting and talking with friends and loved ones, playing music, painting, communicating with one's elders or superiors, gardening, and sleeping. Right-nostril breathing is the preferred state for bathing, learning new things, debating, eating, defecating, motivating others, strenuous haṭha yoga, and hard physical labor.

As without, so within: The human body, the yūpa, temples, and many deity images all display an abundance of Earth energy and tamas in their nethermost regions; a surfeit of the rajas of the Water, Fire, and Air Elements in their middle parts; and a predominance of the heavenly light of Space and sattva at or near their crowns. Each of these embodiments expresses an upward aspiration, a dream of re-union with unqualified consciousness, even as each retains its firmly rooted earthy foundations.

While we could conceivably angle our building with an unusual slant, the vast majority of structures are better when built vertical, stretching straight up from the plane in which we have limned our diagram. The building's vertical axis is the extension upward of its stable center. By suggesting movement that is solely skyward, that is up but not out, verticality promotes stability. Let a building lean, even slightly, and viewers will sense that the building is moving laterally. This may be good for tourism, but not for steadiness; few people would be interested in visiting the Leaning Tower of Pisa if it were straight, but fewer still would want to live or work in it as it is, or in a building similarly inclined. Get the verticality right, and the horizontality will take care of itself.

The Brahma Sthāna

Any structure, be it human body or human creation, should strive to incarnate the pure light of consciousness at its center. Vāstu insists that the central area of any structure should be well lit, and relatively empty of furniture. Unoccupied Space in this locus acts as a conduit for prāṇa, light, and other positive energies, ensuring their smooth flow to residents within.

The central core of any structure or diagram, of any temple or city—the central channel for light, heat, air, and prāṇa as they move in and out of the surrounding form—is termed the *Brahma Sthāna* ("place of divinity"). The Brahma Sthāna acts as the base of the "vertical axis of consciousness" that rises in external space like a sacrificial post from the earth and like a caduceus within a human. To provide space for the free circulation of these life-nourishing energies in the structure, the Brahma Sthāna should always be left unoccupied.

The ancient Britons respected this principle in their sacred stone circles, such as those at Avebury and Stonehenge, which display certain key characteristics: circularity for power, stone for stability, defined

Relentless tilt

centers, open to the sky. In temples and churches built throughout Europe in later eras, the sanctum sanctorum, or high altar, was often placed in the main hall's most central space. Otherwise, that space might be kept relatively empty, to encourage attention to rise into a dome or steeple situated high above, as with York Minster's great lantern tower. In that cathedral, light streams down on worshippers through an array of lofty windows as if from the Lord's throne itself.

The central area of a building intended for secular use, such as a house or office, should (where the climate permits) be kept similarly open to the outdoors, or at least should be dominated by a sky lit atrium. The floor marking the location of the Brahma Sthāna should either be kept vacant, or should speak to the glory of one of the Five Elements. A pool or fountain may in certain circumstances profitably occupy this central space; the main court of the Frick Gallery in New York City provides an excellent example of how well a fountain can serve as a room's focal point.

The Water Element's creative energy admirably reflects the creativity on display at the Frick. In other circumstances, a richly decorated carpet—an accoutrement that is an acknowledgement and homage to the Earth Element—might be a better choice for the central adornment. Hunting or skiing lodges are often structured around a central blazing Fire. Whatever the means, Vāstu's goal is to provide a central Space for the Air Element to circulate, both atmospherically and pranically, while discouraging people from hogging the energetic core by planting themselves there.*

While the center should remain unoccupied, a building's inner space overall should attract people, and make them feel welcome and comfortable, or focused and productive. One of the reasons for the success of the Pentagon as a structure (if notoriety be taken as a token of success) may well be its sizable inner courtyard, which draws to the building's center the attention of its occupants, thus providing a stable center to the building and enabling the occupants the ability to focus their minds.

Cities and towns should, like rooms and houses, be built around a central focus—a square or common, temple or tabernacle, seat of

---

*One way in which triangles can be profitably employed in structures is to use them to form a pyramid. A pyramid formed of four truncated triangles is an acceptable Vāstu shape, provided that it has a clearly-demarcated Brahma Sthāna, and that its flattened top has a perimeter that equals the perimeter of the Brahma Sthāna of the base.

Boulders ennobled by placement

government or other place of unique beauty or power—that defines the municipality for its citizens. Humanity's first big buildings, the symbols of the culture and enterprise of the individuals and organizations that built them, were temples, reflecting an era in which the priestly class (*brāhmaṇas*) predominated in cultural and social life. Such cities expanded out from their temple-foci. In Ur of the Chaldees, the locus took the form of a ziggurat; in Central and South American cities, the seminal structure was, characteristically, a pyramid. Many European cities once radiated outward from their cathedrals; a few, like Vatican City, still have this arrangement. The city of Santa Fe, New Mexico, is structured around a central plaza.

When the warrior class (*kṣatriyas*) gains ascendancy in a civilization, the general populace is guided to build cities around a fort, castle, or palace. The ancient layout for the city of Tokyo provides one such example of this schema. The Alamo, a fortified religious mission at the heart of the city of San Antonio, Texas, reflects both the spiritual and defensive motivation.

The newer cities of the world, particularly in the United States, are built around "downtowns" that house the markets and commercial centers where capitalists (*vaiśyas*) congregate. And during the communist era, Moscow's Red Square and Beijing's Tiananmen Square were transformed (at least in name) into monuments to the working classes (*śūdras*). Whoever the rulers, and whatever the rules, a city needs a center, lest it become a place where there is no "there" there.

A city's central focus needs ample space in which to establish its anchoring, if it is to serve as a true center. New York City's Central Park is clearly big enough, and centrally located enough, to serve this purpose. Pioneer Square in Portland is smallish, but so is the downtown that it supports. The Liberty Bell and Independence Hall sites could have served Philadelphia similarly, but the city's planners allowed the defining energy of their most precious monuments to be choked by permitting construction to intrude on the space around the sites. The Boston Common was once an adequate municipal atrium, but that was back when Boston was far smaller and the Common was proportionately larger. Washington, D.C. has its Mall, which functions well in its purpose but is, sadly, in continual danger of further encroachment.

The city of Seattle has a dramatic aqueous feature, Lake Union, at its heart. Surrounding the city (when the clouds lift long enough for these to be visible) are the Cascades to the east, Mount Rainier to the south, and the Olympics to the west. Encircling Lake Union, emphasizing it as a place worthy of attention, are such landmarks as the Space Needle; the Locks, providing protection for the city and a transition for ships moving from salt water to fresh water; Gas Works Park, a 19-acre green space on a northern shore of Lake Union; Seattle University; and the downtown area.

Seattle thus overcomes a Vāstu negative (being long and skinny) by having a strong central focus that will never be superseded by buildings (the seaplanes that take off and land on the lake rather beautify it, as do some, if not all, of the sailboats and houseboats). With surrounding sheaths consisting of an inner circle of dramatic manmade structures and an outer circle of dramatic natural formations, the city's vital core is further protected and solidified.

Smaller towns should also have well-defined centers that are empty of buildings other than temples or churches, palaces or castles, courthouses or commons. The center should always be of a size appropriate to the settlement that surrounds it, housing perhaps not a lake, but at least a small body of water; perhaps not a forest, but certainly a central grove.

The Vāstu Puruṣa

The roots of the human yearning for borders surrounding us, and for an inner protective dwelling space within which we can bask, are established by our experience of being sheltered and guided in the womb. Thus, Vāstu's version of the blueprint, the system's seminal geometrical design, shows the form to be created within a diagram-womb assembled from circles and lines. Drawn on the surface of stone, wood, metal, or canvas, this plan is often termed the *pañjara* ("cage" or "skeleton"). The pañjara is a cage that restrains and channels the creative energies, a skeleton over which an image fills out as it comes to life. This blueprint is a stable square that encloses a dynamic circle, a group of lines that provide the discipline required to transform curvy dynamism into true creativity.

Stretching a construction over a pañjara has always been a sacred activity, one that literally confines divinity within walls and that demands supreme concentration from its creator (*śilpin*):

"For the Indian artist, the *śilpin*, the creation of an image is, in part, a religious discipline. Entering into a state of concentration by means

*Diana Eck, *Darsan*, p. 52

Noble obelisk

Park patrician

Water, earth, sky

of yoga, the śilpin is to visualize the completed image in the mind's eye. According to the śāstras, the śilpin, before beginning a new work, undergoes a ritual purification and prays that he may successfully bring to form the divine image he has seen."*

An Indian temple contains at its center the image of the deity to which it is dedicated, a deity who incarnates puruṣa, the Formless, Ultimate, Transcendent Awareness. Puruṣa also resides at the center of Vāstu's diagrams. Extending outward in all directions from that center is its surrounding space, which represents prakṛti, the field of all creation. The bond that develops automatically between the center and the contained space represents the self-awareness of mahat. Within this square, ahaṁkāra's three great attributes—*sattva* (poise), *rajas* (transformation), and *tamas* (resistance)—array themselves.

A Vāstu diagram's center also shelters an earthly personification—and rendering—of puruṣa: the *Vāstu Puruṣa*, who is the embodiment of the spirit and the consciousness of the space that we wish to define. An ancient Vāstu myth recounted in the *Bṛhat Saṁhitā* describes how once, after a rather demonic *bhūta* ("being") had obstructed heaven, earth, and the space in between with its body, the gods grabbed the demon and pinned it to the earth. The god who restrained a particular limb of the bhūta became the presiding deity of that limb, and that appendage took on the presiding deity's qualities. Thus pacified, the bhūta became benevolent, and was awarded the name *Vāstu Puruṣa*. When he requested food, the gods chose to award him all the offerings made by those who undertake the construction of an edifice.

The word *bhūta* means "element" (in a "Five Great Elements" sense) as well as "being." The being who became the Vāstu Puruṣa was the embodiment of raw matter (vastu = matter), made from the "unenlightened" Five Great Elements. The bhūta was a demonic force so long as it remained selfish, tamasic, and uncooperative, which suggests that, until we stake out our space, mark it, measure it, and establish order within it, its spirit will remain formless and uncontrollable for us. The action of "pinning" matter down to the ground renders it favorable to us, says Vāstu, as long as we revere and honor it by respectfully honoring the Five Elements.

The Vāstu Puruṣa Maṇḍala

Pūrvottara din-mūrdhā puruṣo 'yam avāṅgmukho 'sya śirasi śikhī |

This Vāstu Puruṣa, who lies prone on the site, has his head turned toward the northeast.

Bṛhat Saṁhitā, 53:51a, p. 470

The sanctified body of the Vāstu Puruṣa is what supports whatever we build on a parcel of land. It is to him that a Vāstu master offers thanks and praise before beginning construction on a site.

In the sacred layout the Vāstu adept uses, the Vāstu Puruṣa lies face down with his head into the northeast. His splayed knees and elbows occupy the southeast and northwest corners of the square box in which we encase him, and his feet occupy the southwest. This archetypal topography creates the Vāstu Puruṣa *Maṇḍala*, the geometrical design (*maṇḍala*) that we use for construction planning. In Sanskrit, the word *maṇḍala* actually means circle, but like other maṇḍalas, the Vāstu Puruṣa Maṇḍala has a caged circularity, the roundness converted into the more stable square form. The tamas of matter (vastu) is thus transformed, by the rajasic activity of the architect-creator (puruṣa), into a blueprint (maṇḍala) for sattvic equilibrium. Rightly oriented, the Vāstu Puruṣa Maṇḍala can help us organize and align our living and working spaces with great precision.

One reason to anthropomorphize the Vāstu Puruṣa is to give us a divine visage to worship when we wish to honor a plot of land. Another is that humans have a marked tendency to see living beings in "non-living" things: "It doesn't take much for us to interpret an object as a human or animal figure," writes Alain de Botton. "A piece of stone can have no legs, eyes, ears or almost any of the features associated with a living thing; it need have only the merest hint of a maternal thigh or a babyish cheek and we will start to read it as a character." (de Botton, p. 82)

Yet another reason for this anthropomorphic view is to remind us that our constructions (be they hotel rooms or space stations) actually endeavor to bring to life a space and the structure it hosts. Buildings may not be protoplasmic, but many of the same limitations of protoplasmic life also apply to living spaces.

One such limitation is that of the *marma*, a critical energy point that must not be "damaged" by being built upon. Marmas arise at the intersections of the Vāstu Puruṣa Maṇḍala's many lines. Each of these lines is a nāḍī, a vessel in which prāṇa moves, a "breathing channel" for the Vāstu Puruṣa. Currents of prāṇa meet where the nāḍīs meet, and to build upon one of these junctures is to obstruct those currents.

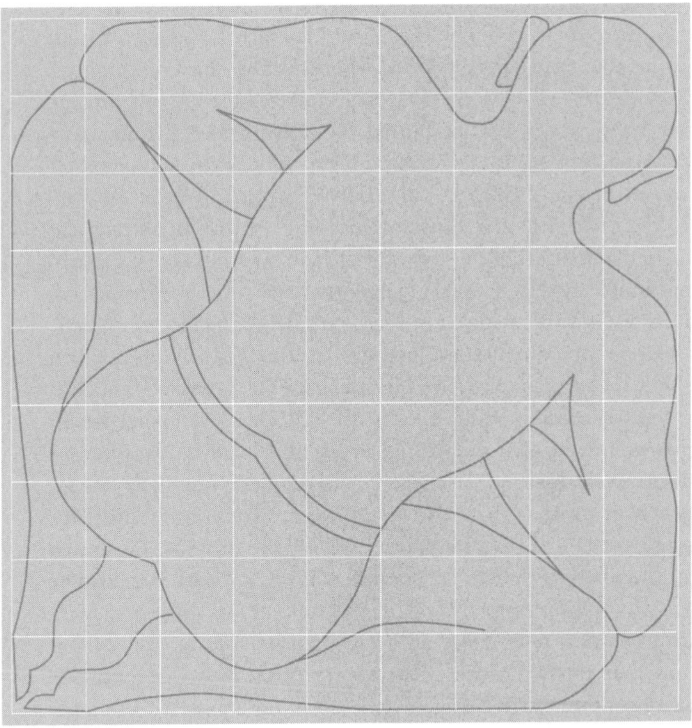

Vāstu Puruṣa

In terms of prāṇa, the most significant of the Vāstu Puruṣa's limbs is the *Brahma Nābhi* ("divine navel"), which appears at the center of the maṇḍala. Like the umbilicus of any fleshly being, the Vāstu Puruṣa's navel is his talismanic souvenir of zygotic singularity, the "root" from which arose his umbilical cord "stem," the "axis mundi" that joined the sky of the womb to the earth of the growing fetus. Prāṇa enters us through the umbilicus while we sleep in utero; after we're born, the navel is the body's center of pranic activity, the central focus for a plethora of intersecting nāḍīs. The Brahma Nābhi is thus the Vāstu Puruṣa Maṇḍala's chief marma.

The Vāstu Puruṣa's limbs indicate which portions of the space being designed are best assigned to which functions. Loss of a limb means loss of that limb's function. *Bṛhat Saṁhitā* relates that when Vāstu Puruṣa is "endowed with all the limbs in fine shape, the occupants of the house will be blessed with honor, wealth, and happiness." When, however, he is missing his head, one of his arms, or his feet (i.e., if one of the quadrants of the floor plan for a house, or even a room, is absent or distorted), various miseries are foretold for the inhabitants. In particular, a headless Vāstu Puruṣa (a space in which the northeast quadrant is deformed) is said in the *Bṛhat Saṁhitā* to make the master or mistress of the property "fall from all virtues." (*Bṛhat Saṁhitā* 53:67b, p. 475) A clearly demarcated perfect square or rectangular floor plan that fits within the truncated area in question—be it a room, a whole house, or a large parcel of land—protects those virtues instead, by allowing the Vāstu Puruṣa to have a space where he can be whole.

All manner of configurations can do harm to Vāstu Puruṣa. If you draw a square or rectangle around the perimeter of a structure's outside wall, then wherever the wall deviates from this ideal perimeter—even for the best of reasons—the Vāstu Puruṣa suffers an injury, a bite. A corner that was truncated or recessed to accommodate a stately tree, or to enhance or reduce exposure to sun or wind, affects Vāstu Puruṣa for the house as a whole. An external stairwell whose entryway juts into a room afflicts both the Vāstu Puruṣa of the room, and that of the whole house.

Furniture does not "chop off" Vāstu Puruṣa's parts, unless that furniture is an integral part of the structure. In the latter situation, this built-on furnishing will damage only a room, not the whole building, unless it also compromises the symmetry of the exterior walls. A stairwell that juts into a room prunes that room's Vāstu Puruṣa, as would a large, peculiarly-situated walk-in closet that is integrated into a room's walls.

Fortunately, Vāstu Puruṣa is quite adaptable—he will gladly shrink or swell to fill the largest square or rectangle that can be sketched onto a surface. If one of a structure's external corners is missing, Vāstu Puruṣa can be redrawn to a smaller, more symmetrical perimeter (with the resulting imperative that those portions of the building that "stick out" after the reduction may need to be sequestered from the rest of the structure in some way); "virtual walls" (fences, hedges, etc.) can be added to compensate for missing physical walls; or Vāstu Puruṣa can be expanded outward, and the new space thus added can then be enclosed within a symmetrically shaped verandah.

Vāstu Puruṣa similarly fits most comfortably into rooms that are already square or rectangular, but will gladly adjust to whatever area he is assigned. All asymmetrical areas will need to be "squared."

Roga	Nāga	Mukhya	Bhallāṭa	Soma	Mṛga	Aditi	Diti	Śikhī
Pāpaya-kṣma	Roga	Mukhya	Pṛthvī-dhara	Pṛthvī-dhara	Pṛthvī-dhara	Aditi	Apah	Parjanya
Śoṣa	Śoṣa	Rudrajaya	Pṛthvī-dhara	Pṛthvī-dhara	Pṛthvī-dhara	Apavatsa	Jayanta	Jayanta
Asura	Mitra	Mitra	Brahmā	Brahmā	Brahmā	Aryaman	Aryaman	Mahendra
Varuṇa	Mitra	Mitra	Brahmā	Brahmā	Brahmā	Aryaman	Aryaman	Ravi
Puṣpa-danta	Mitra	Mitra	Brahmā	Brahmā	Brahmā	Roga	Roga	Satya
Sugrīva	Sugrīva	Indrajaya	Vivasvān	Vivasvān	Vivasvān	Savitṛ	Bhṛśa	Bhṛśa
Dauvārika	Indra	Bhṛṅga-rāja	Vivasvān	Vivasvān	Vivasvān	Vitatha	Savitṛ	Nabha
Pitṛ	Mṛṣā	Bhṛṅga-rāja	Gandharva	Yama	Gṛhakṣata	Vitatha	Pūṣan	Anila

Vāstu Puruṣa Maṇḍala

Temporary or permanent partitions can turn a large, irregular room into a square or rectangle—or some combination of squares and rectangles—by means of tables, chairs, sofas, settees, screens, panels, plants, or partial walls. The small compartments and detached spaces thus created can host other plants, jars, vases, statues, baskets of pinecones, audio speakers, or pretty much anything else fit to be immured behind partitions.

Irregular rooms that are too small to respond well to such "pruning" offer a greater challenge. Sometimes such a room's furniture can be so arranged as to produce the appearance of geometrical regularity, or perhaps a well-placed mirror or piece of art may provide some balance. As a last resort, one can consider more heroic measures, such as breaking down weirdly angled walls and adding new, more symmetrical ones.

Vāstu Puruṣa Grids

The Vāstu Puruṣa lives within his Vāstu Puruṣa Maṇḍala, stretched out atop a square Procrustean grid made of smaller cells that help us plan out what should go where within the room or the house in question. Even if we intend to erect a rectangular structure, the initial site-plan is usually drawn in the form of a grid of little squares, which are then extended outward proportionately into a host of little rectangles to create the desired floor plan. If you have a rectangle that is 4 units x 8 units in area, for example, you would take the square Vāstu Puruṣa Maṇḍala and stretch it out so that it became 4 x 8 as well. Then each of its smaller squares would be stretched out to the same 1:2 proportion, keeping each small rectangle associated with the same quality/body part of the Vāstu Puruṣa.

Rectangles

Vāstu prefers the rectangle as a floor plan for most secular buildings. The text Śilparatna *mentions rectangles of 1:2, 2:3, and 3:5 proportions, ratios that happen to be derived from the popular Fibonacci series (1, 1, 2, 3, 5, …), which tend at the farther end of the series to a ratio of 1:1.6.*

The most commonly used ratio of breadth to length is probably 1:2. Some regard a 1:3 proportion as being particularly desirable, because the perimeter of such a rectangle is a multiple of eight, and Vāstu is fond of the 1:3:8 ratio.

Another concept, called guṇāmśa, *examines every proportion between 4:5 and 4:28 (i.e., 4:5, 4:6, 4:7, etc.) and permits all to be used except the so-called padona ratios: 4:7 (1:1.75), 4:11 (1:2.75), 4:15 (1:3.75), 4:19 (1:4.75), 4:23 (1:5.75), and 4:27 (1:6.75). Why these ratios are forbidden is unknown, though probably it has something to do with a widely followed tradition in India that holds quantities, times, and ratios that are a quarter less than a whole to be generally inauspicious.*

The 4:28 (1:7) ratio makes for a very long, skinny, ungainly building that inefficiently encloses space (granted, such a structure may be useful for stables,

Rectangles galore

strip malls, and the like). A rectangle that is 1 foot wide and 7 feet long has a perimeter of 16 feet, but an area of only 7 square feet, whereas a square with the same perimeter (4 feet by 4 feet) contains an area of 16 square feet. The 1:7 rectangle thus encloses less than half the area than a square of the same perimeter. Rectangles in proportions of 1:8 and above enclose even less area, and are correspondingly less practical.

The key Vāstu treatise known as the *Mayamata* describes 32 types of such site-plans (called *pada-vinyāsa* or *Vāstu-maṇḍala*), from the 1 x 1 cell that is a simple square, to the 2 x 2 cell diagram comprising four squares (*padas*), to the 1024 cells of a grid that has 32 cells on a side. Each grid's every cell has its own quality of awareness, its own personal intelligence—many different energies arise from the act of demarcation.

The *Mayamata* specifies that the 1 x 1 square be used for fire altars, the 2 x 2 through 6 x 6 grids for seats, daises, and thrones, and the 7 x 7 through 11 x 11 for houses, pavilions, and temples. 12 x 12 through 19 x 19 grids are meant for temple complexes and villages, and towns and cities employ the largest grids of 20 x 20 through 32 x 32. The two most suitable plans for residences are the 8 x 8 and 9 x 9 grids, which yield 64 and 81 cells respectively. The builder or planner would overlay the chosen grid on top of the diagram of the area where the construction is to take place, and then begin delineating the placement of individual sections, be they rooms, parts of a temple, or divisions of the city.

The 8 x 8 grid is given the special name *Maṇḍūkapada*, and the 9 x 9 is called *Paramasāyikā*. Of these two, the 9 x 9 Paramasāyikā is usually preferred, particularly because it facilitates alignment of the Maṇḍala with the Nine Planets of Jyotiṣa (which we will soon introduce), but also because it has a resonance with our numbering system, with its nine digits. For evidence that the 9 x 9 square holds a special place in human archetypal thinking, consider the Sudoku puzzle, which has recently gained worldwide popularity. Sudoku challenges players to place the numerals from one to nine in such a way that each appears exactly once in each of the puzzle's rows, columns, and smaller 3 x 3 squares.

At the center of a completed puzzle, a Sudoku diagram is filled with numbers. The center of any Vāstu Maṇḍala is instead always the seat of the Brahma Sthāna, whose precise middle is the bindu, the point of greatest divinity and power. For an 8 x 8 grid, the Brahma Sthāna is taken to be the innermost 2 x 2 = 4 squares; for a 9 x 9 grid, the innermost 3 x 3 = 9 squares make up the Brahma Sthāna.

Each of the names associated with the Paramasāyikā Maṇḍala's cells represents a *deva*, or deity, a personality that reflects the numerous qualities that the space embodies (the word itself literally means "shining one" and is related to the word *divine*, and to *Deus*, the Latin word for God). A *deva,* or *devatā,* is a particularized expression of the One Consciousness, a representation of a facet of Reality that sports a specific name and form.

India's Seers have long sculpted their perceptions of Reality into sacred images, teaching that, though there is but One Reality, this True God has Many Faces, each a personality of the Godhead. Each divine persona is ostensibly independent, but behind each mask appears the True Visage of the One. From the perspective of the Ultimate, each deity is a limited expression of divinity, but from the point of view of the Multiplicity that we inhabit, each deity can also be taken as representing the Supreme.

Performing pūjā (ritual worship) of a deity is a way of inviting the deity to actively intervene in your life. Worship of the ten directions (north, northeast, east, southeast, south, southwest, west, northwest, up, and down) involves showing respect for them, the same sort of respect that you would offer to any important personage whose goodwill you valued. If you appreciate the ten directions for the role they play, your gratitude for their presence in your life will encourage them to align with you even better.

Vīthis

We can group the squares that envelop a Vāstu Maṇḍala's Brahma Sthāna into three "belts," known as *vīthi* (or *pada*). The Brahma Sthāna itself forms a central vīthi; it is surrounded by:

Deva or *Daivika* ("divine") *Vīthi*
Manuṣya ("human") *Vīthi*
Paiśāca ("goblin") *Vīthi*

The Vāstu Puruṣa's Vīthis are the several layers of his body's "tissues," and the multiple square cells symbolize his individual components (vessels, organs, joints, and the like). Together they map the well-textured complexity of his energetic being.

The Brahma Sthāna, or *Brahma Vīthi*, is the building's most intimate space. Within the cosmos that we are creating, be it a room, house, or larger locale, this is the space most protected from the outer world, the personal space of whoever that room, house, or parcel of land belongs to.

Immediately outside the Brahma Sthāna is the Deva Vīthi. This is divine space, shining with the light of the Brahma Sthāna, the inner sanctum. By intervening between us and the light and awareness of the Pure Center, this benevolent space makes its powerfully radiant force available to us in a form that we can assimilate. The Deva Vīthi is "familial space," whose noble energy inspires the residents of the home to work together as one by focusing their awareness on the pure central reality. Only those who are "family" (consanguineous or otherwise), those who will support us come what may, should be permitted to spend much time here.

The Manuṣya ("human") Vīthi is the next ring, whose position between the Deva Vīthi and the Paiśāca Vīthi reflects the position of humans in this world as intermediaries between the "gods" and the "demons." Here, the awareness nurtured by this Vīthi is twofold: inwards toward the family and Reality, and outwards toward the guest, the stranger, society, the unknown. This ring reflects the Janus-faced nature of all humans as being part solitary and part social creatures.

Outside the Manuṣya Vīthi lies the Paiśāca Vīthi, which represents the unknown, the unfamiliar, the unpredictable, the potentially dangerous. In Indian myth, the *piśāca* of Paiśāca Vīthi is an evil spirit who feasts on human flesh. Powerful untamed energies occupy its cells, forces that—because they are indifferent to us at best, actively inimical towards us at worst—promote chaos in our lives. This Vīthi serves as the abode for all those who are not part of our home, beings who, not being "family," may think of us as prey and "gobble us up," literally or figuratively. Vāstu advises us to keep the Paiśāca Vīthi in any grid unoccupied, to provide prāṇa with space in which to circulate, and as a buffer against the "goblin" energy of the outside world.

In the context of a room, keeping the Paiśāca Vīthi unoccupied means keeping furniture and other items from touching the walls. A

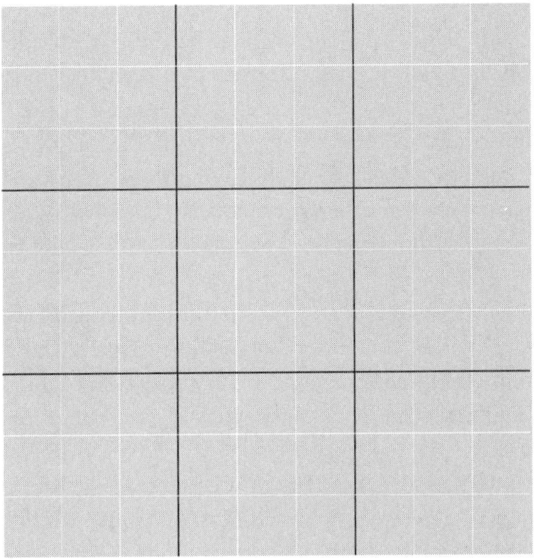

9 x 9 grid

Modern Maṇḍala

house's Paiśāca Vīthi is the permanent open space that surrounds it, a band of empty ground around its perimeter, between the house and the property's retaining wall (if there is such a boundary). This "belt" provides an opportunity to intercept visitors at the front gate, where their bona fides may be evaluated before letting them near the house. A house's veranda provides another intermediary stop where guests can be greeted and feted, without the need to admit them into the family's private quarters.

In many cities where land is at a premium, both Indian and Western alike, these outer rings are condensed into a front room, sitting room, or parlor—a room set aside for entertaining those who, though not intimates, require more than just a rendezvous at a restaurant or other neutral location.

We avoid encouraging paiśāca traits in a larger tract of land, like a city or an estate, by keeping the area's Paiśāca Vīthi free of buildings. In a maṇḍala diagramming a walled city, this might be accomplished by including a moat; for a modern city, the same can be achieved with an outer green belt; for an estate, perhaps a belt of trees and shrubbery that hug the outer compound wall.

For a 9 x 9 grid, the Brahma Vīthi (Brahma Sthāna), which is the innermost 9 squares out of a total of 81 squares, occupies 11.1 percent of the grid's total area; this space should remain vacant along with the Paiśāca Vīthi, the outer envelope of 32 cells (39.5 percent of the total area). These 9 + 32 = 41 cells comprise slightly more than 50 percent of the entire maṇḍala (however large it may be). In other words, no construction on any plot—and no furnishing of any room—may cover more than half of a 9 x 9 Paramasāyikā Maṇḍala used to plan its development. This constraint ensures an adequate supply of space for the circulation of light, air, and energy in and around any edifice.

Marie's Living Room, On The Grid

Marie's rectangular living room measures 18 feet (216 inches) from east to west and 14 feet 6 inches (174 inches) from north to south. This gives us a theoretical area of 261 square feet to work with—theoretical because of the presence in the room's southeast corner of two short stairways, each 3 feet 4 inches wide, one proceeding downward to the level of the front door, the other proceeding upward to the level of two of the bedrooms. Both jut slightly into the room, reducing its available area by about five percent (and mangling Vāstu Puruṣa's right hand and arm in doing so).

To conjure Vāstu Puruṣa onto this slab of space, we first lay down the desired grid. For a 9 x 9 Paramasāyikā Maṇḍala, we stretch Vāstu Puruṣa's square into a rectangle (as explained above), then divide each side of it into nine equal portions of 2 feet (24 inches) by 1 foot 7 1/3 inches (19 1/3 inches). Each of the 81 identical rectangles thus formed covers an area of 464 square inches (about 3.2 square feet).

Of these, the innermost nine squares (which cover an area of 6 feet by 4 feet, 10 inches, or 29 square feet) form the Brahma Sthāna, which Vāstu directs us to keep empty. This is a good spot for Marie to locate her Persian or Turkish carpet, or something similar, as a way of keeping the area open (at least when the dog is not around). If keeping that area completely open seemed particularly wrong to her, she might consider placing something in the vein of a low coffee table there. This would not precisely fit the bill, from the perspective of giving the room's prāṇa its freest rein, but it would still serve the purpose of keeping people (and the dog) off that space.

The Paiśāca Vīthi, the wall-hugging belt of space that must also be kept empty, theoretically extends 2 feet into the room along the east and west walls, and 1 foot, 7 1/3 inches into the room along the north and south walls. The Vīthi's extent is "theoretical" here because Marie may find, when she again asks herself the question, "How full should this room be, and how empty?" that creating this precise configuration would make the Paiśāca Vīthi too wide to give the room the right "feel." She had previously estimated that her living room should be about 70 percent full and 30 percent empty, whereas Vāstu prescribes that the fullness-emptiness ratio for a room organized with a 9 x 9 Paramasāyikā Maṇḍala be more like 50-50. Marie will have to determine for herself, using her breath, her hara point, and whatever other tests she finds germane, the arrangement that feels most "right"; through these assessments, she can determine that ideal percentage of fullness that encompasses sufficient furniture to make the room utilitarian while preserving ample circulation space for people to inhabit it comfortably, to *live* in it.

As she arranges her furniture, Marie will want to pay attention to the most significant of the room's marmas, those points where the Vāstu Puruṣa Maṇḍala's many lines intersect. She will be wise to avoid "afflicting" these points by having them support any heavy items, though they may be able to serve as locations for small prāṇa-enhancing articles, like plants or light fixtures.

Exercise Nine: The Vāstu Puruṣa Maṇḍala

To experiment with the Vāstu Puruṣa Maṇḍala yourself, overlay it on a diagram of one of your own rooms. Measure the room's dimensions, draw a sketch of the room, divide it into nine parts on each side, and create the grid by adding in the appropriate lines and Vīthis.

Once you have your diagram—or diagrams, if you find it easier to consider the marmas and Vīthis separately—sit on the floor of the room, in its Brahma Sthāna, facing east or north. Focus your awareness on the qualities of the room's individuality, its "personality," or set of traits. Breathe calmly, deeply, trying to let your awareness "meet" the room's awareness, its "roominess" or "pranic sentience." Try to get a feel for how the lines of force extend and connect around you, by comparing your own experience with how they're depicted on the diagram(s); note those areas where the energy is palpable, as well as those where the reality of the room's prāṇa does not seem to follow those paths.

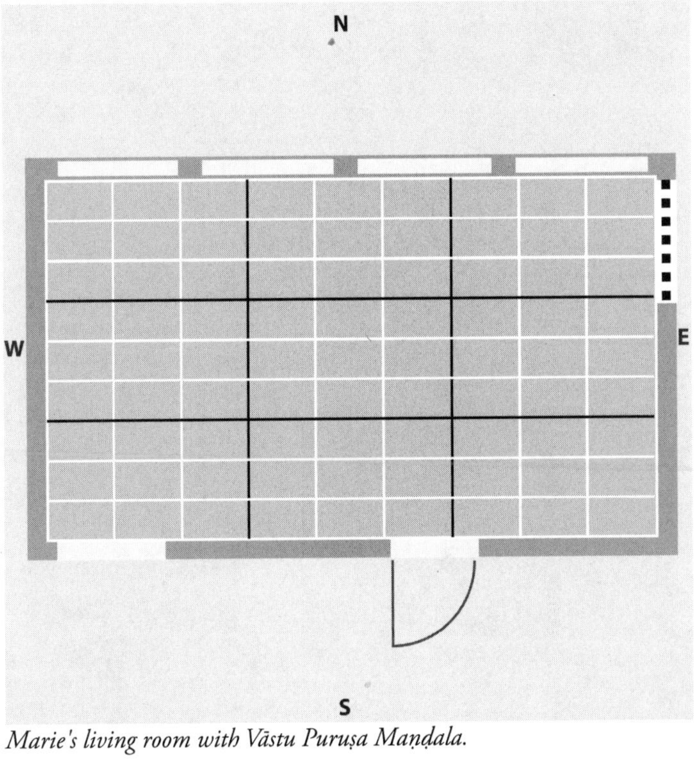

Marie's living room with Vāstu Puruṣa Maṇḍala.

6 Directions

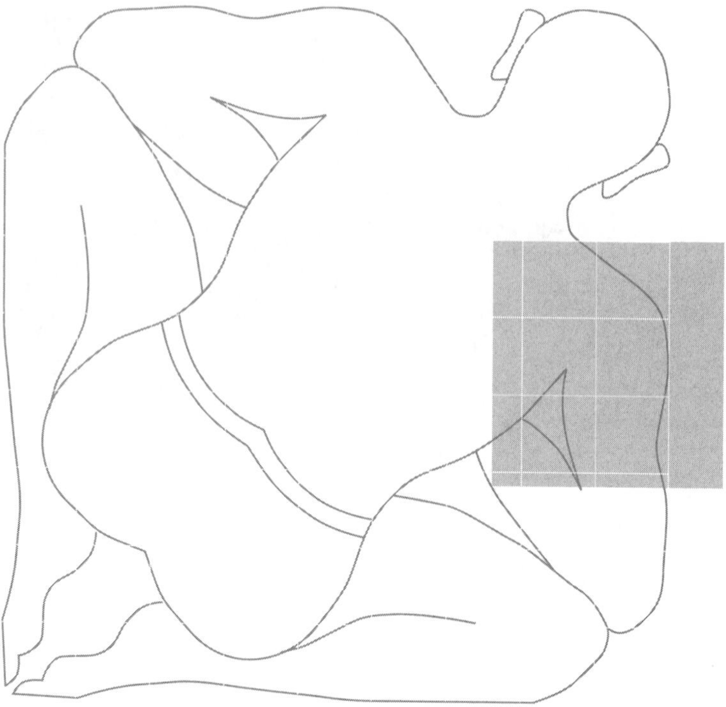

Directionality

Every structure should have a well-defined center from which the energy it contains can radiate. Centrality begets axiality, and axiality begets *directionality*. Our spaces "learn" from the directions with which they align, meaning the associated directions give our spaces certain qualities. Life on Earth developed within the spatial grid that the cardinal directions generate, and these directions continue to be truly "cardinal" in the lives of all protoplasmic beings. Vāstu teaches that rooms and buildings ought to be aligned closely with these four chief directions because each has very particular characteristics that can affect our well-being, state of mind, and ability to succeed in life's endeavors. We will thus be well advised to become fully versed in the characteristics of the directions when we are designing or modifying a space.

East

East is the first, the key direction; *orientation*, in fact, literally meant "aligning with the east" when the word first emerged in the 1830s. East is the direction of the rising sun, on whose unending contributions of light and heat life depends. The sun regulates all forms of human endeavor by providing us with directionality, which aligns and structures both space and time (since the sun defines day and night, and the seasons of the year). Presenting us with a firm, unwavering "eye" in the sky, the sun offers us our most perfect representation of the unrepresentable Ultimate Absolute. By rising high into the firmament, the sun transcends the limited verticality of tall trees and lofty mountains with a "light-column" that penetrates downward from heaven to earth.

Most importantly, the Sun provides us with our prāṇa. In the words of a Vedic text, "It is by the rays of that Sun that all these creatures are endowed with vital breaths, and therefore the rays extend downwards to these breaths."* The central, sacred Brahma Sthāna of a Vāstu diagram symbolizes this Sun, from which emanates light, breath, and life itself.

Numerous cultures have worshipped the sun as God incarnate, and in India—since the Vedic era or before—people have worshipped the sun by such means as reciting invocations like the Gāyatrī mantra to dispel the darkness of ignorance and gain discernment, and by performing yogic Sun Salutations, to cultivate health, strength, and awareness.

**Śatapatha Brāhmaṇa* II.3.3.7

By serving as the sun's "nursery," the site of its rebirth each morning, east represents life's beginnings. To face a building toward the east is to "educate" that building's space in all that east stands for—youth, strength, beauty, wholeness, freshness, hope, promise—so that these traits may develop in the lives of those who own and occupy the structure. *Pūrva*, the Sanskrit term for east, means, "that which comes first," reflecting Vāstu's firm conviction that, among the four cardinal directions, east is best.

West

The sun sets—it "dies"—in the west. As it moves toward the western horizon, the sun withdraws its light from the world. The morning sun's light waxes with each passing moment, while the sun's light wanes with each passing minute of the late afternoon. West is thus the direction of endings, of the decline and conclusion of activities, of departures, of detachment from the world, of life's closing stages. In Sanskrit, west is *paścima*, "that which comes after."

To face a building toward the west is to "educate" its space to encourage some variety of disconnection from the wholeness of life. When influenced by this westerly tenor, some individuals disconnect from the material world and embrace the spiritual; other west-influenced people retreat from the spiritual, and move toward materialism. California, the quintessential "Western" state, has long been fertile ground for its inhabitants to pursue both tendencies.

Death is an integral part of life, and often one creation (whether it be an entity, system, or structure) must die before another can be born. Occasions may arise in life when nothing other than west will do. It's wise to think twice, though, before deliberately "educating" your dwelling space to promote endings rather than beginnings—to advance change at the expense of continuity—by setting the front door, the portal through which you greet the day and the world, to face west.

North

The symbolism of north and south, more complex than that of east and west, is also based in large measure on the sun's apparent behavior. As Earth circumambulates its star, its movements cause the sun's apparent rising point to shift on the horizon. The sun's rays become stronger, and the days longer, as the sun's point of arrival on the horizon appears to move north (in the northern hemisphere). In the northern hemisphere, the year's longest day arrives when the sun reaches its most northerly point (June 21 or 22, nowadays). Shortly before and after this peak, the sun appears to stand still in the sky for several days, unable to move further north and not yet ready again to move south. We call the apex of this solar choreography the *summer solstice* (solstice = sun stands still), the longest day of the year.

After the summer solstice, the sun begins its apparent southward movement. Each day the intensity of its rays weaken, and the days shorten, until, in the northern hemisphere, the sun reaches its southernmost point, on December 21 or 22. During the days before and after this *winter solstice*, the shortest day of the year, the sun again appears to stand still before again turning north. The sun gains power and influence between the winter and summer solstices, and its power and influence wane between the summer and winter solstices. Midway between the solstices comes the *vernal* and *autumnal equinoxes* (equinox = equal night), when night and day are of equal length everywhere on earth.*

The period from December 21 to June 21 is known in Sanskrit as *uttarāyaṇa* ("the advancement toward the north"), and the June 21 to December 21 period is known as *dakṣiṇāyana* ("the progress toward the south"). Uttarāyaṇa is the "morning" of the year; the minutes of daylight that the northern hemisphere receives increase daily during uttarāyaṇa, just as the light of a typical day increases during morning, from dawn until noon. Dakṣiṇāyana is similarly the year's "afternoon," during which the day's length decreases, just as the sun's power decreases during the time from solar noon until dusk every day of the year. The summer solstice is our planet's high noon, in northern and southern hemisphere alike, and the winter solstice, in either hemisphere, serves simultaneously as "sunset" for one year and "sunrise" for the next.

In Sanskrit, it is said, *Kālo hi bhagavan*: "Time is indeed God," and, "God is indeed time." Properly timing an event increases the likelihood of a successful result, and for millennia, authorities in India have suggested that most major life events should be timed to occur during uttarāyaṇa, the period when the sun's strength is increasing. In Sanskrit, north is *uttara*, "that which is better."

---

*All this is true solely for the northern hemisphere. The situation is precisely the opposite in the southern hemisphere, where the winter solstice occurs in June, the summer solstice in December, and the vernal and autumnal equinoxes in September and March respectively.

South

East is auspicious by virtue of being the direction of sunrise and morning for the day; north is auspicious as the direction of sunrise and morning for the year. When we face the dawn, the time of new beginnings, we open ourselves to sattva—to calm, poise, equilibrium. East is so central to sukha that the Sanskrit word for south is *dakṣiṇa*, "the right side," which indicates that south sits at our right hand and implies that we are facing east.

East and north (and northeast) thus represent the future as assuredly as west and south, the directions of eventide and sunset for the day and year respectively, represent the past and the soon-to-be past. West and south also relate to tamas, inertia, loss of momentum. Southwest, representing as it does both south and west, epitomizes in Vāstu all that relates to tamas, all that is dark, shady, heavy, and nocturnal.

The subtropical and tropical nature of India's climate reinforces this connection of south with tamas and north with sattva, for sweltering heat makes movement almost impossible between morning and evening during the subcontinent's long, hot summers. Peninsular India's relatively mild winters promote a level of focus and activity that is out of the question when the weather turns torrid.

Further testimony to the accuracy of this north-sattva and south-tamas correlation comes from seers who long observed within themselves the effects of the pull from Earth's magnetic lines of force. They found that (at least in the northern hemisphere) a northward orientation encourages more spirit-oriented life experiences, while southern magnetism promotes greater groundedness and earthiness.

This resonance between life and the northern direction is significantly enhanced by the eternal presence in the northern sky of the polestar, Polaris. The northern pole of the Earth's axis of rotation points almost directly at Polaris, which makes the heavens appear to rotate around the star, and makes it a reliable guide to north. The polestar's relative immobility garners it the Sanskrit name *Dhruva* ("fixed, stable, immovable").*

---

*Vāstu developed in India, a subcontinent that occupies the northern hemisphere. Vāstu has only recently been introduced into the southern hemisphere,

North and east (and northeast) are clearly Vāstu's preferred directions, particularly for a structure's main entrance. *Bṛhat Saṁhitā* expresses this directional predilection by stating that the Vāstu Puruṣa "has his head turned toward the northeast."

But northerly exposures and entrances are more appropriate for India than for most of the temperate northern hemisphere, and certainly for the subarctic regions, where north is commonly (and rightly) equated with cold, darkness, forced immobility, and death, and south is revered as the direction whence arises heat, light, change, and life. The ancient Chinese oriented their world along the north-south axis, placing the yellow of earth at the center and the red phoenix—the bird of sun, summer and youth—in the south. The white tiger of autumn, which represents old age, appears in the west, and the black tortoise, the "warrior" of the north, signifies death. The blue dragon sits in the east, which, as in India, represents spring, and birth.

How you elect to dispose your dwelling in relation to north and south ought thus to depend chiefly on your latitude. In much of India, a southern door is an invitation to death by baking, for the blazing tropical sun will be able to cook you all day long, all summer long, if your door and main windows are subject to its rays. Some Vāstu "experts" in fact claim, with dogmatic certainty, that south is wholly inauspicious, a source of all evil. Despite the evident benevolence of a southern exposure and the increased warmth that it offers in the cold north, these diehards insist that no building in any country should ever have a southward-facing entrance, that all existing southern entrances in all buildings should be immediately closed, and so on. This sort of inflexible, authoritarian interpretation of Vāstu's principles is preposterous even in India, where some people have done well even with south-facing houses and properties. Experience must always supersede theory, in Vāstu as in other Vidyās, whose wisdom has developed out of generations of collected experience.

---

far too recently to permit us to speak confidently of the relative value of north to south there. South is, in the southern hemisphere, clearly superior to north from the point of view of the sun's location and the year's seasonal shifts, but not necessarily from the perspective of the influence of Earth's magnetic lines of force. As experience with Vāstu accumulates Down Under, a clearer picture should develop as to whether south should, in the southern hemisphere, receive the same veneration that north receives in the northern.

The Four Puruṣārthas

Prāg-dvāraṁ sukhadaṁ vidhi paścimaṁ puṣṭi-vardhanam |
Dhanadañ ca uttara-dvāram yāmyañ ca mokṣadam ||

An eastern door gives sukha, a western door development,
a northern door abundance, a southern door mokṣa.

Traditional Vāstu saying

One way to look at which direction your door (and thus your life) should face is to consider which goal of life (*puruṣārtha*) you most want to pursue. Each of us, consciously or unconsciously, is trying to achieve four goals in life: *dharma*, *artha*, *kāma*, and *mokṣa*.

Dharma is "doing what you are born to do," following your ideal path through life, doing what feels most right to you, in every way. A spiritual path is a dharma. A profession can be a dharma, particularly if it's your true calling. Following the path of your personal dharma is the most reliable way to ensure sukha in your life. If overall sukha is your priority, then it's good if your dwelling faces east.

Artha is the goal of legitimately accumulating possessions as you fulfill your dharma, by collecting your paycheck, for example, or accumulating profits from a lawful business. If pursuing material prosperity is your chief aim in life, then you should dwell in a north-facing house.

Kāma (desire) is the aim of using your accumulated possessions to satisfy legitimate desires, like procuring a new car, or buying Christmas and birthday presents for your relatives. One way to facilitate a desire-gratifying life, a life that generally promotes growth and prosperity, is to tenant a west-facing residence.

Mokṣa (liberation), the ultimate goal, involves realizing that there is more to life than merely performing duties, accumulating possessions, and fulfilling desires. Mokṣa entails disengagement from worldly life and is abetted by a south-facing abode; it may in fact be useful to orient a retirement cottage, retreat cabin, or hermit hut to the south. South is however the least productive direction in which to orient a home for those who prefer to engage with the world.

When a structure is closely aligned with the four cardinal directions, the four "intermediate directions" appear at the four corners of the square or rectangular space thus established. The intermediate directions mainly derive their Vāstu significances from the movements of the sun, whose apparent motion has it rising on the eastern horizon substantially to the north of east in June and to the south of east in December. North and east both being benevolent directions, northeast is regarded as being doubly auspicious. Southeast is less advantageous, being made up of equal parts of the desirable east and the unwelcome south. Sunset likewise commutes between northwest, a semi-desirable direction, and the doubly-negative southwest, which from the Vāstu perspective has little good going for it.

When we include the orientations of "up" and "down" to the navigational set comprising the four cardinal and four intermediate directions, we then amass a full complement of ten directions, in three dimensions. As a direction, up is associated with the sun and the heavens, where live the celestial deities and whence comes our spiritual inspiration. Down is connected with the earth, and our physical existence and appetites. Because of their sunnier dispositions, north, east, and northeast are generally upward-trending directions; south, west, and southwest generally trend downward.

We orient our Vāstu Puruṣa Maṇḍala to these ten directions by converting the round compass rose into a quadrangle:

"The cycles of the sun are pinned to the four directions and in this way the circle of the sun's rotation is squared. In the world of appearances the plane of earth is round, circumscribed by the circle of the horizon. When structured by the cardinal points, determined by the movements of the sun, it is converted to a square and in this respect is called 'four cornered' (*caturbhṛṣṭi*)."*

As the earth spins around its axis and circles the sun, the directions are marked by the two solstices (which are the furthest points that the sun "travels" toward the north and the south) and the two equinoxes (which delineate the directions of east and west). These four "corners" of the year define a geographic (or astrological) square or rectangle within which the sun's eternal movement cycles. In Vedic symbolism,

*Adrian Snodgrass, *The Symbolism of the Stupa*, p. 101

the circle represents the mutable, flux-filled terrestrial realm, and square represents the immutability of heaven. Vāstu symbolism inverts the Vedic order to present the square as a symbol of the Earth Element's stability, whereas circle stands for the dynamic Air Element. Vedic or post-Vedic, on heaven or on earth, squares are stable and circles, mobile.

The Vāstu Puruṣa has his head in the northeast. Orienting the Vāstu Puruṣa Maṇḍala accordingly, and dividing it into four equal quadrants, gives us:

This quartering arranges the Five Great Elements in space, with Fire

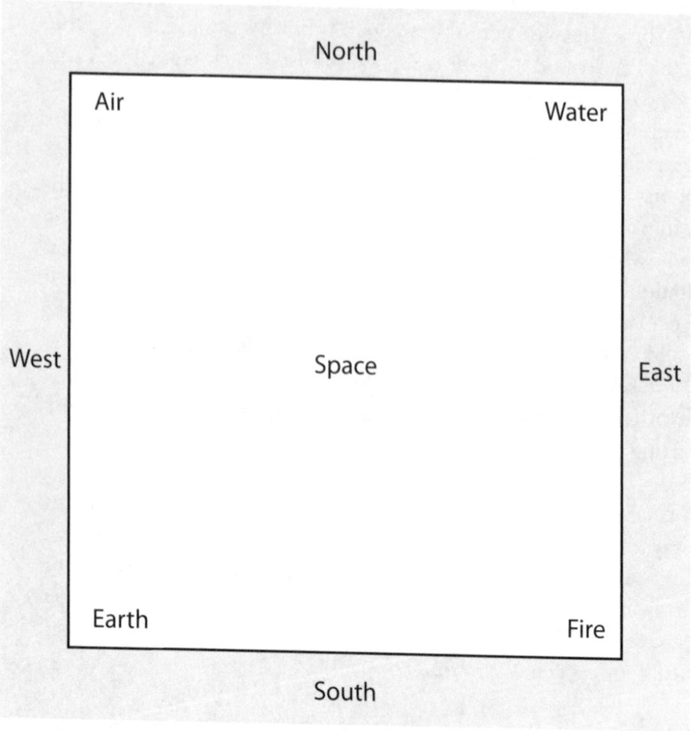

in the southeast, Air in the northwest, and Water in the northeast. Southwest represents either Space or Earth—authorities disagree. The fifth (either Space or Earth) of the Five is situated at the stable center of the schema.

By occupying the realm that extends from the earth into the

atmosphere, terrestrial life "unites" our planet with its sky, along an axis that is defined for any Space by its center, the hub of its activity, its heart. When a structure's center is well balanced and well integrated, Space and Earth enter into a relationship of health and harmony there. Vāstu always prefers to leave the center of a room, building, or city unoccupied, to provide a meeting place for this consummation of earth and sky. Setting aside "empty" Space in the center provides room for prāṇa to circulate throughout the spaces of the house and grants its inhabitants the harmony that a healthy Space-Earth liaison generates. When well situated on Earth, a maṇḍala's center best facilitates the self-expression of Space.

Space and Earth enjoy a substantially reduced potential to form a healthy relationship in the southwest, a direction that (being the offspring of south and west) is much more likely to encourage instability and unbalanced activity than constancy and purposeful action. Tamas is inertia; inability or unwillingness to adapt; refusal or resistance to reconcile. Stubborn rejection of change is an "Earthy" sort of tamas, heavy and insensitive; "Spacey" tamas appears in situations where change is as free-flowing as the wind, but the changes made do not endure. Southwest embodies a double portion of tamas, half "Earthy" and half "Spacey," two components that tamasically refuse to cooperate with each other. The "Spacey" bit of southwest promotes flighty tendencies in those who frequent this quadrant, as Space tries to get Earth to move; and southwest's "Earthy" bit encourages a retreat into numb habit, as Earth digs in its heels attempting to "ground" Space.

The collision of Space's irresistible force with Earth's immovable object creates a third tamas vector, of irremediable difference. Vāstu addresses southwest's thrice-troubled energy by siding with Earth's innate stability, directing that extra Earth be placed in the southwest, in the form of tall, heavy things like trees, hills, closets, and cupboards, to anchor and steady those irreconcilable influences as best one can.

The Vāstu Puruṣa and the Three Guṇas

The dynamic tension generated between the problem that is tamas and the potential that is sattva is known as rajas, and the influence of directionality induces these Three Guṇas to predominate in distinct portions of our maṇḍala:

With the chart thus subdivided, our spatial grid becomes a space-time

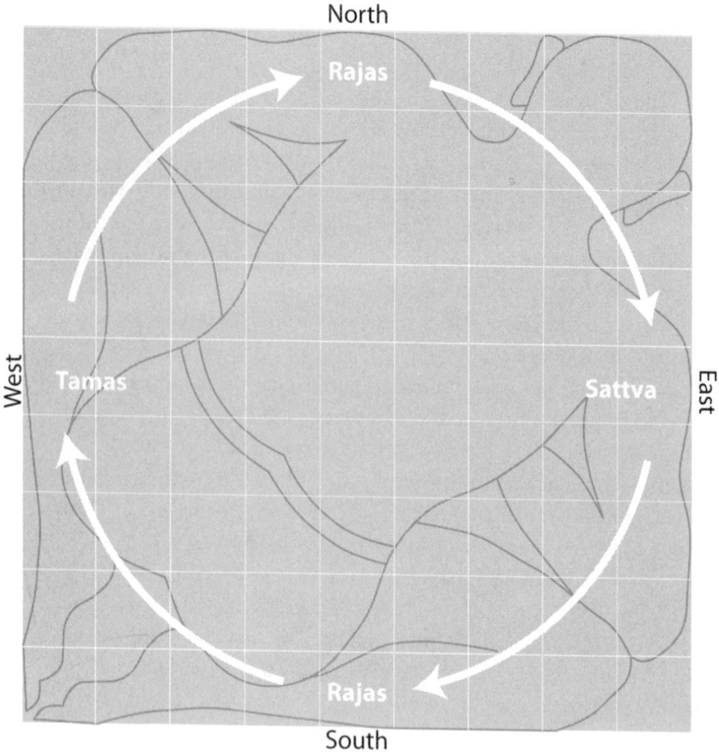

diagram that correlates, within the confines of our stable square, the natural tendencies of the directions with the natural predispositions of time.

Energies move within a structure as ceaselessly as Earth rotates on its axis and circles its sun. Our sun's daily influence emerges, with its ascent, in the east. That influence then flows south (in the northern hemisphere the sun shines on us from the south—moss grows on the north sides of trees there because it likes the shadier and damper conditions), then west, and then north (at midnight, when the sun is invisible to us), before becoming easterly again, at its next rising. Movement in the above diagram is similarly clockwise: sattva becoming rajas, which is transformed into tamas, which changes back into rajas, which again moves to sattva, ad infinitum.

The caduceus, the yin-yang symbol, and the *svastika* (or *swastika*) are reverberant ancient emblems that each represents the "good space" that opposing forces generating endless motion can create, when they're

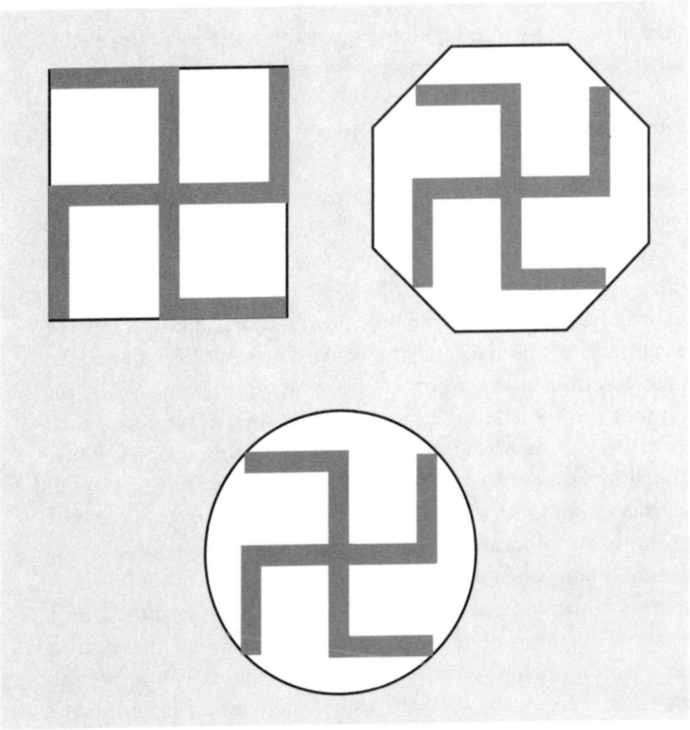

harmonious (in Sanskrit, the word svastika means, roughly, "Let this be good!"):

"The svastika, commonly used as an aniconic representation of the Buddha, is also homologous with the wheel. … Like the wheel, the svastika represents movement about a fixed and unmoving axis and, like the wheel, it is a symbol of the generation of universal cycles from a forever-Present Centre. It represents the generation of currents of energy, and is a symbol of the action of immutable Principle, the 'unmoved mover,' within manifestation."*

We can inscribe svastikas in any of Vāstu's three basic shapes: square, octagon, or circle.

The Nazis took the svastika hostage, using it to symbolize their own

*Snodgrass, op. cit. pp. 83-84

perverted ideas of unity through brutality; efforts are now under way to rehabilitate it, and return it to its proper position of honor.

The Circulation of Elements & Traits

Our diagram's northeast quadrant represents the pre-dawn period, the hours of the day that are most sattvic, most meditative; these moments are when the world is calm and quiet, readying itself for the new life that the nascent day will bring.

At dawn, the focus moves from northeast to east. Sunrise is the first active moment of the day, and the activity of rajas amplifies as the sun proceeds from east toward southeast. At solar noon, when the sun sits more or less due south in the sky, the day's rajas peaks. Tamas begins its increase just after noon, particularly in the tropics (where only Englishmen and mad dogs go out in the noonday sun). As the sun journeys from south to southwest, any residual rajas-based activity moves in the direction of tamasic inertia. Who does not feel a low in the late afternoon, when the light begins to die?

The day's tamas concentrates in the southwest, during the pre-dusk hours, the antipodean opposite to the sattva maximum that accrues in the northeast before dawn. Late afternoon is the time of least focus during the day, the time that is generally lowest in purposeful concentration (and often highest in jittery nervous energy). These least productive hours of the day are associated with the southwest quadrant, as Space's drive to expand wrestles with Earth's inertia.

As southwest continues on to west, the moment of sunset, tamas begins to accelerate toward rajas as we mobilize ourselves to cope with the onset of the hours of darkness. Rajas is maximal in the northwest just before bed. Then, as activity and rajas slow and finally shut down for the night, northwest moves on at midnight to north, then to northeast, and the cycle starts anew.

Your aim, as architect of your environment and its ambiance, is to create a space that resonates with the energies of time and direction. In this context, you will, almost always, want to maximize the harmonizing influence of sattva and minimize the unresponsive lethargy of tamas.

For thousands of years, Indian tradition has thus stressed that the sattvic pre-dawn hours offer the best time of day for prayer and meditation, since these activities characteristically promote (and are promoted by) sattva. Facing north, east, or northeast while meditating can potentially enhance the sattva-generating effects of your contemplation. The "sattva effect" can be boosted yet further by sitting in the north, east, or northeast corner of your prayer room, a position which will offer even greater sattva enhancement should it be located in your home or office's northeastern quadrant.

Southeast and northwest both supply the dynamism of rajas but, by and large, the action that southeast promotes is better focused and more efficacious than that of northwest. By virtue of following northeast in the cycle, southeast enjoys some of the flavor of sattva's balancing energy; northwest follows southwest, which flecks its rajas with tamas. Also, Fire is the Element predominant in the southeast and at midday, while Air predominates in the northwest and at midnight; both of these are lively, on-the-go elements, but Fire is warmer, more centered, and more nourishing than is Air.

Moreover, the performing of exploits during the day, the time when humans evolved to be active, is less likely to aggravate the organism than is remaining awake and vigorous at night, when nature intends for us to sleep. Northwest is a lunar direction, good for the qualities and activities associated with the moon. To stay up all night long from time to time, particularly under the pearly luminosity of a full moon, may inspire succulent poetry to fall from your lips, urge your imagination to new creative heights, and make romantic trysts sublimely juicy. But habitually remaining wakeful at night will exhaust your body's energy, dull your mind, and generally imbalance your system. Dreaming is the form of rajas that is most appropriate for the midnight hours.

The moon may make the sap rise, but the sun cooks it into boughs and branches. Similarly, India's Vidyās take the many factors that compile our lives and "cook" them into a satisfyingly luscious experience of living. Any kind of "cooking" is done with Fire, which makes cooking your own meals, particularly when your kitchen is located in the southeast of your dwelling, a good way to nourish your life generally—particularly now, with the outside world eternally tempting us to live fast, and eat on the run.

Doṣa Circulation

Orientation also influences the doṣas, for direction and doṣa can both be expressed in terms of the Five Elements. Fire, for example, appears in the southeast and in pitta. All else being equal, there is an above-average likelihood that pitta will increase in either your body or mind (or both) if you predominantly eat, work, sleep, and spend the major part of your day in the southeast quadrant of your space.

Similarly, Air appears in the northwest and in vāta, and those who primarily orbit around the northwest quadrant of their space are likely to find vāta increasing within them—all other variables being held equal. The Watery kapha is likely to increase in those who tenant the Watery northeast quadrant of their spaces to the effective exclusion of the other quadrants. Southwest, which reflects the influence of both Earth (kapha) and Space (vāta), tends to enhance overall the force of vāta, as a result of some impediment to prāṇa's free flow, often due to a kapha obstruction.

Time also comes into play: Northeast will encourage kapha most during kapha-predominant periods of the day, like the hours of early morning and early evening. Southeast will be at its pitta-promoting peak at midday and midnight, and northwest will spur vāta to soar rapidly during the late afternoon and pre-dawn hours.

In addition to the day and night doṣa succession, Āyurveda recognizes three other "seasonal" cycles: the seasons of the year, the phases of an individual lifespan, and the stages of digestion. A fertile woman has one extra: the menstrual cycle. Doshic influence is evident during each of these stages.

Time and Doṣas

Kapha predominates

during the day

from dawn to midmorning

for the first few hours after sunset

in spring (after accumulating during winter)

between birth and the end of growth

immediately after eating

between the end of menstruation and the moment of ovulation

Pitta predominates:
at night
from midmorning to mid-afternoon
during the midnight hours
in summer (after accumulating during spring)
from the end of growth until menopause
(or the male equivalent thereof)
during the digestive process
from ovulation until the flow begins

Vata predominates:
at dawn and dusk
from mid-afternoon to dusk and
during the pre-dawn hours
in autumn (after accumulating during summer)
after menopause
during assimilation and excretion
during the menstrual flow

Dikpālas

The ten directions (*dik*, *diśā*) are innate properties of Space, which—because Space is a form of matter—makes them material substances. They are substantial enough to be thought of as space's attire; naked wandering Indian holy men are sometimes spoken of as being *digambara*, "clad solely in the [ten] directions."

The Five Great Elements became associated with the directions long ago, in the Vedic era or earlier, when the rishis were engaged in establishing connections between aspects of the material and immaterial realities. These Seers codified these connections in personalized forms known collectively as *devas* (deities). Most of the deities popular today in India were introduced well after the Vedic era, including particularly the Trinity of Brahmā the Creator, Viṣṇu the Preserver, and Śiva the Destroyer (the square, octagon, and circle, respectively, in Vāstu symbolism). Certain Vedic deities have, however, held onto their importance as direction-lords. The names of these *dikpālas* (the Regents of the Ten Directions) vary from text to text; here is the most commonly accepted list:

East (*pūrva*) is presided over by *Indra*, king of the *devas*.
Southeast (*āgneya*) is presided over by *Agni*, Fire personified.
South (dakṣiṇa) is presided over by *Yama*, lord of dharma and death.
Southwest (*nairṛtya*) is presided over by *Nirṛti*, the power of chaos and dissolution.
West (*paścima*) is presided over by *Varuṇa*, lord of Truth, Order, and Vastness.
Northwest (*vāyavya*) is presided over by *Vāyu*, Air personified.
North (*uttara*) is presided over by *Kubera*, god of wealth.
Northeast (*īśānya*) is presided over by *Īśāna* (or *Īśvara*, "The Great Lord") or *Soma* ("Nectar Incarnate"), and is associated with the Water Element.
Vertically above (*ūrdhva*) is the sky, where the planets congregate, ruled by Brahmā, the Creator, and also Brahman, the Absolute, the source of peace, concord, and life itself.
Vertically below (*adhas*) is the realm of *Ananta* (or *Śeṣa*), the thousand-headed serpent who is the source of all natural resources and all worldly pleasures.

Brahmā the Creator is the embodiment of the creative power of Brahman the Absolute; Brahmā possesses attributes and confers attributes on others, while Brahman remains ever attribute-free.

Ananta, or Śeṣa, who rules the downward direction, supports the earth on his thousand hooded heads. Snakes are notorious for being powerful and uncooperative, but divine intervention caused this particular snake-being to be transformed from a potential destroyer into a protector. *Śeṣa* means "residue"—a residue that becomes a residence once it's bound down.

Śeṣa is usually bound down at the time when a building's foundation stone is laid. An astrologer will determine a spot where Śeṣa is regarded as being present, and a wooden or metal peg will then be driven into the ground there. This "nailing down" of the Serpent fixes position, establishes directions, and makes the chaotic, cosmic: "Before its transfixing the Serpent moves in cyclic motion, proceeding from the East to the South-West and North, completing the cycle in the course of a year, moving one degree each day. By pinning the Serpent, time is fixed, transformed to the timeless. The world is made stable."*

---

*Snodgrass, op. cit. pp. 83-84

This process of "binding down" a potentially dangerous force recalls, of course, the process by which the Vāstu Puruṣa is pinned to the ground. One Tibetan story conflates these two myths by making the Vāstu Puruṣa appear as the "earth-bellied snake deity," who sports a hood of snakes and a man's torso.

Restriction is also associated with the regents of the south, southwest, and west. Varuṇa, lord of the west, whose name comes from a root meaning "to restrain," is the Vedic deity who measures. Varuṇa limits, circumscribes, kills the day; by measuring it, he provides it with its end.

Varuṇa wields a noose, as does Yama, lord of the south. Even Nirṛti, the southwest lord, is associated with binding and releasing. All three regents thus reflect mythologically the themes of constraint and termination that Vāstu astronomy suggests for these directions, themes that typically leave most people ill at ease.

Vāstu Puruṣa consequently lies face down with his head into the northeast, bowing low to Īśāna, "The Great Lord" who rules over that direction, whose energy is that of life. Accordingly, Vāstu prefers that most buildings face the life-giving east or north, and are aligned squarely with the cardinal directions. Most modern constructions do not, however, align with the compass rose, which makes it more difficult for the energies and significations of the directions to express themselves easily and with natural clarity. Such misalignment may mean that your home will find it more difficult to ingest clear, benevolent directional energies from outside, and will "leak" some of its energy into its surroundings.

If your residence is not square with the cardinal directions, measure the angle by which it varies from true. A building whose frontal façade faces mostly north (to be precise, less than 20° off of north, in either direction) can be considered to be, effectively, northern. A building that is more than 25° off north in an easterly direction should be considered to face northeast; if more than 25° off north towards the west, view it as northwest.

A home that falls in the "twilight zone" between 20° and 25° occupies an amorphous "neither this nor that" region whose energies will have difficulty deciding which direction to identify with. To remedy such a situation, you might superimpose clearer energetic expressions and boundaries, with bright colors, clear lines, and spare furnishings helping to delineate the qualities you want; you can also establish clearly-defined and demarcated Vāstu Puruṣa Maṇḍalas both within and outside of the house, or add on a properly aligned extension into the northeast. As a last resort, consider finding another place to live, one that holds the directions in greater esteem.

Here Too, Confluence

It's generally true that people with excess kapha can benefit from the motivation and stimulation of southeast and northwest, and that vāta can often find needed balance and relaxation most readily in the northeast, and the requisite warmth in the southeast. Pitta benefits from the challenge of northwest, the stability of northeast, and the coolness of both. The southwest portions of rooms, buildings, properties, and continents are as generally unbalancing to the doṣas as their northeast portions are generally harmonizing.

But this is only generally true. The directions and how you use them do affect your physical condition, but your state of health also depends, of course, on what you consume and how you act. A diet of spiced sausages, coffee, tequila, and tobacco will send your pitta through the roof no matter how resolutely you may cling to your northeastern chaise each morning. A black tea, raw veggies, and rice cakes regimen will likewise put you into vāta orbit no matter where you set up your desk or how you arrange your plants, or how religiously you sit to meditate at dawn and dusk. A daily cheese-and-mayo-on-white-bread lunch—with ice cream for dessert—will put you into kapha limbo, regardless of how ceaselessly you shuttle between the sleepless realms of southeast and northwest.

When you find it impossible or impossibly inconvenient to rearrange your living space to align ideally with the directions—especially in homes that are not directionally well aligned—you can still ameliorate the situation by returning to basics. The most basic of life's principles is to strive always to live in concordance with prāṇa. Begin by evaluating yourself—your own doṣa and guṇa predilections, your strengths and weaknesses. Discover who you are, and it will become clear to you what you need to do to bring yourself into alignment with your environment. Experiment, and keep experimenting; try out alignment methods to determine which ones work best for you. Some people will get their best results from dietary changes; others will find color coordination to be the most potent amelioration. Make sure that in the course of enhancing an influence, you do not aggravate another quality, and don't try to "nail down" alignment before you're certain that it is indeed worthy of becoming permanent. In all circumstances, look to prāṇa, the ultimate source of your sense of sukha.

7 Planets and Confluences

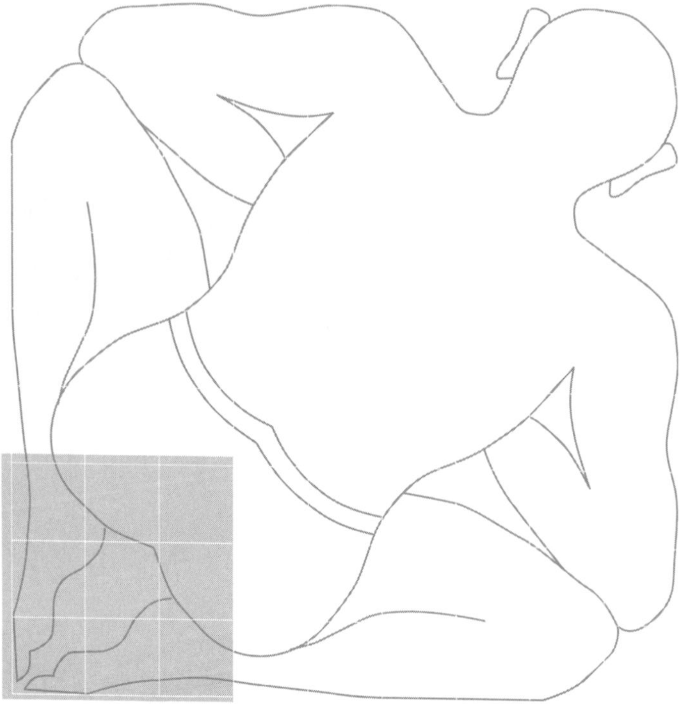

The Nine Grahas, the "Planets" of Jyotiṣa

As well as providing orientation, the directions offer space a means of establishing a sequence, just as hours, days, and years bestow sequence upon time. One salient difference between space and time is the fact of time's incessant forward march. Were we to evaluate the directions solely via the approaches offered to us by the Elements, guṇas, doṣas, and regents, which represent static realities expressed in different idioms, we would neglect the dynamic prospects afforded to us when we consider the directions through a perspective that includes the time axis as well. We shall consequently now add another viewing angle on the directions: the Nine *Grahas* ("planets") of *Jyotiṣa*, the Indian system of astrology.

Ever since humans became sufficiently self-aware to conceptualize, they've looked upwards into the heavens for guidance in the understanding and regulation of time and space. Although we now know that the earth moves around the sun, we on Earth perceive that the sun, moon, planets, and stars seem to move around the earth. The path of this seeming motion for each of these celestial bodies, which is the plane of the Earth's orbit around the sun, is called the *ecliptic*, and the apparent movements of these celestial bodies are confined to a belt in the sky called the *zodiac* which, seen from Earth, extends approximately eight degrees to both the north and the south of the ecliptic.

In our world, time is measured by the appearance and disappearance of light. One day equals one cycle of sunlight and darkness; one lunar month covers the cycle of one "moon" waxing into fullness and waning again into newness. One year is 365 days during which the sun moves from its luminous minimum to its maximum and back again.

Although there is only one ecliptic and as a consequence only one zodiac, the latter is given two different names to differentiate between two ways of measuring along the same circle: the *tropical zodiac* and the *sidereal zodiac*. Each circle of these zodiacs contains 360°, and each is divided by astrologers into 12 equal segments of 30 degrees each. The 12 divisions of the tropical zodiac are known as *signs*, and the 12 divisions of the sidereal zodiac are known as *constellations*.

Two Zodiacs

The portion of the sky that we call the zodiac is the same for both Jyotiṣa and the Western system of astrology; what differs is where the two systems locate the point referred to as 0° Aries, the position where the zodiac is understood to start.

The tropical zodiac fixes 0° Aries at the point in the sky where the sun is found each year at the precise moment of the vernal equinox, which occurs on the day during the spring when day and night are precisely equal in length around the world. Western astrology uses the tropical zodiac almost exclusively.

Jyotiṣa, on the other hand, almost always employs the sidereal zodiac, which fixes 0° Aries at a point in the sky according to the positions of certain stars. The two systems differ because Earth's axis perpetually shifts in space, wobbling like a spinning top. This causes the position of 0° Aries in the tropical zodiac to retreat in space slightly each year. Stars also change their apparent position in the sky in the sidereal zodiac, but so much more slowly that we can consider the sidereal 0° Aries to be, compared to the tropical 0° Aries, invariable.

From the sidereal perspective, the placement of a celestial body as it relates to a zodiac sign always corresponds to the astronomical constellation of the same name; when Jupiter is calculated to occupy astrologically the sign of Cancer in the sidereal zodiac, you'll also find it in the sky in the constellation of Cancer. When, however, Jupiter occupies the sign of Cancer in the chart for the tropical zodiac it may (depending on its position in that sign, which will depend on the year you observe it) actually be found in the sky in either the constellation of Cancer or in the constellation of Gemini. Three thousand years ago, a Jupiter in the tropical sign of Cancer might have appeared in the constellation of Leo; six thousand years hence, it will possibly turn up in Pisces; and so on.

Debate continues over the precise value of the ayanāṁśa, *the correction factor that must be subtracted from the planet's tropical longitude in order to obtain its sidereal longitude (longitude = position of the planet along the circle of the zodiac). The most common ayanāṁśa in use in Jyotiṣa is the Lahiri ayanāṁśa. Below is a table of approximate Lahiri ayanāṁśa values for the last century, in ten-year intervals:*

Year	*Ayanāṁśa*
1900	*22°28'*
1910	*22°36'*
1920	*22°45'*
1930	*22°53'*
1940	*23°01'*
1950	*23°10'*
1960	*23°18'*
1970	*23°26'*
1980	*23°35'*
1990	*23°43'*
2000	*23°51'*

The ayanāṁśa for intervening years can be obtained by simple calculation.

Example: If you were born in 1955, 5/10 of the difference between the ayanāṁśas for 1950 and 1960 must be added to the ayanāṁśa for 1950. Since that difference is 18' - 10' = 08', and since 08' x 0.5 = 4', the ayanāṁśa for 1955 is approximately 23°14'.

To transform your tropical horoscope into a sidereal chart using the Lahiri ayanāṁśa, you must take the position of the rising sign and of each of the planets in your tropical horoscope, and subtract the ayanāṁśa from these positions. The rule is:

If the tropical longitude of a planet is greater than the value of the ayanāṁśa, the planet occupies in the sidereal zodiac the same constellation indicated by the sign it occupies in the tropical chart. If in your tropical horoscope, that planet's longitude is less than the value of the ayanāṁśa, the constellation it occupies in your sidereal birth chart is the sign previous to the sign it occupies in your tropical chart.

Each sign spans 30° of the celestial arc. If you were born in 1955, and the longitude of your rising sign, Sun, Moon, or any other planets was greater than 23°14', it occupies in the sidereal zodiac the same constellation as it would in the tropical chart; if its longitude was less than 23°14', its constellation in your sidereal chart will be the one immediately previous to the sign it occupies in the tropical chart.

For example, should the rising sign of the person born in 1955 appear tropically at 27°32' of Scorpio, it will occupy the sidereal constellation of Scorpio, because 27°32' is greater than 23°14'; subtracting the ayanāṁśa from the tropical longitude gives us the precise degree position, which is 4°18' (27°32' - 23°14' = 4°18').

Suppose though that your rising sign sat at 07°22' of Scorpio. It would be awkward to calculate this by subtracting 23°14' from 07°22'. However, because each sign spans 30° of the celestial arc, we can also express the point "07°22' Scorpio" as "37°22' of Libra." We can then subtract 23°14' from 37°22', which gives us 14°08' in the constellation of Libra.

The size of the current ayanāṁśa ensures that most people will discover, when they do the arithmetic for each of the positions in their horoscopes, that their Suns are no longer in Capricorn, but rather in Sagittarius; that their Gemini Moons are now Taurus Moons; and so on. These changes cause needless disquiet for many who, having become comfortable with the idea of "being" a certain sign, now feel confused about having to "become someone new." The truth of the matter is that Jyotiṣa interprets charts very differently than does Western astrology, for the two are different languages. You can still be an Aquarius in the Western system—and a Capricorn in Jyotiṣa—without any substantial inconsistency in being who you are.

Jyotiṣa, which began long before the invention of the powerful telescopes that have introduced us to the planets beyond Saturn, focuses on those lights that the ancients could see. Its Nine Grahas consist of the two luminaries (the sun and moon), the five planets that are visible to the naked eye (Mercury, Venus, Mars, Jupiter, Saturn), and Rāhu and Ketu, the two lunar nodes. The nodes are the points in the sky where the plane of the moon's orbit around Earth and the plane of the ecliptic (the plane of Earth's orbit around the sun) intersect. Though they are neither visible nor corporeal, these nodes, which are the points where eclipses occur, nonetheless influence significantly with their shadows, and so are deemed to be planets.

Once our ancient cultures developed writing and recorded history, certain adepts began to identify correspondences between the positions and movements of these Nine Grahas in the firmament and affinities and events on Earth. With the awareness that light determines time came the awareness that light, like all other substances, possesses attributes. Over a long period of study, each of the grahas accreted to itself a personality, a set of traits that has come to describe and define its influence on worldly life. Taken together, these Nine Grahas (each a decisive influence on the Space we inhabit but each incomplete in its own way) add up to the sum of all possibilities in human life.

Jyotiṣa, the *Jyotir Vidyā*, is known as the "lore of light" because each of Jyotiṣa's grahas represents a pattern of qualities that can either "illuminate" us or "cast us into darkness." Each of us, according to the individual astrological makeup mapped out in our horoscopes, is more susceptible to being "illumined by the light" or "shaded by the shadow" of one particular attribute pattern—whether it be mercurial, venereal, martial, jovial, saturnine, lunatic—at any particular moment. These individual patterns enjoy such strong mutual affinity that they together behave as if they formed a conscious living being, one that can "possess" people and act through them. The Sanskrit word *graha* comes from a root that means "to grasp." When a planetary archetype takes hold of you—when it becomes solidly established within you—your choices, actions, and experiences become colored by that set of traits. You will see the world in substantially the same way that the planet "sees" it, and you will act, more or less, in conformity with its tendencies.

Graha and *gṛha*, the Sanskrit word for house, are derived from the same root. A house is thus a space that influences your life by gripping you firmly (for better or worse). As we have seen, directionality is one of the most important routes via which a home can grip you. Though five chief styles of Jyotiṣa (*Pārāśari, Jaimini, Nādi, Tāntrika, Tājika*) offer more than one system for correlating the Nine Grahas with the directions, the following is the scheme that Vāstu employs most often:

East is presided over by the Sun.
Southeast is presided over by Venus.
South is presided over by Mars.
Southwest is presided over by Rāhu and Ketu, the Moon's Nodes.
West is presided over by Saturn.
Northwest is presided over by the Moon.
North is presided over by Mercury.
Northeast is presided over by Jupiter.

This series recapitulates in many ways the correlations evidenced by the Regents of the Ten Directions (as explained in Chapter Six). In the east, the person of the Sun, the regal, leonine, lord of the planets, fittingly reflects the east's association with Indra, the lord of the celestials, ruler of the heavens. Mars, the fierce but righteous warlord, shares the south with Yama, the god of death and duty. Saturn, who governs the archaic as well as rectitude and justice, rules in the west along with the ancient Vedic deity of righteousness, Varuṇa. Wealth and commerce are conflated in the north with the appearance there of both Mercury and Kubera.

The intermediate directions provide us with correspondences between the planets and the elements. Venus rules the southeast, where lives Fire, and Moon is regent of the northwest, the province of Air. Jupiter is assigned to the northeast, which is Water's domain, leaving southwest, which symbolizes Space and Earth, to be the bailiwick of the Nodes.

Though invisible and incorporeal, Rāhu and Ketu, the Moon's Nodes, influence the earth and its inhabitants nonetheless. Being themselves shadows, embodiments of darkness, their influence is strongly tamasic. Saturn, who in mythology is the son of the Sun and Shadow, also denotes tamas, but brings to it an added measure of discipline due to his identification with Varuṇa. Mars is tamasic, but can, like Yama, facilitate the furthering of dharma.

On days when the Moon pattern is strongly influencing your mind, you will tend to act in an emotional, dreamy, lunar kind of way. The Saturn pattern will render you sardonic and contracted, the Jupiter pattern expansive and philosophical, the Mercury pattern communicative and mercurial, and so on. When a direction becomes significant in your world, by virtue of being the direction in which your front door faces, for example, or in which your head points when you sleep, the traits of the planet that rules that direction will become more prominent in your life, for better or worse.

Exercise Ten: The Front Door

Walk around your home and try to get a feel for how different things would be if your front door were someplace other than where it is now. You'll want to move consistently in one direction (clockwise is probably best), trying as you go to use all five senses to note what would change if you greeted the world each day from another perspective.

One person I know owns a house whose front door opens in a direction good for him to go out, and in a less-than-beneficial direction for him to enter. When he first moved to the residence, he would feel so uneasy entering the house that he always wanted to leave again. His wife had the opposite experience: She always hated to leave the house, but loved to return. When they described this situation (one having a strong affinity for staying in, and the other, for going out) to their astrologer, he advised her to walk backwards out of the house every day when leaving, and told him to back into the house when he returns from outside. This simple change of habit allowed the situation to even out, and both are now happily content in their comings and goings.

Planetary Significations

Every human is a living microcosm of the universe, a self-enclosed universe whose every constituent mirrors some constituent of the incalculable creation that is external to it. The Nine Grahas system offers us yet one more means through which we can encourage "mini-cosmic" selves to align with the macrocosm. This system is particularly useful because every aspect of existence can be traced to at least one planetary pattern.

The simplest of the planetary correlations is also the most ubiquitous, and is becoming increasingly prominent in our digital society: the nine integers of our numbering system. In Jyotiṣa, numbers are most commonly allocated to planets in the order that they are associated with the days of the week, with Sunday considered the first day.

1. Sun
2. Moon
3. Mars
4. Mercury
5. Jupiter
6. Venus
7. Saturn
8. Rāhu
9. Ketu

When you consider the following partial list of planetary significations (some of which are shared by more than one planet), remember that the digit associated with the planet figures substantively in its connotations:

1. The Sun rules:

East
Sunday
deep dark red; orange
vegetation in general
tigers, lions, deer, horses, geese, swans
pitta
the sense of sight
gold, copper, ruby, garnet
the soul
the father, males, powerful people, heads of state, government officials, physicians
sattva (trending toward rajas)
firmness, steadiness, nobility, individuality, generosity, grandeur, dignity, power, authority, leadership, creativity
chronic skin diseases or eye troubles, difficulties with father, altercations with the authorities, overweening pride, egotism, self-centeredness, pomposity, ostentation

2. The Moon rules:

Northwest
Monday
milky white
all manner of vegetation (this is one example among many of a category or item that is ruled by more than one planet)
antelope, hare, partridge, cranes, and water creatures of all types
vāta and kapha
the sense of taste
silver, bronze, pearl, moonstone
the senses and the emotions
the mother, females, farmers, gardeners, caregivers (nurses, hoteliers, food providers, etc.)
sattva (trending toward rajas)
receptivity, sensitivity, imagination, good memory, good habits and conditioning
swellings in the body, water retention, difficulties with mother, emotional upheavals, hyper-sensitivity and overreaction, fickleness, changeability, difficulty getting in touch with feelings

3. Mars rules:

South
Tuesday
bright red
inorganic matter, including minerals, in general
roosters, raptors, and other birds of prey; rams and monkeys
pitta
sense of sight
copper, coral, bloodstone
power and strength
siblings, chefs, armed people (police, army, security, etc.), people who cut (surgeons, butchers, barbers), people who work with heat and metals (such as engineers, metallurgists, welders)
tamas
goal-directed energy, strength, courage, passion, action, the competitive spirit, vim and vigor
conditions of excessive "heat" in the body such as ulcers and rashes,

rashness, accident-proneness, conflicts of all sorts, legal problems, difficulties with siblings, lack of courage, anger, irritability, haste, foolhardiness, impatience, inconstancy, inconsistency, lack of drive, an "all-or-nothing" attitude, obsession, violence

4. **Mercury rules:**

North
Wednesday
green
animals in general, and cats in particular
flying creatures like birds; in particular, parrots
vāta, pitta, and kapha
the sense of smell
brass, emerald, peridot, green tourmaline
the rational mind and speech
maternal uncles, educated people, students, accountants, astrologers, artisans
rajas (moving toward sattva)
rationality, intelligence, wit, cleverness, skill, dexterity, verbal and mental ability, skill at study, shrewdness, versatility
nervous and mental disorders, lack of ability to communicate or to study, aloofness, amorality, over-intellectualization, difficulty in thought and communication, volatility

5. **Jupiter rules:**

Northeast
Thursday
yellow
animals in general, especially the horse and elephant; also two-legged creatures, like pigeons, swans, and humans
kapha
the sense of hearing
gold, yellow sapphire, topaz, citrine
knowledge and fortune
children, wise and learned persons, counselors and advisors, clergy, judges
sattva

growth and expansion, humanitarian and spiritual outlooks, wisdom, optimism, faith, geniality, generosity, joviality, humor, idealism, good powers of judgment, mildness, tenderness, benevolence

obesity, liver diseases, difficulties with children or teachers, difficulties in having children, overconfidence, overindulgence, extravagance, immorality, greed

6. **Venus rules:**

Southeast

Friday

radiant white, and variegated colors

vegetation in general

cows and buffalo; two-legged creatures including peacocks, parrots, and humans

vāta and kapha

the sense of taste

silver, diamond, white sapphire

desires and yearnings

the spouse, performers (artists, actors, musicians), persons dealing in beauty, culture, and pleasure (fashion designers, decorators, restaurateurs, etc.)

rajas (veering toward tamas)

affection, friendliness, love, gentleness, sociability, harmony, balance, elegance, gracefulness, refined sensuality, tolerance, lenience, an easygoing and accommodating nature

diseases of the sexual organs, marital problems, laziness, vanity, sentimentality, vice and sensual corruption, lack of taste and refinement

7. **Saturn rules:**

West

Saturday

black, violet, indigo, dark blue

inorganic matter, including minerals, in general

flying creatures like birds, especially crows, vultures, cuckoos; also elephants

vāta
the sense of touch
iron, lead, sapphire (especially blue sapphire), lapis lazuli
sorrows and misfortunes
subordinates, old people, people who deal in old things and dead things (historians, morticians, leatherworkers, etc.), people who deal with products from the earth (miners, drillers), laborers, renunciates, monks, isolated and "odd" people (vagrants, the homeless, etc.)
tamas (maturing toward sattva)
authoritativeness, discipline, responsibility, conservatism, practicality, realism, durability, constancy, consistency
pain (especially musculoskeletal), timidity, diffidence, anxiety, fear, bad dreams, poverty, instability, shame, delays, humiliation, inhibition, loneliness, isolation, depression, mental or physical rigidity, stinginess, disappointment, resignation, melancholy, lack of trust, suspicion, doubt, a hard-hearted nature, meanness, mercilessness

8. Rāhu rules:

Southwest
ultraviolet
inorganic matter, including minerals, in general
gulls, snakes, camels, donkeys, wolves, rodents, mosquitos, scorpions, and other poisonous or annoying insects
vāta
lead, hessonite garnet, agate
the maternal grandparents, eccentrics, the inspired and imaginative, fanatics, the isolated, the insane, the possessed, unusual people of all sorts
tamas
originality, individuality, independence, insight, ingenuity, inspiration, imagination
timidity, anxiety, hallucinations, confusion, escapism, neurosis, psychosis, deception, addiction, vagueness, illusion, delusion

9. Ketu rules:

Southwest
infrared
inorganic matter, including minerals, in general
owls, snakes, camels, donkeys, wolves, rodents, mosquitos, scorpions, and other poisonous or annoying insects
pitta
lead, cat's eye, chrysoberyl, turquoise
the paternal grandparents, eccentrics, the inspired and imaginative, fanatics, renunciates, the isolated, the possessed, unusual people of all sorts, the insane
tamas
universality, idealism, intuition, compassion, spirituality, self-sacrifice, subtlety
accident-proneness, anger, irritability, impatience, inconstancy, eccentricity, fanaticism, explosiveness, violence, unconventionality, amorality, iconoclasm, impulsiveness, emotional tensions

Once you understand these significations, which are but a fraction of the spheres of influence that have been elucidated for the Nine Grahas over the centuries, you can make your space work for you more efficiently—when these correlations are used wisely.

Planetary patterns influence how you think, what you say, how you behave. When a planet's traits are numerous and pronounced in your surroundings, you are more likely to display that planet's whole trait pattern, including its temperament, in your interactions with the world. Consider, for example, that corner of your room or house ruled by a particular planet: If that area has paint or wallpaper of that planet's hue, the other attributes in that pattern, including particularly the planet's temperament, will all get augmented, to varying degrees, in every aspect of your world.

If you can "digest" a planetary pattern well, you'll find it easier to access that planet's positive significations, the qualities of which you can develop in your life by judiciously developing the segments of your space ruled by that planet. "Digest" a pattern poorly, though, and the pattern's negative correlations are more likely to blossom in your temperament. Should you find yourself falling prey to several of a planet's negative indications, you should be very cautious about enhancing the power of the planet in question by making its corresponding direction and other characteristics prominent in your home or office.

For example, should Mercury's pattern agree with you, you can freely emphasize the northern direction in your life, by positioning your desk so that you can read or study (Mercurial activities) facing north, particularly on Wednesdays (Mercury's day). Or you could dedicate a northern room of your home to a home business that involved accounting, or the tutoring of students (both Mercurial pursuits).

Situating your front door in the north will significantly strengthen Mercury. If that is not feasible, then you can render your northern walls prominent by decorating them with healthy green plants (green, and particularly the hue of leaves, is Mercury's color), by using them as a backdrop for a large, well-polished brass object (Mercury rules brass, and immaculateness), or by hanging the parrot's cage there (Mercury rules birds in general; parrots, many of whom are green, are Mercury birds). You might also employ aromatherapy, particularly using fragrances that are a grassy green, like oil of vetiver. Money no object? Then shower yourself with emeralds, peridots, green tourmalines, and other green gems.

If, however, Mercury's energy is (for whatever reason) hard for you to digest, you will be better off making its correspondences less prominent in your home or office, strengthening instead a planetary pattern that is more beneficial for you. Even so, it's better to avoid stimulating any one planet's energy too strongly, lest you unbalance yourself. In particular, you should always be cautious about enhancing the dark, tamasic, heavy planets that rule south, southwest, and west: Mars, Rāhu and Ketu, and Saturn.

A competent Jyotiṣa astrologer can look at your horoscope and tell you precisely which planetary patterns you will find most easily "digestible," and which you are likely to have trouble assimilating. If you don't have access to such an expert, then study the correspondences between the planets and what they rule, develop a feel for how the planetary patterns relate to you, and rely on your breathing and your gut reaction to tell you which patterns will serve as your ideal cup of tea, and which will be more likely to throw you (or others) off balance.

Confluence

Studying correspondences permits us to identify times and spaces in which *confluence* occurs. Confluence, a principle that is fundamental to all the vidyās, suggests that *when many factors with similar traits appear together, they will strongly support one another.* A west-facing front door made of black wrought iron represents a triply confluent Saturn influence; a yellow sapphire set in gold doubly promotes Jupiter. Positive confluence promotes "good space"; negative confluence multiplies imbalances.

Recall the standard horror movie scene in the ancient (Saturn), lonely (Saturn) castle decorated with suits of steel (Saturn) armor in which a cold (Saturn) dinner is served in a cavernous (Saturn) dining hall whose stone (Saturn) walls are hung with ancient (Saturn) and dilapidated (Saturn) tapestries and rugs. This hyper-confluence of Saturn ensures that our misgivings will be borne out, and that the anxious, justly suspicious guest will be terrorized mercilessly and persistently by the mean, hard-hearted, implacable host.

In the Ayurvedic context, a vāta-unsettling confluence would occur if you had a constitutional tendency for vāta excess that was buttressed by a strongly placed vāta-aggravating Saturn and/or Rāhu in your horoscope. Perhaps you also live in the vāta-promoting climate of a windy desert. If you also consume vāta-disturbing food and observe vāta-enhancing nightlong sleepless vigils during autumn, the most vāta-promoting time of year, you will generate an overpowering confluence for vāta imbalance. If you persist in your vāta-rousing ways in such circumstances, illness becomes almost inevitable. Avail yourself instead of a positive confluence of vāta-controlling diet and activities, and introduce vāta-managing vāstu features into your home and office environment, and you may yet stave off vāta-induced infirmity.

Exercise Eleven: The Nine Planetary Patterns

In Exercise Three, "The Body Container," you experimented with finding a confluence of the Five Elements in your environment. Repeat that exercise, now looking for confluences that indicate the predominance of one of the Nine Grahas. Familiarity with these Nine Planetary Patterns can markedly enhance your space-organizing capabilities.

Each morning, when you first leave your residence, note the first thing you see that reminds you most forcefully of one of the Nine Grahas. It should be striking: a crow staring you straight in the eye, an accountant jogging down the road while talking on his mobile phone, firemen on their way to a fire, a procession of ants parading by. This iconic image will often reflect the planet that rules that day of the week.

Once you have your "vision" for the morning, be on the lookout for further demonstrations of that pattern during the day. On a Saturday during which crows continually appear in your sightlines, you may find your attention being drawn steadily to the west while you wait, delayed, attracting panhandlers, your path blocked by a construction crew driving iron pilings into an excavation at a building site. On such a day, you'll know that Saturn is affecting you strongly, since these experiences, visions, and substances (crows, delays, iron, etc.) are strongly Saturnian. If you find this agreeable, then you should make it a point to wear black and park yourself on a steel bench to watch the sun set, which will reinforce the temperament that Saturn promotes. If you find yourself wishing instead to be a bit freer of Saturn's influence, you'll do better to perform Sun Salutations, visit the arboretum (ruled by the Moon), go horseback riding (Jupiter), paint a picture (Venus), meditate while facing northeast (double Jupiter), or do something else that can lighten Saturn's heavy energy.

Or, you may find yourself in a plush restaurant on a Venusian Friday evening, where you and your sweetie are about to consume a sumptuous meal with abundant libations, serenaded by a handsome gypsy violinist. In such a situation, you would do well to remember to maintain some discipline in the midst of your extravagance, to prevent a Venusian pattern of overindulgence from developing. You could do this by facing west, the direction of the disciplinarian Saturn—but that might also cause Saturnian frustration to sprout. Probably you will be better off to sit facing east, northeast, or north, to encourage the energies of the Sun, Jupiter, or Mercury to assist you in your resolve for restraint.

Many people are so taken with the idiom of the Nine Grahas that after they learn it they never speak any other language; others can't ever seem to get the planetary patterns into their heads, but relate well to the Regents of the Ten Directions. Some find it difficult to relate to deities or visual archetypes, but get inspired by the mathematics and geometry of maṇḍalas and yantras; others rely on the principles of Āyurveda, including the Three Doṣas. Yet others resist any expressions but those couched in terms of the Three Guṇas, or prefer to use the Five Elements to structure their perceptions of the world.

All these tongues are valid means of Vāstu expression, identification, and implementation. You will ordinarily do best to express your Vāstu self in the language that agrees with you the most. Sometimes this idiolect is obvious; if not, you'll have to experiment. Should you wish to try out more than one means of expression before settling on a favorite, choose one at a time and become substantially familiar with that system before you try to experiment with another.

Whatever mode of interpretation you choose to use, remember that all of Vāstu is based firmly in the understanding, assessment, and manipulation of the "fitness" or "unfitness" of space. Vāstu speaks in "prāṇa language," and only when your prāṇa feels "right" about something should you conclude that you've discerned that degree of fitness that will encourage cooperation. Never convince yourself intellectually or emotionally of the fitness or unfitness of a situation without checking it against the gut feeling of your prāṇa as well. Pranic reality, an essential bellwether of Vāstu, is real!

As you add new ways of perceiving the world to your perceptual repertoire, you'll discover correspondences that you could never have otherwise suspected might exist. Being aware of more such correspondences offers you additional ways to tie down the "things" of your life into a multi-dimensional relationship web. Anchor your life more securely, and you enhance stability in yourself and your house alike—even if it does happen to face south!

The Jyotishical Door

Though Vāstu's modes of expression are manifold, the patterns that Jyotiṣa and its Nine Grahas elaborate tend to foster insights of greater Vāstu specificity and sophistication than do those derived from other vidyās; hence Vāstu's long history of being taught within Jyotiṣa's curriculum of study, and Vāstu's preference for employing Jyotiṣa-related techniques in its architectural calculations.

Jyotiṣa's first Vāstu consideration is the front door, for the main door of any dwelling activates one of the Nine Grahas. The front door is the gateway through which we proceed into the world, and via which the world enters; it influences our lives each time it opens and closes. As a man or woman thinks, so he or she becomes, and what you see in the morning, through your front door, often sets the emotional and spiritual tenor for the rest of your day. Ideally, you look out onto the manifestation of reality that you most want to come to resemble—like the sun.

We've already examined some of the life themes that can come to the fore when a house's main door faces one of the cardinal directions. These themes reflect to a substantial degree the "attribute profiles" of their ruling planets: Sun is most dominant when the front door faces east, Mars when it faces south, Saturn when facing west, and Mercury when north.

Confluence operates here as well. One sort of confluence relates to doors and gates that are secondary to the main door. For example, Saturn's influence will be strong if the door to your apartment opens into the west. It will be even stronger if the main entrance to your apartment building also opens into the west.

Another measure of planetary influence, and of confluence, concerns the precise location of your door as it appears in its wall. Each portion of that wall is ruled by one of the Nine Grahas, and the planet that rules the wall segment of the front door will have a substantially magnified influence in your life.

To determine which planet rules the front door of your home, first measure the length of the front wall of your house or apartment. Divide this length by nine.

Now use this length to divide the front façade of your home into nine equal portions, assigning a planet to each portion. If your house faces either east or west, start assigning from the northern corner and

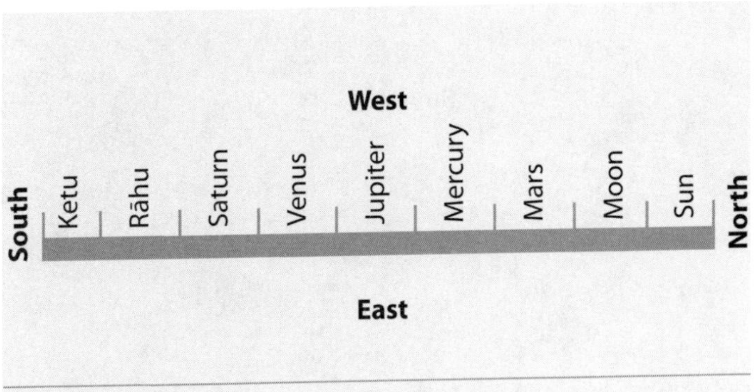

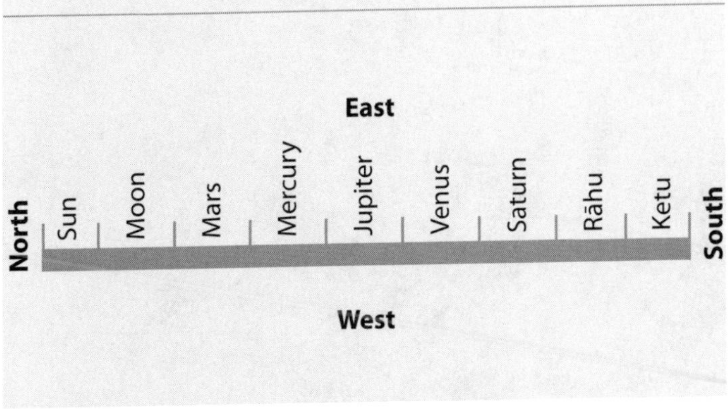

go to the south. Should your house face either north or south, start from the east corner and proceed to the west.

Here are the portions that correspond to the planets, from north to south or east to west:

Sun
Moon
Mars
Mercury
Jupiter
Venus
Saturn
Rāhu

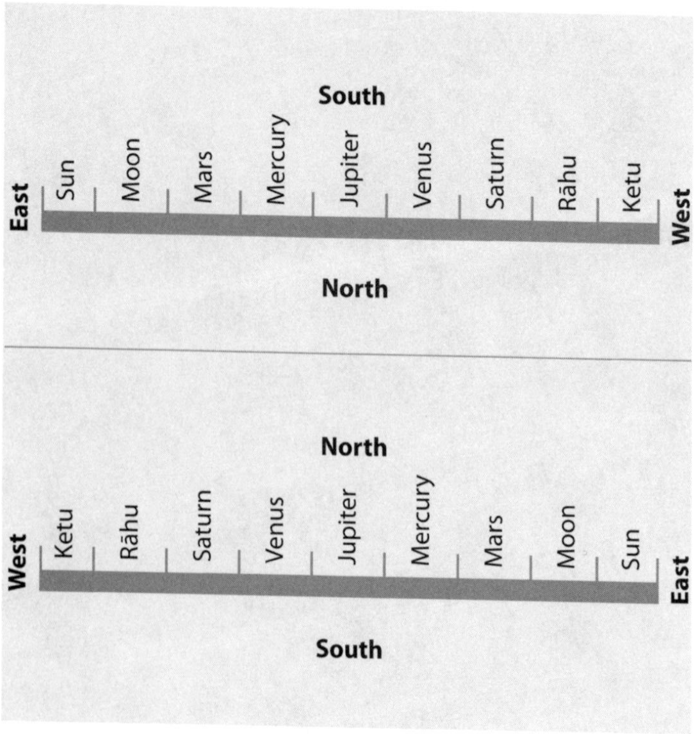

Ketu

A front wall that measures 72 feet is made up of nine portions of 8 feet each. If this wall faces east (or west), the Sun portion of the wall extends from its northeast (or northwest) corner 8 feet towards the south. The wall's Moon portion occupies the 8 feet of space that is just south of the Sun's portion; its Mars portion is the 8 feet immediately south of the Moon's portion, and so on.

A north- or south-facing front wall that is 63 feet long has nine segments that each measure 7 feet; a door that occupies the precise middle of the wall, its margins 28 feet from either corner, is a Jupiter door. That wall's Mercury section is just east of Jupiter, and its Venus portion is just west of that central location.

Whatever planet rules the front door wall segment will contribute mightily to the flavor of your life experiences while you inhabit that dwelling. This sort of analysis can grow to be a subtle, sophisticated

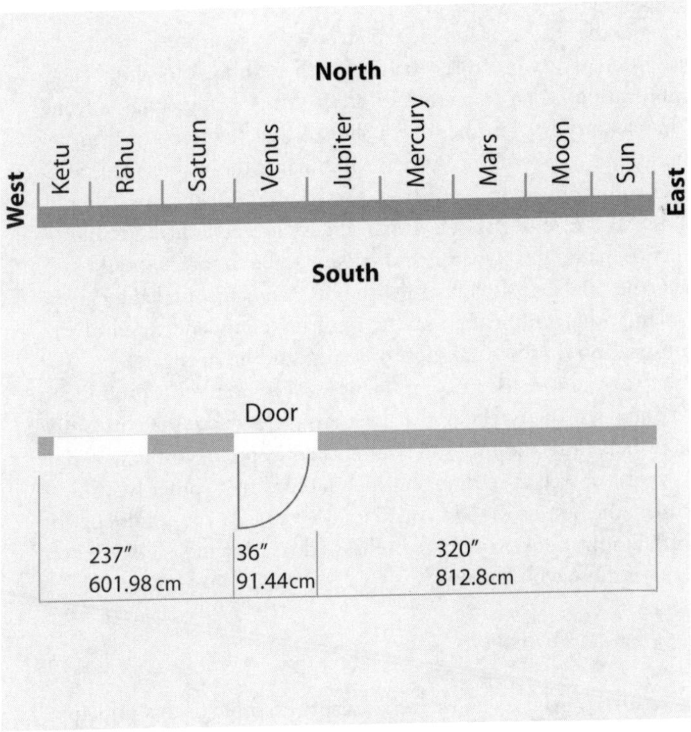

dialogue between your horoscope and your home—one further layer of the relationship between you and your world that you will do well to tend.

As a general rule, your door should appear in a section of the wall ruled by an auspicious planet (Moon, Mercury, Jupiter, or Venus).* Auspicious planets tend to promote sukha in life, by encouraging enjoyable, life-enhancing, prosperity-promoting, desire-fulfilling attitudes and events,

*As usual, opinions vary. One authority asserts that a main door in Mercury, Jupiter, or Venus is good regardless of the direction your residence faces, but a main door in Moon is good only on the east and south sides. *Bṛhat Saṁhitā* employs a completely different approach, proposing that Moon, Mars, and Mercury are good on the east, Mercury alone is acceptable on the south, Mercury and Jupiter are appropriate on the west, and Mars, Mercury, and Jupiter will do on the north. Yet another authority opines that the door must usually be in the fourth segment from the extreme right as you stand outside the front of the house facing it.

according to the attributes and life experiences they nourish.

Take Mercury, who rules (among other things) business and communication, as an example. All other things being equal, a front door in Mercury (i.e., in the fourth slice of wall as measured from its northernmost or easternmost corner) will enhance the business prospects and the communication abilities of that house's inhabitants. Should the house also face north, which is Mercury's direction, the resulting confluence makes this dynamic more likely to be in force. Should said house be painted green, trimmed with brass, and surrounded by green leafy plants, the confluence and the resulting confidence level of the prognostication for financial success become all the stronger.

In such a situation, Mercury's influence will be even more prominent on Wednesdays, the weekday that Mercury rules (note that the order of the planets in relation to wall segments corresponds to the weekday progression), as well as on days on which (according to other Jyotishical principles) the Sun or Moon is ruled by Mercury. As the confluence of Mercurial indications on a home swells, so does Mercury's influence on the lives of those who live there.

Marie's Front Door

Let's return to Marie's house for a real-life example of this principle. The residence's front wall, which faces pretty much north (Mercury's direction), measures 593 inches (49 feet, 5 inches, or 15.06 meters). Dividing this length into nine sections gives us 65.9 inches (167 cm). Marie's front door, which is 36 inches wide, appears 320 inches (26 feet, 8 inches, or 8.13 meters) from the house's northeast corner, and 237 inches (19 feet, 9 inches, or 6.02 meters) from its northwest corner. The door thus straddles the fifth and sixth ninths of the wall, but as only about a quarter of the door appears in the fifth, we can consider the door to fall within the area of the sixth of the nine segments.

That sixth division being ruled by Venus, an auspicious planet, we can conclude that Marie's front door is likely to promote benevolent, sukha-enhancing life experiences for her. (It would have this portent even if we took it to fall within the also-auspicious, Jupiter-ruled fifth division.) Its location in Venus's portion suggests that the door will promote a Venusian sort of sukha, including admiration for and delight in music and other arts, appreciation for and enjoyment of good food, pleasure in adornments of all sorts, a general atmosphere of tolerance and sociability, and the like. Precisely how these qualities will manifest in the lives of the house's residents will depend on what Venus promises in their individual horoscopes.

Marie's door thus benefits her twice: by facing north, and by occupying the portion of the wall associated with an auspicious planet. This is a sort of confluence of positive indications, which will reinforce one another even though they don't represent the same planet's pattern. Some of the indications of Mercury and Venus do overlap (both rule parrots, artisans, and matters relating to vocalization), but more to the point is that both planets supply generally benevolent and desirable energies to the dwelling and its dwellers.

A door in Mercury's sector on that north wall would certainly have provided, through a specifically Mercurial confluence, a stronger corroboration for Mercury's portents. This would have been good only if the family could easily digest that concentrated Mercurial energy; this might be the case at least for Marie's husband, who works in the Mercurial profession of accountancy. If, however, Mercury was not a good planet for one of the family members, a Mercurial confluence could turn its promise of benevolence into an impediment, perhaps even a curse.

Strong energy in a space can generate potent results, which will be desirable or undesirable depending on how well you can wield that energy. Until Marie is certain of how far into the Mercurial world she dares to stray, she is better off not proceeding too far in that direction. Rather than augmenting one planetary pattern at the expense of the others, she will be more likely to enhance her sukha by encouraging an amicable balance among them.

Negative Confluence

Your sukha will benefit, substantially or slightly, when your front door occupies a portion of your front wall that is ruled by one of the benevolent planets. Your sukha will similarly be blighted, to some extent, when the door occupies a portion of the main façade ruled by one of the more malevolent planets. Do not panic, though, and call the wrecking ball to knock yourself a new portal just because your entrance's location is less than ideal. Even if your portico's position happens to activate one of the disorderly planetary patterns—Ketu, Rāhu, Mars, or Saturn; Sun is rather neutral here—the direst indications of such planets will develop only when clear confluence encourages them to do so.

In such a situation, it's vital to refrain from encouraging this kind of negative confluence. A Saturn door for a west-facing house will provide a double negative that becomes even more likely to bode ill in the presence of other Saturnian indications (a house made of stone, or sheathed in lead). Too much Saturn, and you may find yourself becoming isolated from the people and things that give your life its savor. You may even find the vāta in your body increasing (Saturn being a vāta-promoting planet), making you more prone to illnesses instigated by vāta excess.

Similarly, the Martian energy attracted by a Mars door will double for a house that faces south (Mars's direction), and will become yet more difficult to manage if such a house is painted red and surrounded by a sharply pointed fence and perpetually aflame tiki torches. Few can, in the long run, digest such a strong confluence of Mars-ness. If, in addition, your Martian house is triangular in shape, and you happen to be a surgeon who breeds falcons, those who are wise will steer well clear of you, cognizant that you are a major Martian accident waiting to happen. At the very least, this confluence will likely create a powerful pitta imbalance in your body, which will (unless dealt with promptly) display itself in the form of some "hot" physical disease or mental imbalance.

Though various strategies can often be used to cope with a strong negative confluence, such coping may have to continue in perpetuity, since every time you open your door, you reinforce the confluence, positive or negative, that the door epitomizes.

The Front Door

Mārga-taru-koṇa-kūpa-stambha-bhrama-viddham
aśubhadaṁ dvāram |

It is unfavorable for a door to be pierced by a road, tree, corner, well, pillar, or watercourse.

Bṛhat Saṁhitā, 53:67a p. 481

The front door is in many ways the prima donna of the home, and like any other attention-seeker it hates to be overshadowed, in any way. It should not be obscured behind a hedge or any other sort of foliage, or located behind a boulder or some similar obstruction. Sizable shadows that cut across the front door are also unwelcome.

For that matter, you want nothing inauspicious to be in line with the front door on the inside of your residence. When you open your front door to come into your home, you should not be greeted by toilets, sinks, or other water drains; neither should you be received by stairs or the open maw of your laundry room or storeroom. Should you have such rooms directly in your front door's line of sight, keep their doors closed, or open just a crack. Another option is to conceal them behind screens.

The same care should be taken in regard to what you encounter when you leave your home. You don't want to walk out of your abode each morning to be greeted by a drainage ditch, cemetery, garbage dump, slaughterhouse, funeral home, or the like. Roads with high traffic flows and major intersections in front of your house are undesirable for many reasons, but even infrequently trafficked crossroads can disrupt the free movement of prāṇa. T-junctions are particularly potent in this regard; a road that Ts in front of a house acts like a śūla, *an energy "spear" aimed right at the heart of your dwelling. Driveways can act as spears, as can lampposts, utility poles, transmission lines, and even the sharp angles of buildings across the way.*

Spears are mainly a concern in regard to your front door, or to the door that you use most, but they can also afflict large windows. In those cases when the oppressing entity has some measurable height, like a streetlight, you need not worry about a "spear" that is at least twice as far from your front door as it (the "spear") is tall. For those that are nearer (and for roads), some remedy is needed. Often, obstructing the view of the offending "spear" is sufficient to nullify its malevolence, which you can do by utilizing a hedge or fence (one that's far enough away from the front door so as not to throw any shadow on it). Where this fix is not possible, placing a sacred geometrical design, like a yantra, on or near the door may help. Where there is strong negative confluence, the situation may become difficult to resolve.

The front door of a home in India is always decorated, often with leaves and flowers, or with the patterns called rangoli that are drawn or stenciled in front of the threshold with rice or chalk powder. Deities are also popular, and are usually stationed on a perch above the lintel; in addition, the door itself can be carved or painted. Make sure that the image you select for your door is one that is both benign and reflects who you are as a family. Marie's front and back doors each came complete with bas-reliefs of aboriginal warriors on their inner surfaces; after her family moved in, the one in the untamed southwest quadrant was spared, but the front door, and its accompanying fighter, were promptly (and rightly) sold.

A foyer or vestibule is a useful front-door transition zone, separating house-space from the external world. Residents and guests alike should remove their shoes there, that they may not track up the house, and that the home's energy might "work" on them more easily.

Confluence in the Conference Room

Here is a specific confluence scenario: Suppose you own a business, and one day you decide that your board of directors requires a "motivation infusion." You might reasonably conclude that a good way to motivate them would be to surround them with a success-promoting color during your weekly corporate deliberations. Knowing that red is said to encourage success, you might be tempted to redden your conference room décor.

Feng Shui loves the strong, vigorous color red, the color of the active, forceful planet Mars, and asserts that red promotes success. Vāstu agrees, with the reservation that activating Mars can at best promote success in general, since an active approach to any endeavor is more likely to bring results than is a laissez-faire attitude.

Your personal experience of Mars will, however, depend on how well you can "cook" that Martian energy into a tasty broth. Judiciously stimulated, Mars can provide the vitality, passion, and courage to confront and surmount obstacles in your quest to achieve worthy objectives. The heat, hurry, and tamas of an overstimulated Mars temperament, though, will lead competition to deteriorate into conflict, frustration to explode into fury, and haste to churn out mainly waste.

Your decision to redden your conference room would in itself suggest that Mars was already working rather too strongly through you, because Mars's policy of active confrontation rarely promotes concord. However, subjecting your directors to "red conferences" might actually work, at least for some time, particularly while your business is in a phase of expansion that can turn Mars's energy of conquest in the direction of market share domination.

But should you, in a moment of Martian keenness, decide to move the conference room into the southern portion of your building, you will increase Mars's power there exponentially (particularly if your building happens to have a southward-facing front door). And should you further direct all the men to wear cherry ties and shirts to meetings, and the women to wear power suits of scarlet, you will activate this already powerful confluence of Martian energy to an extreme degree.

Should you then choose to sit facing north to chair the meeting (so that in order to face you, everyone else has to face south), and hold your meetings on Tuesdays (Mars's days), you would also be wise to install metal detectors at the doors. The intense Martian blaze that you will thus stoke will, like a "red flag to a bull," trigger Mars's tamasic traits of domination, aggression, and violence, and could goad your crimson compatriots to strike at one another's throats.

You may still succeed at managing the free-for-alls that will ensue, provided that you don your samurai armor and lay about freely with your scimitar (Mars rules sharp objects). But how long will it be before these continual clashes wear down you and your directors? If you insist on leading subordinates by force, at least consider activating the Sun instead. The Sun, like Mars, resorts to punishment or threats of punishment as its method of persuasion, and is similarly forceful, compelling, and insistent in its negotiations. Solar and Martian people also respond best to these tactics.

But east, the Sun's direction, relates to birth and new beginnings, while south, the direction of Mars, relates to death. Chastisement from the Sun is thus more likely to provide some beneficial result, to act as the "start of something good," than is a reprimand from Mars, who operates more commonly in "kill or be killed" mode. A conference room in the eastern portion of your office building is thus most often a better choice than is one on the south side, though it will still require an autocrat or a paternal figure (the Sun signifies the father) to "rule the roost." Bright red should give way to dark red, orange-reds, saffron, and gold, and you will need to lead, not by confronting, but by dazzling your underlings with the brilliance of your personal power (and keeping them in line via the chain of command).

When you tire of heat, you might consider cooling down the fervor of your forums by activating the silvery Moon instead. Moon uses temptation—incentives of various sorts, including bribes on occasion—to get its way, and Lunar people respond most readily to similar enticements. Locating your conference room in your building's northwest corner, painting it a shade of ivory, trimming it with silver or bronze, filling it with vegetation and scenes of the seaside, installing a fish tank replete with seaweed along one wall, serving dairy products and other white foods to your conferees, and appealing generally to their senses and emotions—all these will magnify the Moon's alluring influence in your discussions, particularly if you meet on Mondays. Should you manage this lunar energy well, you will encourage receptivity, support sensitivity, and enhance your collective powers of imagination.

The Moon is, however, a very inconstant planet, one that changes its form and position on a nightly basis. Should you "wipe out" while attempting to surf the Lunar wave, you may get dragged under by hyper-sensitivity, overreaction, and fickleness.

You might then turn to Mercury or Saturn, the planets of diplomacy. Mercury and Saturn freely accept and use craftiness, including Machiavellian stratagems, the spreading of rumors, and the use of spies, to achieve their ends. Schedule meetings on Wednesdays (Mercury) or Saturdays (Saturn), in rooms to the north or west (respectively), and you strongly encourage office politics to gain a prominent place in your decision making, particularly if you generate Mercurial or Saturnine confluence via hue and décor. If your corporate culture emphasizes fair play and moral rectitude, this approach may succeed; overdo these influences, though, and you'll find cunning expanding into guile, deviousness spreading unchecked, and unethical strategies of negotiation, including blackmail, rearing their heads during your consultations.

If the northern and western portions of your office are your only choices for a conference room, you'll generally be better off choosing north, which will at least encourage the natural skill at communication that is Mercury's forte. West promotes instead the sort of suspicion, isolation, and resignation for which Saturn is known best.

Your two optimal choices for a conference locale are northeast (ruled by Jupiter) and southeast (ruled by Venus). Both Jupiter and Venus naturally prefer to make and accept direct, honest requests, and mild, polite appeals to reason, and to give and receive good advice. Both directions permit the conferees to benefit from the strong, waxing rays of the morning sun (to obtain the benefit of which you should consider scheduling your meetings early).

Northeast is the better direction of the two, since it facilitates the Jovian's naturally philosophical, optimistic, altruistic outlook to prevail, particularly if meetings are held on Thursdays in a room whose décor is rich in deep yellows and golds. Meetings in the southeast, especially if on Fridays in a room of radiant white embellished with multihued furnishings, will promote friendliness, though participants may spend more time socializing—or dining and drinking (Venus rules sensuality)—than actually working. Add further correspondences, and a richer confluence will make the influence of Jupiter or Venus ever stronger.

Southwest, the least esteemed of the directions in general, is also least valued as a location for a conference room. Southwest activates the energy of Rāhu and Ketu, the shadowy "planets" that promote exaggeration, misperception, and confusion. Southwest encourages all varieties of misunderstandings, and can make meetings deteriorate into yowling matches, or cause them to break up before they ever begin. This will be particularly the case in businesses that are founded on the use of shadowy energies, such as Web-based enterprises or motion-picture and TV ventures; those companies that focus on some form of "wildness" (head-banging music, intoxicants of all sorts, etc.) will be similarly subject to such premature deterioration. Southwestern rooms may, however, prove fruitful as "think tanks"—areas set aside for brainstorming—since Rāhu rules insight, ingenuity, inspiration, and imagination. As with the other planets, intensification of these indications will occur as a result of confluence.

In dining room, bedroom, kitchen, or office, as in conference room: Planetary patterns matter in every space. Enhance your awareness of these patterns, understand how your spaces can adjust to them, and you become less subject to their potentially pernicious effects. Minor design changes like repainting walls and shuffling furniture will rarely revolutionize your life on their own, but they may act as easy first steps on the road to "good space"; each positive change you make will encourage sukha to materialize and persist, nourished through confluence.

Yet More Directional Guidelines

Each vidyā offers its unique perspective on the world, and when you evaluate a space, you'll want to examine that space's every angle from many perspectives, to ensure that you're acquainted with as much of it as possible. You'll want to examine a space's every feature with the same care that you would examine every facet of a gemstone you were thinking of buying, since flaws can hide beneath otherwise unblemished exteriors. Knowledge is power; a little knowledge can be a dangerous thing (especially when it inspires you to make decisions that display more brashness than insight), but greater knowledge commonly brings about more power, at least in the Vāstu world.

The positioning of the Vāstu Puruṣa with his head turned toward the northeast provides us a clear intimation of how Vāstu directs us to orient our space. We organize our lives based on the eternal turning of the world and the evolution of its traits, expressed most palpably in the seasons of time and the temperaments of space. The northeast quadrant represents the direction in which our lives are headed. Northeast stands for sattva, the future we aim for, the goal we cherish, the concinnity we envision. By turning our faces to the dawn, we embrace the light of sattva, with its promise of brightness, renewal, and potential.

The southeast and northwest stand for rajas, for activity occurring in the present moment. Southeast and northwest correspond to where we now stand, the space and time that we currently inhabit, the stage on which we act out our roles. To position something in one of these two quadrants is to put it front and center in our daily lives.

The southwest quadrant is the domain of tamas, of the past, where we have come from. Southwest offers us ancestral inheritance, the weight of tradition, the support of memory. What goes in the southwest is what we want to use to bear us up, to place at our backs for protection. Putting your back to the south, west, or southwest lets your ancestors "back you up."

Vāstu's archetypal image is thus this: Men and women facing the light of the future as embodied by the sun, arraying their current lives at their left and right hands, backed up by their recollections and customs, beliefs, and principles. If, like India's ancient sages, we were of an anthropomorphic bent, we might espy in the contours of this archetype the shape of a humanoid being, with the sagacious, perceptive head in the northeast, the maneuvering hands southeast and northwest, and the (hopefully) well-settled lower body in the southwest: the very stance taken by the Vāstu Puruṣa.

This style of orientation has its origins in commonsensical self-preservation. When in a jungle surrounded by wild animals, you would be wise to sit with an open space in front of you, that you might catch sight of whatever might head your way well before it could reach you. You would want a tree or boulder at your back, to lean against, and to protect you from attack from behind. And you would keep your arms free, ready to act at a moment's notice on your behalf.

Vāstu suggests that you adopt a similar plan of action for your sojourn in the jungle of human society. Consequently, it dedicates the northeast portion of a home or office to *unobstructed vision*, the southeast and northwest to *focused action*, and the southwest to *consolidation*.

Northeast

Northeast is the direction of the Water Element, of sattva, and of Jupiter. Light that enters a home, office, garden, or other space from the northeast has a sattvic, Jovian flavor, the flavor of *Soma*—"Nectar." Northeast directs our future creativity to sweet, pleasant ends, and is a good quadrant in which to contemplate sattvic activities. Spend more time in the northeast and, all else being equal, you will become more sattvic.

Jupiter's kapha takes on a bit of the Sun's pitta nature and Mercury's pliant character to produce a kapha predominant, pitta secondary region of space for the Water Element. The fire of pitta combines with the intelligence of sattva to prevent the Water Element from becoming too heavy and cold. From this perspective also, northeast is the best among the directions.

Water, which is essential to all living beings, represents all that is creative in life. To situate water in the east, north, or northeast of a territory, building, or room—in the form of a stream, pond, well, or fountain—is to promote inspiration in that entire space.

The northeast quadrant of your home is the best region in which to dedicate some space to "sattva enhancement." This "serenity nook" could be a room or a corner of a room that is used exclusively for prayer, meditation, or worship rituals. Your nook might shelter something as complicated as an ornate altar, or as simple as an image of a person, place, or thing that you venerate.

Yellow, Jupiter's color, further enhances the generosity of spirit that northeast implies. When you paint the room that occupies the northeast corner of your house a mild yellow or a gentle gold, you strengthen its Jupiter confluence in the form of the mild, benevolent Jovian decorum and graciousness that naturally gravitates there.

A home office adorned in yellow stimulates creative thinking. To facilitate the transforming of ideas into realities, you can add in a little saffron red, to request the Sun to contribute some focused, purposeful activity to that space. Blending in some green will augment instead the intellectuality of the rajasic Mercury, which may enrich meaningful discussions.

Jupiter also represents the animal kingdom—horses and elephants in particular. To shelter a horse or elephant in your backyard and tend to it carefully can dramatically enhance Jupiter's influence in your life (though large animals are also substantial responsibilities that can easily become terrific headaches). Fortunately, you can achieve a similar effect by spending time around someone else's horses and elephants, or by looking after images of those animals in lieu of the animals themselves. Even a horseshoe may serve.

Jupiter rules pigeons and swans as well, so cooping your racing pigeons in the northeast quadrant of your property, or positioning a swan lake there, will yet further expand Jupiter's amiable influence in your life—as will locating images of these birds in that portion of your apartment.

Southeast

Southeast is the direction of the Fire Element, of rajas, and of Venus, the other of Jyotiṣa's "great benefics." Light that enters into a living space from the southeast will take on a southeastern, rajasic, Venusian tang. Southeast being the proper "home" of the Fire Element, the southeast quadrant of a space is the right area in which to establish fire: overtly, by locating the kitchen stove or fireplace, or both, in your home's southeast portion and indirectly by placing electrical and electronic equipment (computer, TV) in a southeast room or alcove, or in a room's southeast corner (electricity being a "fiery" energy).

The naturally mild, harmonious, vāta-and-kapha energy of southeast-lord Venus is easily outshone by the broiling energy of the eastern Sun and the southern Mars, yielding a predominantly pitta effect in this Fire-dominated quadrant. The strengthening of Venus in the southeast can, however, promote good doshic balance, which again awards southeast second place in the best-direction contest.

"Present-time creativity" resides in the southeast and northwest, and spending serious time in those quadrants, or even facing southeast and northwest when in another quadrant, will automatically activate and boost your overall activity level. Rooms in these two quadrants are best dedicated to dynamic activities like cooking, which can be exceptionally creative when done in a merry, sensuous, carefree Venusian fashion.

Venus, who in India is said to be a "king among poets" (*kavirāja*), rules eloquence, and southeast can support expressiveness in cuisine, conversation, and composition alike. A kitchen, music room, or painting atelier becomes even more Venusian when painted radiant white or in gaily hued shades, spectral qualities that Venus rules. Colorful and visually alluring accoutrements, like drapes or wall hangings made from the strong, durable, decorated fabrics that Venus favors, also enhance southeast's transformative power. The tints selected will determine whether that rajasic activity is flavored more with the equanimity of sattva (dark reds and oranges, for Sun) or the resoluteness of tamas (bold, bright, brashness-heightening reds, for Mars).

Venus rules all sorts of entertainments, which highlights the value of listening to good music while cooking, and makes performing artists (actors, musicians) akin to Venus incarnate. Fashion designers and interior decorators also follow archetypically Venusian professions; employing them to titivate your spaces will please Venus doubly.

Sun and Venus alike rule the vegetable kingdom, which suggests that the southeast quadrant should house its share of plants, particularly those that yield white and very fragrant flowers. This goes for the garden as well, for Venus rules blossoming trees.

To establish an appropriately resonant connection with the animal kingdom, you can hang your parrot cage in your kitchen's southeastern corner, or station a peacock (another Venusian fowl) on your southeast roof. You can ornament a southeastern space with cow or buffalo motifs or, if your situation permits, even station an actual cow or buffalo there. Should you lack the zoning or yardspace to house such large creatures, you can also sit in this portion of that space, facing southeast, and visualize yourself tending one of them.

Southwest

Southwest is presided over by *Nirṛti*—the power of chaos and dissolution—by the Earth Element, by tamas, and by Rāhu and Ketu, the Nodes of the Moon. Light that originates in the southwest will take on a southwestern, tamasic tinge. This light, and the energy it brings in its wake, is the most difficult for the average person to "digest" well, being at once chaotic and stiffly resistant to change.

The vāta that Saturn and Rāhu share combines with the pitta of Mars and Ketu to produce in southwest an energy that strongly enhances the force of both of those very active doṣas. Vāta is the most difficult doṣa to bring into and keep in balance, and pitta is almost as recalcitrant. The vāta-pitta overabundance here, coupled with the natural tamas that Saturn, Mars, Rāhu, and Ketu all display, combine to remind us of how difficult balancing the energy of the southwest can be, particularly when it becomes strongly activated.

Vāstu's answer to this problem is to encourage inactivity in the southwest, calling it the best direction in which to store items and information, to perform routine activities, to position heavy furniture. The stability that Earth offers us makes southwest the perfect location for the master bedroom, with its heavy bedstead that invites us to sleep (a pastime that promotes tamas, just as tamas encourages drowsiness).

A southwestern bedroom encourages sleepers to revisit, just before they fall asleep, the events of the day. Such bedtime reflection invokes the power of Nirṛti to "deconstruct" our recent experiences into digestible fragments, which we may then ruminate on in our contemplations and dreams. Understanding past events helps us refine our abilities for future living and experiencing. The southwest direction is a potent catalyst for such insights, for southwestern creativity is the creativity that relates to and is derived from past experience.

We can and should make use not only of the wisdom of our own experiences but of those of other family members as well, for the southwest direction also relates to ancestors, "those who have gone before." Our forebears generously offer us the wisdom they gleaned from their life experiences, asking in return only that we "respect our roots." To put photos of your parents and grandparents in the southwest corner of a room, or the southwestern section of a house, is to open yourself to their inspiration.*

Passing time in a southwest quadrant, or facing southwest as you sit in your home or office, will automatically activate this creativity related to bygone times, but will not necessarily enhance your present-time perceptivity. It may merely lead you into nostalgia, if your memories are so powerful that they drag you back to live in the past. Moreover, memories are rarely perfect, and the powers of delusion and confusion that are Rāhu and Ketu will tend to encourage you to "misremember," to use your memories to reinforce aspects of yourself that you would often be better off dismantling. Vāstu hence suggests southwest chiefly for activities like storage and sleep that are best performed without focused mental action.

Rāhu and Ketu rule ultraviolet and infrared respectively, but rooms that are decorated in phantasmagoric images and smoky, swirling shades (as one might find in a rave club or psychedelic shack) will also enhance their indications. So will images of gulls, owls, snakes, camels, donkeys, wolves, rodents, or poisonous or annoying insects like scorpions and mosquitoes. Adding bright red into the mix will append a southern, Martian edge to the already tamasic energy of the Nodes; black, violet, indigo, and blue highlights will emphasize the western, Saturnian variety of tamas. Blend in some eccentric, idiosyncratic people, and you have a recipe for pure southwestern extremity.

Southwest rules the mineral kindgom, which makes the southwestern quadrant of your home or office the ideal spot for that sculpture of agate (Rāhu) or turquoise (Ketu) keepsake. Your pet rock, crystal collection, ceremonial sword (Saturn rules iron, and Mars, sharpness), copper (Mars) artifacts, and knick-knacks of coral (Mars) and lapis lazuli (Saturn) should all find homes in the south, southwest, and west areas of your space. Outside, southwest makes a good direction in which to establish a rock garden, or to locate a heavy sculpture, particularly if this corner of your yard has a slight natural elevation. Letting this garden quadrant go feral is also a good option, for the Nodes rule wildness.

---

*Some say it's wise to avoid keeping any mementos of the dead in one's house. There are certainly occasions when this would be true, as when the dead person was particularly notorious, or when the current householder is particularly susceptible to being swayed by external influences. Usually, though, the benefit to be derived from respecting one's predecessors supersedes any inauspiciousness that the presence of their likenesses might convey.

Northwest

Northwest is the direction of the Air Element, of rajas, and of the Moon, the ruler of the mind. Northwest is the quadrant of eternal movement, of perpetual change; its light enjoys the rajasic flavor of the capricious moon, who shifts her shape and size as she speeds across the sky, appearing each night in a new *nakṣatra* (lunar constellation).

Northwest displays a clear vāta predominance, for Moon, Saturn, and Mercury all indicate vāta. Moon's secondary kapha, and Mercury's willingness to promote any of the doṣas, takes some of the edge off what would otherwise be a purely erratic, restless vāta experience. Still, northwest energy is second only to southwest in its reluctance to fall naturally into step with the rest of the cosmos.

Northwest's energy waxes and wanes like the moon, for northwest is an amalgam of the Moon with the fixity of Saturn/west and the duality of Mercury/north. North being ruled by Kubera, the god of "wealth and indulgence," the northwest quadrant is a good place to locate that sort of treasure that is often in flux. To this end, Varahamihira's *Bṛhat Saṁhitā* proposed that the "treasure-room" and "granary" of the house be positioned in the northwest. Cashbox and grain bins alike display the mildly paradoxical character of remaining full by virtue of an unending in-and-out flow, like a river, a barrel of port, or a hotel room. Despite the perpetual turnover of their contents, such "temples of transience" remain (we hope) continuously filled. The northwest quadrant is thus ideal for a guest bedroom, which a good host reallocates as soon as it empties.

One recent book on Vāstu suggests that northwest is a good location for a guestroom because the restlessness that the Air Element foments will stir up a wind to "blow guests away." Unfriendly implications of this strategy aside, you cannot guarantee that your visitors will be "blown away" by the northwest "wind." What if they find your guest room far more inviting, comfortable, and stimulating than their previous, possibly even more volatile, accommodations?

The same book asserts that it is wise to station your TV in the northwest corner of a room, in the northwest quadrant of your home, to prevent you from spending too much time staring at it. But suppose that facing northwest as you stare at your TV makes you so restless that you become immobilized, unable to pick yourself off the couch because you feel so soothed by the hypnotic images unspooling before you? Using instability to cure instability is a tricky task, in Vāstu as in life in general.

A television would be good in the northwest if you can "dip into" it from time to time, sampling its ever-changing wares like you sample the contents of your cashbox and your food stores, keeping your finger on the world's pulse without becoming captive to its apparitions. Northwest is also a good location for the medicine chest, particularly because the Moon also rules caregivers. A medicine chest is another container that is always being refilled, one that you "dip into" occasionally, for a different product each time (we hope). Communication devices like phone and fax often do well being situated in the northwestern region of a room or structure, for similar reasons.

A northwestern room becomes even more lunar when painted white. Black, violet, indigo, or blue trim will move the energy in the western, Saturnine, fixed direction, and green frills will move it onto a more northern, Mercurial, two-trends-at-once track. Living greenery encourages both Mercury and the Moon, for the Moon governs plants and their succulence. Images of lunar beings, like the partridge or crane, the antelope or hare, or of water creatures, will strengthen the Moon yet further.

8 Organizing Spaces

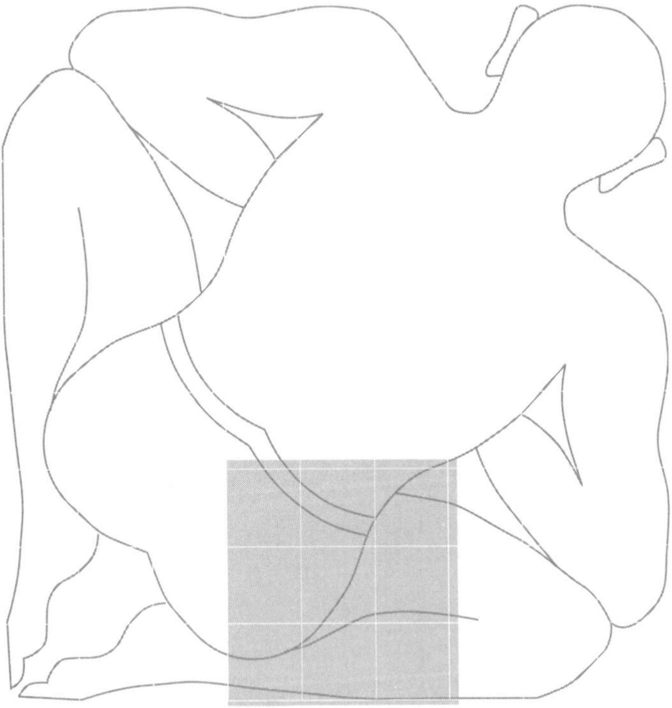

Marie's Living Room, Directionally

Even now our level of Vāstu fluency permits us to compose simple Vāstu sentences, statements that accurately describe situations in space and what might be done to rectify or improve them. Your own initial Vāstu phrases will probably be unsophisticated, but they will (so long as they are accurate) set in motion an evolution of understanding that will enrich your every future Vāstu expression.

Your possibilities for "educating" and invigorating your space are limited chiefly by your imagination, but that "education" will proceed more smoothly if you will, in your plans for your house and its rooms, design always for balance between the purpose you intend for a space and that space's natural traits. Much of the time, space will cooperate with you more readily when you direct awareness and alertness generally to the northeast, allot steadiness and solidity chiefly to the southwest, and divide the most active of your activities between southeast and northwest.

What jumps out at Marie and me, as we survey her living room from a directional point of view, is how weak that room's southeast corner seems. The two small staircases that project into the room disfigure Vāstu Puruṣa's right hand, the hand he uses to perform auspicious activities. When whole, Vāstu Puruṣa encourages the whole space he rules to be cooperative; when one of his limbs is missing or distorted, though, the space that that room represents is substantially compromised, and will need remediation.

A deformed right arm for Vāstu Puruṣa weakens the focus and integrity of the energies that call the southeast quadrant home: the Fire Element, rajas, and Venus. The two staircases, moreover, stimulate the natural instability of rajas, whose penchant for activity is enhanced by all that is transitory—thus, the stairways contribute a pronounced flavor of transience to the room. Compromising the power of Venus inhibits creative expression; weakening Fire (the "problem-solver" among the Five Elements) tempts any condition of imbalance to persist. An excess of rajas with no clear outlet will usually manifest in the mind as frustration, and in the body as vāta. One example of a Vāstu statement that would reflect these energetic proclivities is: *Those who frequent this room will tend to find accumulating within them vāta-induced frustration and lack of focus, brought into being by the inhibition of creative expression that the room's distortion will promote.*

This analysis is actually a "diagnosis" of Vāstu Puruṣa's condition in that room, expressed in the vāta-pitta-kapha of Āyurveda and the sattva-rajas-tamas of Sāṁkhya. As with you and me, so with Vāstu Puruṣa: the Three Doṣas govern his physical health, and the Three Guṇas, his mental health. The bodies and minds of those who inhabit a room will be inclined to resonate with the body and mind of that room's Vāstu Puruṣa; how he feels is how they will tend to feel.

Our statement of assessment is also a sort of "weather forecast" for the room, an indication that people will be disinclined to spend much time in this room, and that those who do are likely to find a strongly vāta- and rajas-provoking wind circulating therein. How much this wind will affect a resident, and in what way, will depend on how prone that person is (by constitution, current condition, and season) to vāta aggravation in body, or rajas activation in mind. Climate, diet, habitual pursuits, season, attitudes, and horoscopic factors also each have their own bearing on this proclivity. Usually, the best way to estimate the extent to which a setting will affect you is to monitor your breath while you sit within it getting a "feel" for its nature. Now is thus a good time to return briefly to Exercises One, "Breath Awareness" and Two, "The Gut Feeling." Performing them again will refine your internal "breath monitor," so that you may discover an accurate picture of your home's "subtle atmosphere."

Remedying the Living Room

In Marie's case, the warm, wet climate that is typical of South Florida works against vāta by strengthening Fire. The fact that the compromised southeast corner of the living room opens right onto the kitchen and that room's repository of Fire also helps. The piano's presence adds to the mix, as does the sound system, which occupied the northwest corner until the first phase of Marie's "renovation" shifted it into the master bedroom. Though some Vāstu commentators maintain that "fiery" electrical equipment should always be set up in a space's southeast quadrant, this is true only in a general sense. Where a southeast quadrant is compromised, northwest forms a good alternative for such gear, by virtue of being the opposite end of the northwest-southeast diagonal. In Jyotiṣa, two planets that sit opposite one another are said to strongly "aspect," or influence, one another; here the sound system's energy "aspects" the weakened southeast corner, thereby strengthening it.

Moreover, sound has a strong impact on vāta; harmonious, comforting sounds help to bring vāta under control, while intensely dissonant noise aggravates vāta all the more. A sound system could thus benefit Marie's living room from the perspectives of Fire, Air, and Venus alike, provided that it contributed balancing, not stimulating, sounds. In practice, however, while Marie's stereo did frequently play calming music and chanting, it more commonly had a stimulating effect on the occupants of the room.

Of course, a heightened vāta-force in a room will encourage restlessness in visitors and residents alike. If she wanted, Marie could encourage vāta to accumulate in her living room, and could then use that room to entertain guests who she'd like to see headed on their way. The room's vāta would then tend to whisk those visitors out the door as quickly as it swept them in. Though this strategy might reduce Marie's burden of socializing, the negative implications of creating a vāta-cauldron at the center of her home are likely to outweigh the benefits of being able to promptly send visitors on their way.

Replacing the sound system with the large chair from the same furniture set as the sofa, and then pointing it directly at the compromised southeast corner, was in this case a good choice. Though this was a weaker remedy overall than that of using audio, the stability it creates is more welcome than a further manifestation of flux. Other strategies that could also aid Venus to feel less afflicted, and strengthen the room all-round, would be to cover the walls with a fresh coat of light-colored paint; to put up colorful wall hangings or images of Venusian beings; to introduce more plants into the room; and to generally dedicate the room to entertainment—which is, after all, a living room's reason for being.

Remedying Your Rooms with What We've Learned Thus Far

You can use this sort of analysis on each room of your own dwelling, composing statements about how a particular irregularity might affect it, then considering ways in which to compensate for the imbalance.

Exercise Twelve: Remedying Imperfections

Overlay one of the rooms of your home, preferably one that is not a perfect square or rectangle, with the

Vāstu Puruṣa Maṇḍala. Evaluate the implications of whichever quadrant is compromised by considering the qualities associated with its ruling element, planet, trait, and doṣa. Test your hypothesis with your breath, your gut, or whatever other means you find most reliable.

Then create a plan for dealing with the imperfection. Since neither you nor your home will ever be totally perfect, Vāstu aims to establish a situation that is the most sattvic and sukha-promoting, given your range of constraints. It's often useful first to write down all the approaches that might produce good results, even the ones that are least practical (like knocking down all the walls in the room, and replacing them with "Vāstu-perfect" partitions).

Once you've made your list, select the most practical and the simplest of your suggestions, and implement at least one of them. After you've administered your "remedy," again evaluate (using your preferred method of evaluation) how the room feels, and what—if anything—your remedy has accomplished. Keep making additional adjustments until the room's space feels substantially more balanced than it was before you began.

Organizing The Home Space

Before you sort out each of the rooms in your residence by bringing their respective individual Vāstu Puruṣa Maṇḍalas into relative balance, you should first consider how aptly they are arranged, according to directionality, within the Vāstu Puruṣa Maṇḍala that governs your residence as a whole. Vāstu Puruṣa's realm actually covers your entire property, including lawns and gardens, but for now, let's apply the Vāstu Puruṣa Maṇḍala solely to your house or apartment's floor plan, to assist us in answering our primary questions:

What can materialize in this space, and how might it do so?

How full should this space be, and how empty?

What items should fill this space, and how should they be arranged?

What qualities should these items possess, to achieve the results desired?

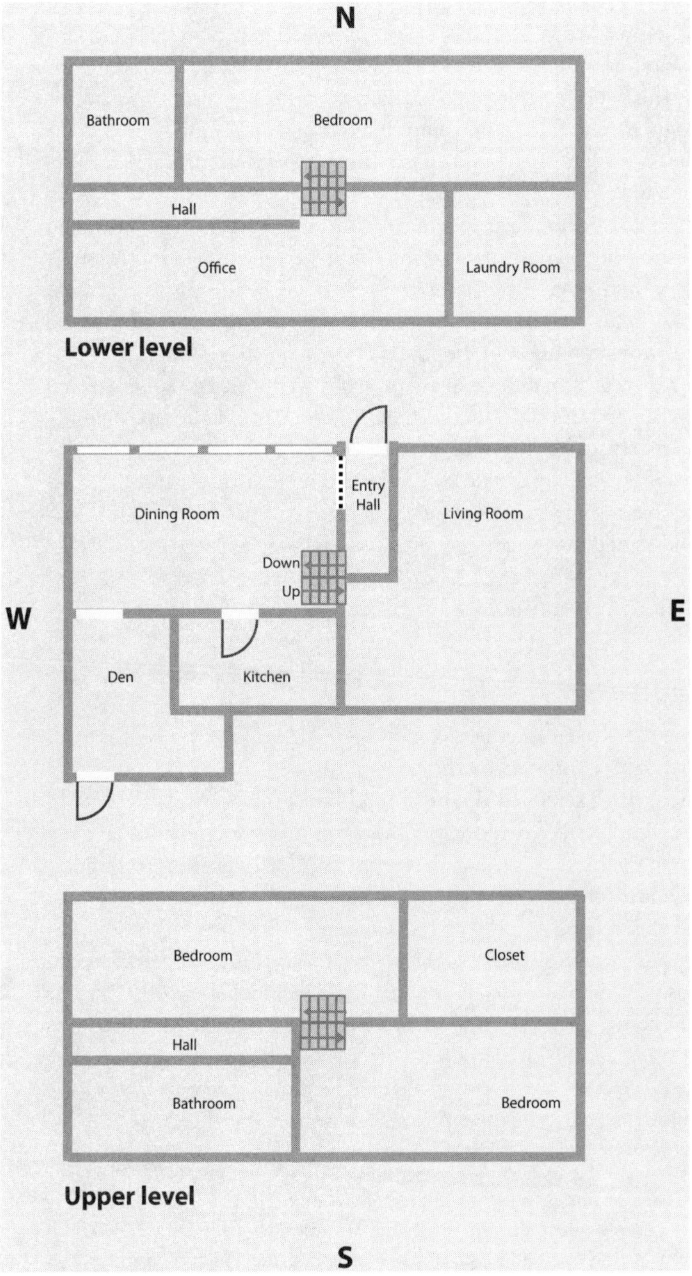
N
Bathroom
Bedroom
Hall
Office
Laundry Room
Lower level
Entry
Hall
Dining Room
Living Room
Down
Up
W
E
Den
Kitchen
Bedroom
Closet
Hall
Bathroom
Bedroom
Upper level
S

To help us answer the first question—what can materialize in this space, and how—we first apply the Vāstu Puruṣa Maṇḍala to the floor plan. This will be easy to do if your floor plan is already square or rectangular, and a bit more complicated if it is not.

The floor plan for Marie's house provides us with a useful real-life example:

The house covers three distinct levels, with an L-shaped extension containing the den jutting into the southwest, the one corner we least want strengthened. Extensions are welcomed in the north and east, and are usually tolerated in the northwest and southeast; but they are strongly frowned upon in the southwest.

To leave the situation as it is would be to encourage southwestern energy to predominate in the house—which would invite ongoing turbulence into the lives of its residents.* We need to address this extension, which we can do by several methods, including:

Completing the larger square/rectangle

Subdividing into smaller squares/rectangles

Completing the larger square/rectangle

To accomplish this, we would draw lines into Marie's backyard that would extend the "house" as such into a larger, more regular figure. The virtual lines could then be made tangible by building an extension (a conservatory, for example) onto the house, enclosing the area with a screened veranda, or adding a covered deck. We could even extend a slatted roof over the area, turning it into a partially enclosed "garden room," with a terra cotta, tile, or flagstone floor. This would create a transitional space, partly outside and partly inside the house.

One advantage of this "expansive" approach would be that it would increase the house's size. A disadvantage would be that the house's central point, the location of its Brahma Sthāna, would be shifted to a point very near the kitchen sink—precisely the sort of location (an area where dirty water drains away) that we would least like to have as the focus for the energy of the entire structure.

---

*Turbulence will be particularly strong when Rāhu or Ketu is prominent in the birth charts of one or more family members; it will display itself particularly during periods when one of the Nodes is activated by transit (*gocara*) or planetary period (*daśā* and *bhukti*, stages of life during which the influence of one graha predominates) in a family member's horoscope.

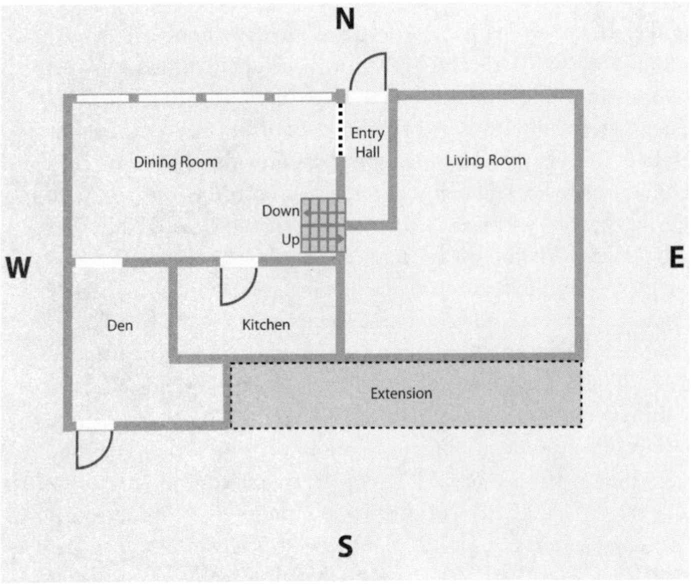

SUBDIVIDING INTO SMALLER SQUARES/RECTANGLES

Alternatively, Marie could erect a barrier, solid and permanent—or flimsy and movable—between the dining room and the L-shaped den, in effect isolating the den from the rest of the house. As it is, the den was a later addition to the house, so it doesn't really "belong" there;* one gets the distinct feeling, on crossing the threshold between dining room and den, of entering a discrete space.

Marie has in fact never been happy in that room, and avoids spending time there. When she and I surveyed the house, she was using a hanging curtain to separate the den from the dining room; at one time, a folding room divider was positioned at this threshold, and Marie had already been thinking of reinstituting the room divider, or maybe even installing a sliding door. Whichever barrier she selects will simply formalize the situation as it exists, respecting reality by making a preexisting tendency more definitive.

*Though we can't know for certain the situation that existed when the previous owners decided to construct this odd addition, it's reasonable to wonder whether one of them, or one of their family members, was being strongly influenced by one of the Nodes at the time.

The den is already its own little world that, without consciously intending to do so, Marie and her family have oriented in a way that reflects the energies of the quadrants. Here, the house's principal TV glowers down bulkily from its perch in the northeast. The telephone graces the northwest, the Venusian southeast provides the room's chief vista, out onto the leafy garden, and southwest hosts the sofa, on which all comers sprawl. Southwest, the corner of densest tamas, has thus been dignified with the divan, setpiece for slouching and sleeping. The Venusian southeast offers the beauty of flowers and fruit, as well as a view to the beckoning entertainments of basketball and table tennis in the backyard. Appropriately enough in this arrangement, northwest houses the room's communication device, and northeast, its "contemplation nook."

The fact that the den's object of contemplation is the television is in keeping with its overall flavor as an entertainment room. Though it's true that the "idiot box" oft mesmerizes its watchers into stultifying states of tamas, its northeast placement will in this context provide its watchers some of that direction's sattva. Since they'll be watching TV in this room anyway, this placement will encourage them to choose programs that are relatively more sattvic. It will also foster attention, so that they are likely to get more out of what they watch than they might if the TV was positioned elsewhere. A room ideally draws attention initially into a point that is high in the southwest (which represents the past, and tamas), then guides that attention toward a point that is low in the northeast (which promotes the future, and sattva); while conventional wisdom would not encourage attention to be directed toward the TV, it might in this case be desirable. One way to cultivate this kind of focus would be to place objects (e.g., pictures of ancestors) high in the southwest corner of this southwestern room, or to decorate those walls with downward-pointing motifs (e.g., hanging on that wall a pointed object, point floorward).

The den has clearly already configured itself into a separate world, and is only waiting, in its southwestern standoffishness, for that solitary status to be made official. We therefore advise Marie to subdivide her floor plan, and permit her den to follow its own destiny (relatively speaking). This will help persuade the den's tamas to remain largely confined to that room alone, allowing the rest of the home to flow toward sattva instead.

Organizing A Large Space

However many rooms an irregular space may contain, and wherever they may be located, the space's overall ambience will be strongly enhanced if the movement of prāṇa within it can be stabilized vis-à-vis its geometry. Thus, unless your own home's floor plan is already configured in a neatly symmetrical square or rectangle, you may want to consider converting it into a regular polygon.

If you live in a house with ample grounds surrounding, extending your home to adjust for a compromised Vāstu Puruṣa is often an attractive proposition. If you live in an urban apartment, adding to your space is likely not an option, and you'll need to subdivide instead, to partition your space into one large area and one or two appendages. Precisely how and where to draw dividing lines when apportioning your internal space will depend on how your space is oriented, and what you plan to do with it. Most of the time you want to maximize both your total area, and the area of your largest partition.

The irregular space shown below, which covers 1040 square feet, is missing its northwest and southeast corners. Let's assume that the structural situation will not permit additions to be made, so that we can't remedy the constriction by extending at those corners, and must partition instead. Four possible ways of dividing this space are shown below, as plans A, B, C, and D.

All four plans produce regular quadrilaterals. From the perspective of wanting the large space to be as large as possible, plans A and B are the most promising of the four, with B's largest space being 720 square feet, and A's being 704 square feet (C's is 576, and D's, 400).

The proportion of length to width is also important, and B's large space, which is 24 feet by 30 feet, has the best proportion, a perfect 1.25:1. A's proportion, at 22 feet by 32 feet, is 1.45:1, which is close to the very desirable 1.5:1. D's large section has a 4:1 proportion, permissible but well outside the 3:1 ratio that is generally considered to be the upper limit of efficient spatial equilibrium. Its long, thin space will not be easy to organize well, which is sufficient to take it out of the running. C's big piece's proportion, at 1.78:1, is also undesirable, as it almost precisely equals the forbidden *padona* ratio of 1.75:1.

A

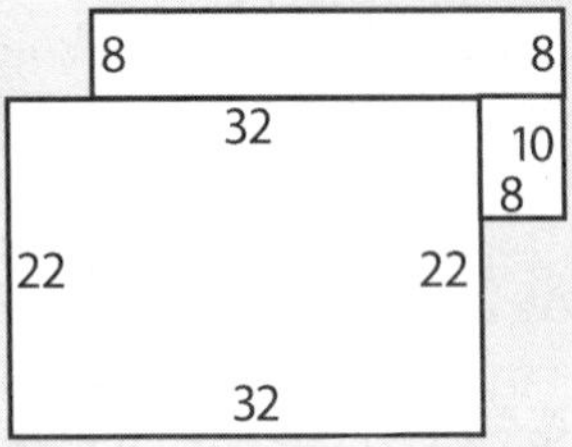
8
8
32
10
8
22
22
32

B

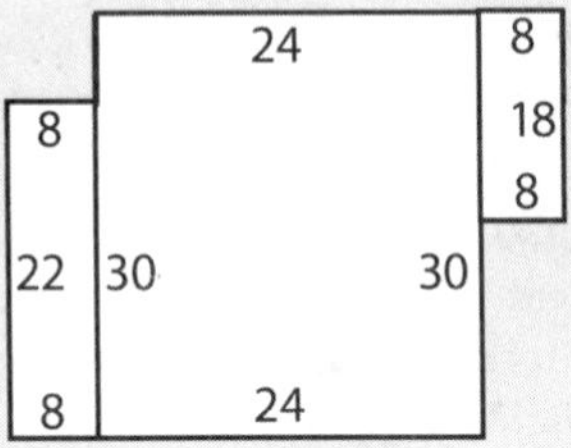
24
8
8
18
8
22
30
30
8
24

C

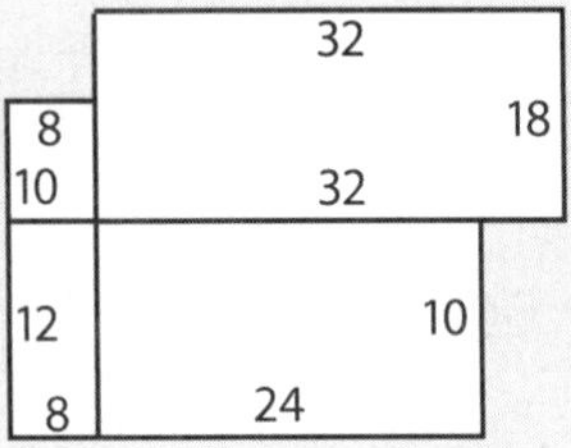
32
8
18
10
32
12
10
8
24

D

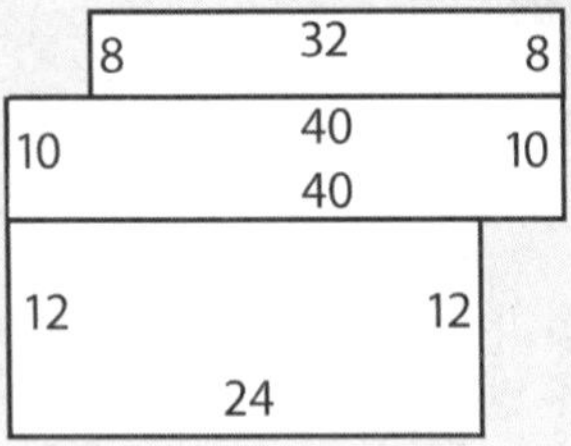
8
32
8
10
40
10
40
12
12
24

B's main space is centrally located, its bindu (center point) being located precisely at the center of the 30 feet x 40 feet rectangle that would be created if we could add the missing pieces to the space to make it symmetrical. This makes the Brahma Sthāna of B's largest piece identical with the Brahma Sthāna of the floor plan as a whole, which is desirable.* Even if we can't put a central skylight there (which is a nice way to highlight the Brahma Sthāna), we can use some sizable light fixture or other prominent ceiling ornament to create the "upward aspiration" that is the Brahma Sthāna's task to embody.

Next we evaluate A, B, and C from the perspective of how the smaller rectangles act as additions to the larger one. In this regard, A is clearly superior, with its northeastern and eastern appendages, which encourages progress toward sattva and the future. B is middling, with one desirable adjunct in the east of north, and one undesirable add-on to the west of south. C, with southwestern and western appendages—both of which are unattractive because they stimulate tamas and the past—can be removed from consideration.

We would now use other factors, such as the position of the main doors and of the individual rooms in the apartment, to draw final conclusions about the best arrangement and choose between plans A and B. All things being equal, we would probably choose A over B, because of the superior advantage of having extensions into the north and east.

Once we make our decision, we would superimpose Vāstu Puruṣa Maṇḍalas over each of the three "autonomous zones" that we have created in the selected arrangement, and then answer our other questions—how full should these spaces be; with what items of which qualities should we fill them; and how should these items be arranged—accordingly.

Organizing a House Full of Rooms

Aiśānyāṁ deva-gṛhaṁ mahānasaṁ cāpi kāryam āgneyyām |
Nairṛtyāṁ bhāṇḍopaskaro'rtha dhānyāni mārutyām ||

---

*Vāstu only rarely advises that the central points of a building and of the squared site on which it sits should coincide, as this concurrence makes the structure's prāṇa too "active." In this instance, though, the structural subdividing weakens prāṇa to some degree, which allows the arrangement to actually reinforce prāṇa.

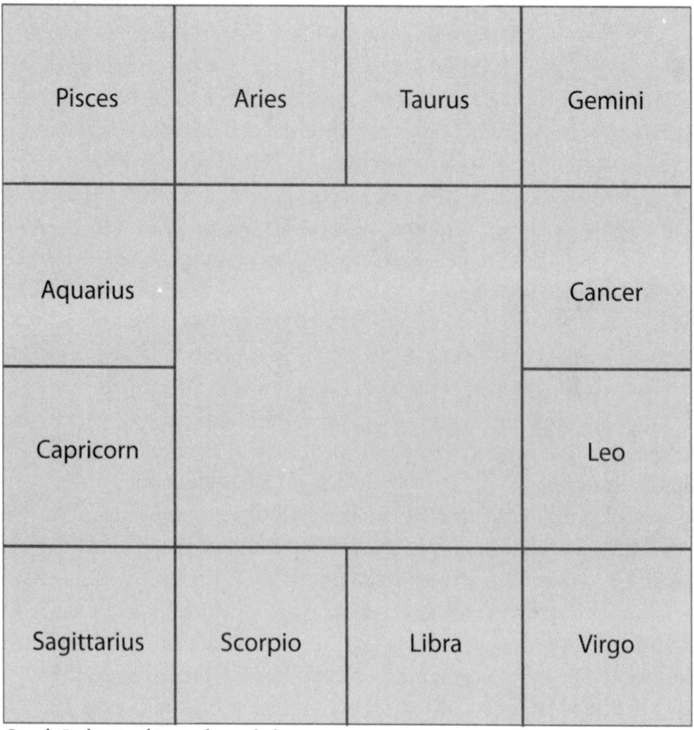

South Indian style astrological chart

> *The worship room should be situated in the northeast, the kitchen in the southeast, the storeroom in the southwest, and the treasure room and granary in the northwest.*
>
> *Bṛhat Saṁhitā* 53:118, p. 495

Vāstu's ideal residence is structured as a hollow square (or rectangle) of rooms surrounding a central courtyard that serves as its Brahma Sthāna. The courtyard is meant to be large enough to serve as the venue for important family events—worship rituals, weddings, performances of music or dance—that both partake of and contribute to the purity and sanctity of that center. A courtyard, said Hassan Fathy, is "the owner's private piece of the sky," the residents' connection to the divinity above.

Like the squares of this South Indian style astrological chart, in which the 12 constellations of the zodiac are arrayed around a central

Kitchen Bathroom Bedroom Dining Room Guest Rooms Garage Recreation Room	Bedroom Dining Room Library/Study Living Room Medicine Chest Financial Center	Meditation Shrine Room Veranda Portico
Bathroom Bedroom Dining Room Library/Study Living Room	Courtyard Atrium Living Room	Bathroom Bedroom Dining Room Living Room
Living Room Master Bedroom Storage Stairs	Bathroom Bedroom Dining Room Kitchen	Kitchen Garage

*Most desirable room locations**

Brahma Sthāna, Vāstu assigns purpose to a residence's rooms according to their location within the omnibus architectural plan.

Vāstu logic helps us augment the skeletal outline of room locations that *Bṛhat Saṁhitā* provides to us. The chart on page 211 presents an outline of the most desirable locations for specific rooms. North is at the top of this diagram, which puts east, of course, at the right.

This diagram offers plenty of flexibility; bedrooms, for example, can appear pretty much anywhere except in the northeast or southeast. Because of the variety of possibilities, you'll want to develop your room

---

*This chart summarizes the generally accepted directives for room placement, and it's important to note that not all authorities agree with these pronouncements. While, for example, *Bṛhat Saṁhitā* assures us that the kitchen belongs in the southeast, other Vāstu texts offer differing perspectives: The 16th-century *Manuṣyālaya Candrikā* testifies that northwest is also permissible, and the text *Mānasāra* even advises north or northeast (based perhaps on the theory that cooking is a sacred activity).

distribution plan with care even if your house is aligned to true east. It's essential to assess potential room assignments with some reliable indicator (like your breath) to discover how "right" those allocations feel to you. A home that is not perfectly aligned with the cardinal directions is deprived of the "automatic allocation" of possibilities that the directions provide, and requires even more of such personalized evaluation and adjustment.

We can derive a rule of thumb from these principles and considerations:

It will be easier to bring the potential of a room to its greatest fruition when it appears in the Vāstu-suggested part of your home than when it is located in an area not recommended by Vāstu, where its potential may remain imperfectly achieved even with appropriate Vāstu adjustments.

Only in those cases where a room in a wholly wrong part of the house also suffers from significant negative confluence would the situation potentially be bad enough to justify making structural changes, or taking the drastic step of changing house. For instance, if your kitchen is in the southwest, and it has no large trees, walls, or tall structures behind it to "back it up"; and if it also has a steep slope that drops away behind it, large windows, a shape that is very large, small, or irregular, etc.—you might want to consider enlisting a contractor or even relocating.

In Marie's home, the kitchen is on the permissible south, the dining room in the southwest but along the western wall, the living room in the northwest but along the western wall, and the garage along the eastern wall. The problematic rooms, from the perspective of their resonance (or lack thereof) with the directions, are the two northeastern bedrooms, the southeastern master bedroom, and the southeastern "family room," which has mutated into a multipurpose space comprising computer room, communication room, library, office, and bedroom.

The Fiery nature of southeast is at least honored in the family room, which hosts "fiery" electronic equipment and serves as a place where family members "cook things up." Andy, Marie's husband, a CPA, prepares accounts there; James and Sarah, the teens, "cook up" plans for adventures with their friends and cousins from this space, via e-mail and telephone.

The southeastern master bedroom is more of a problem, with its eastern and southern windows that let in ample Fiery sunlight in the midst of the sweltering South Florida climate, and its door that provides access to the rest of the house via the Airy northwest direction, which encourages the family to treat the room more as a transit lounge than as a place for repose. The excess of Fire here, spurred on by Air, can aggravate pitta, and make the residents of that room irritable, argumentative, and generally hotter in temperament.

To prevent this, Fire and Air need to be balanced with Water and Earth, through the mediating influences of paint, décor, and artwork, and by placing a large, heavy piece of furniture in the room's southwest corner for "ballast." The excessive stimulation of Fire and Air here will make it particularly important for Marie to point her bed in the most beneficial of directions, and to sleep in an appropriate position (a discussion of the adjustments necessary for the bedroom is below). She has already unwittingly improved the situation by establishing her personal shrine along the bedroom's eastern wall, thereby adding Water, sattva, and the harmonizing energy of Jupiter into the mix. Calming music and chanting is always playing in the room, which is of further assistance.

Another potentially useful remedy for the master bedroom could be a lamp or candle in its southeast corner, a light source that Marie could keep lit when she was present there for any length of time. This may seem paradoxical, since the room is overflowing with Fire energy already; but its Fire lacks the focus that a stove would provide if the room were a kitchen instead of a bedroom. Rather than have the Fire circulating aimlessly there (abetted by Air, which governs and intensifies aimlessness), it's better to offer it respect by giving it a convergence point. The flame helps to "nail down" the Fire energy in its appropriate corner of the room, allowing the other Elements more freedom to express themselves in their accustomed positions.

Of the two northeastern bedrooms, the one on the house's lowest level at least respects the dictum that a residence's lowest point should be in the northeast. The other bedroom, on the house's top floor, lacks this advantage. Both have northern windows only. The lower chamber has a southwestern door, the upper one a southern door, neither of which is particularly welcome. One way to establish a counterweight to the negative influences of these two doors would be to shift the doors to different locations; a less dramatic approach will require careful application of an appropriate Vāstu Puruṣa grid, followed by judicious decorating adjustments and regular observance and application of balancing techniques, including diet and activities that will not promote the influence of Mars (southern door) or the Nodes (southwestern door).

What to Look for in a Room

It's helpful to have an understanding of the ideal layout for each room in your home, and the descriptions below provide an overview. As you read them, remember that none of your rooms are likely to fit the ideal, nor is it necessary that any of them should. You should, however, be alert to those rooms that display a confluence of less-than-desirable traits, and pay more attention to them in your aligning efforts.

Bathroom

Until recently, all toilets and most bathing areas in India were outside the home, a situation that is more hygienic (if less convenient) than indoor plumbing, and better from the point of view of "Vāstu hygiene" as well.

In regards to an indoor bathroom, Vāstu pundits disagree on the placement of the shower or bathtub. Some claim that this element, the bathroom's largest and heaviest fixture, should appear in the southwest corner, the natural home of the large and heavy; others maintain that, in its role as water receptacle, the bathing area should appear in the northeastern corner, the abode of Water.

Another group endorses the presence of tubs and showers on any wall except the northeast. All these options are potentially sound, depending on the context of the rest of the home; but wherever the tub or shower may be, its water optimally drains from there toward the northeast.

A similar disagreement arises regarding the placement of the sink or wash basin: While most say west is optimal, a few opine that the north or east walls are also acceptable.

The best place for toilets is said to be the south or west, with northwest and southeast getting second preference. Everyone agrees that toilets do not belong directly opposite the front door, for prāṇa that flows into the house through that entryway can easily flow right out again, down the gurgler. For this reason, it's best to keep the door of any bathroom or toilet, wherever located, only slightly ajar when not in use; this permits some circulation of air into that room but restricts the loss of prāṇa through it.

Bedroom

Bedrooms on the ground floor usually provide better sleep than those above, though some contend that the master bedroom, the refuge for the head of the house, should be on the house's highest level, so that the master or mistress of the house, like an eagle in its aerie, may look down on his or her world in order to guard it well. The high-altitude perch also evokes the parallel image of a monarch's quarters, arrayed to allow her to look down into the town below the castle. And, indeed, the master bedroom should be castle, haven, place of refuge for the home's ruler.

Keeping all that in mind, one should remember that the master bedroom is usually best positioned in the tamasic southwest, to take advantage of the stability of the Earth Element there, and to promote sleep (the quintessential tamasic activity). Northwest bedrooms are said to be best for guests, who are transient; some commentators suggest that western bedrooms are best for children. Southeast bedrooms tend to promote aggravation of pitta and thus heat in mind and body; northeast bedrooms tend to make body and mind overly Watery, with accompanying emotional hypersensitivity, and propensity for diseases caused by accumulation of kapha.

For reasons of good pranic circulation, furniture should preferably not touch the walls of the house. This is particularly true of a bed, for the reason that while you sleep you rely more on the room's configuration to help circulate your prāṇa than you do while you're awake, when your conscious attention becomes more significant.

As a general rule, beds, heavy pieces of furniture as they are, should be placed along the bedroom's south or west sides. Bookshelves can go in the southwest, electronic equipment in the southeast, and jewelry boxes with dressing table (or your safe for valuables, if you have one) on the north wall.

You'll usually get your best sleep if you sleep with your head pointing east (meaning that, when you lie on your back in bed, the top of your head should point into the east). Sleeping with the top of your head pointed south encourages deep sleep, and helps promote good body-mind integration. Head pointed west? Be ready for an active night, with lots of dreams. Always avoid sleeping with your head into the north unless you're dead or ready to die, or if you want to practice lucid dreaming or astral traveling.

Sleeping with your head into the west or north opposes sleep's chief goal, which is to maximize rest and recuperation. For this reason, it's usually best to go to sleep lying on your right side. This will make the nāḍī associated with your left nostril function more effectively, which will relax your body, since this nāḍī is associated with calming, rejuvenating lunar energy. Everyone shifts sleeping positions several times at night, but if you induce sleep while lying on your right side, so that the left nāḍī is opened, you'll set a pattern for the night that will offer you greater benefit than if you descend into sleep while lying on your left side. Left-sided sleeping activates the right nostril and its nāḍī, whose fieriness does not encourage deep sleep (lie down on your left side after a heavy meal, however, and you'll facilitate the action of your digestive fire). Sleeping on your back tends to aggravate vāta; sleeping on your stomach disturbs all Three Doṣas.

Always remember, though, to apply these rules in the context of the constraints defined by your own personal space! One of my clients was experiencing regular interruptions of nighttime slumber when she slept with her head pointed into the east. The very night that she moved her bed so her head pointed south, she began to sleep all night long without difficulty, and has been doing so ever since. The reason? When she was sleeping with her head into the east, her bed lay between a window and a door, which encouraged a strong current of prāṇa to move through her while she slept. If you value your sleep, make sure that the head of your bed does not line up directly with any door or window!

Also, while asleep or awake, you should avoid pointing your feet toward any sacred picture or object; this bombards the images and relics with "used" energy escaping from your body through your soles, which is disrespectful, and which muddles their purity. This consideration will further restrict the possible placements of your bed, for whether or not you have a room for meditation and worship elsewhere in the house, you ought to establish some sort of small shrine, a "hallowed nook," in the northeast corner of your sleeping space.

While most Vāstu authorities suggest that the bed's headboard should be decorated (in a none-too-ornate style), you should be wary of placing intensely colored art objects, dramatic photos, or other dynamic depictions over the head of your bed. Mirrors don't belong over your head either; in fact, no mirror should be in a direct line with your bed.

Try your best to shut out all light while you are sleeping, as darkness also deepens sleep; but when awake, readily expose yourself to light. Large windows, or a sizable skylight, will admit the early morning summer sun and, on many nights of the month, the bright moon. During the winter you may want to keep your curtains open all night long, so that you can bask in as much natural light as possible. Exposure to the rays of the moon, especially the full moon, is important for everyone's health, particularly those with pitta type constitutions and conditions, and fertile women (moon rays help keep menstrual cycles regular), but you may be better off absorbing those rays in your living room or solarium (or lunarium).

The bedroom should be your place of refuge, and the bed your place of slumber. Do not read in bed, or lie in bed when in a state of worry; use your rocking chair for such pursuits. If you have a television in your bedroom, watch it sparingly, making a habit of listening to soothing recordings on your sound system instead. Do not allow a TV or a computer in a child's bedroom; in fact, if you have adequate space, you should delineate a separate playroom for the children, so that from an early age, they will associate the bedroom solely with repose. At the very least, restrict their more active pastimes and playthings to other parts of the house.

This goes for adults too, of course, such as the man who came to me complaining of fitful sleep. The reason for his tossing and turning was not especially complicated: On his bedroom ceiling, dozens of fighter plane models hung suspended above his bed. Though he initially resisted removing them, he was sleeping much better not long after he did. The violence that the fighter planes implied was one reason for this gentleman's insomnia; another was the fact that anything suspended above you will act as a *śūla*, a pranic spear that "pierces" whatever it points at. Body, prāṇa, and mind alike perceive pointy things as weapons, and no one enjoys having a weapon pointed at them, nor is it a beneficial arrangement from a pranic perspective. Every time you see a "spear," you'll be compelled to wonder, consciously or subconsciously, when it's going to impale you.

Lights that hang down over the dining table may be tolerable, since they let people see their companions and enable everyone to savor the visual cornucopia of the meal; since such lighting elements usually hang above the table's center and away from anyone's head or heart, they do not present a pranic danger. But a light suspended from a bedroom ceiling that points directly at a bed (or worse yet, at a sleeping head), will cause the sleeper to cringe regularly, inwardly if not outwardly, which will not promote healthy sleep.

This prohibition on sharply pointed objects and surfaces applies equally well to other "spears" within the home, like acutely angled walls, and also to every room in the house, not merely the bedroom (though it is particularly important in the bedroom, since when you're sleeping, you're particularly vulnerable to such influences when, being exposed to them over an extended period of time). I know someone in India whose courtyard house has an acute angle pointing directly at her kitchen door. Every time I exit her kitchen, I recoil slightly (if involuntarily) from that "spear." While I'm in the kitchen, I always try to sit so that that "spear" is aimed neither at my back nor my chest. All in all, I avoid spending any more time in that kitchen than I have to, and early on, I discovered that other house residents and guests do the same.

The sharp points of surfaces and objects inside the home can often be remedied by covering them with a curtain, a folding screen, an interior wall, or something similar, though occasionally the walls that create that acute angle will have to come down, and a more benign angle created in its stead.

Dining Room

The dining room can occupy any of the cardinal directions, though most commentators suggest that locating it in the west will provide a certain desirably Saturnian dimension to the act of eating. The dining room's location is certainly less important, in the bigger picture, than is self-control during meals.

Among the most significant of the Ayurvedic rules for eating are:

Wherever you dine, make it a point to face east whenever possible. In this position, your prāṇa is more likely to circulate suitably, since you are thus aligning the Water quadrant (northeast) with your Watery left nostril, and the Fire quadrant (southeast) with your Fiery right nostril.

Ideally, you should be breathing through your right nostril while you eat, as free-flowing air through this nostril testifies to a flow of prāṇa that increases the digestive fire. If the right nostril is closed or is not dominant when you're ready to eat, you can cause it to open by lying on your left side for a few minutes before the meal, or by closing your left nostril with a finger of your right hand and breathing rhythmically for a few minutes through your right nostril. You can also switch the air flow to your right nostril by plugging your left nostril, or by hooking your left arm over the back of a chair for a few minutes.

Eat alone, or with people you know and trust, while sitting, not standing, in an isolated, clean area. Feed all five senses during your meal by providing your dining room with pleasant music, fresh flowers, and the like, and by eating food that is tasty, aromatic, visually attractive, and pleasing in texture and sound.

Concentrate on your meal. Banish TV and radio from the dining room, and if you use your sound system, employ it judiciously, if at all. Observe silence while you eat; sit and chat afterwards. Chew each morsel slowly and attentively many times.

Never eat when not physically hungry, when angry, depressed, bored, or otherwise emotionally unstable, or immediately after any physical exertion.

Avoid exercise or sex within an hour of eating, and sleeping or studying within two hours. If you have overeaten, or are feeling physically weak, lie for a few minutes—without going to sleep—on your left side, to ensure that your right nostril is working to keep your digestive fire well-enkindled.

Before you begin and after you complete your meal, give thanks to Nature for providing you with food, and for the gift of life that permits you to eat it.

Kitchen

The kitchen, which some Vāstu practitioners call "the home's stomach," should be located on the southern side of the house, preferably in the southeast. It can also occupy the center of the east or west sides of the home, but should (according to most authorities) never appear in the northeast, or in the center of the north side. Nonetheless, the dire forecasts that some Vāstu texts make for families whose kitchens reside in the northeast—one book goes so far as to pronounce that such a kitchen will cause "all aspects of life to go up in flames"—are likely to come to pass only in the presence of substantial negative confluence.

One such confluent factor would be a northeast kitchen in which the stove appears along the south, southwest, or west walls (which will have the cook facing in the direction of the malefic planets Saturn, Mars, or Rāhu and Ketu), or along the north wall (having the cook face north is said to promote financial loss). The stove is best on the kitchen's east wall, to align the blaze of the home's cooking fires with the blaze of the sun and to have the cook face that sun's direction of ascent. Natural gas is a better choice than electricity as a modern cooking medium (the classical Vāstu system praises dried cow dung as the best of fuels, giving second preference to wood).

The sink is ideally located on the north side of the stove, at the cook's left hand. A sink in the southwest would provide further negative confluence to a kitchen located in the northeast. Cooking utensils should be stored mainly along the south and west walls, which is also where the dishwasher, refrigerator, and other sizable kitchen appliances should find a home.

Regardless of the kitchen's specific location, its northeastern corner should be kept empty and free of clutter, with no utensils hung there, and no racks permitted, however small. Above all, no brooms, dusters, or wastebaskets should be kept in the kitchen's northeastern segment.

Wherever the kitchen is, and however it's arranged, the potential harm associated with a multitude of misalignments can be undone if the cook sincerely offers food to the Ultimate Reality before, during, and after the cooking process.

Library/Study

A library or study does best on the home's west (the direction of Saturn, who rules old things, like collected wisdom) or north (the direction of Mercury, who rules learning). To face east (Sun), north (Mercury), or northeast (Jupiter) while you sit in the study is ideal, though southeast (Venus) and northwest (Moon) can also work. Wherever you face, do not sit with your back to the door (since then you'll have nothing to "back you up"). Large bookshelves belong in the southwest; computers, scanners, and the like should usually go in the southeast.

Living Room

The living room ideally graces your home's center, and serves as its heart, so you should devote special attention to keeping the room's central Brahma Sthāna open. Portraits or photos of ancestors should be displayed in its southwest section, and its heaviest furniture should be arrayed along the west and south walls, so that those seated there will face east or north. It's better not to have windows, and certainly not doors, directly behind the couch. Ideally, there should be more windows in the north and east than in the south and west. The telephone will do well if it's placed in the northwest, and the entertainment center is best situated in the southeast, with the television in a closed cabinet (or banished to the den). An image of a person, place, or thing that you revere might go well in the northeast.

Shrine Room:

Your shrine room, meditation nook, contemplation corner, or "inner sanctum" is where you go to purify your past, ruminate on your present, and open yourself to your future. If at all possible, dedicate the room in the northeastern corner of your home to this essential purpose. If this is not feasible, combine in one northern or eastern room the shrine with your locus for handling matters monetary and medicinal. When people used to keep all their valuables at home, those valuables were optimally placed for safekeeping in a repository along the north wall. Medicines were traditionally kept in the northern room of the home next to the prayer room, the reason being that meditating over your maladies makes them easier to comprehend and address, and meditating over your remedies makes them more potent.

If you don't have a room to spare, dedicate the northeastern quadrant of one room, such as your bedroom, to your shrine. Let no mundane thing encroach on this sacred space; guard and preserve its purity as devotedly as possible, that it may serve as the province of your home that can be reliably counted on to provide you with inspiration.

Ideally, your shrine room should not share a wall with a bathroom, nor should its door face a bathroom door. It's vastly preferential that toilets, kitchens, and storerooms are not located above or below the shrine room.

Whether you assign an entire room or only a part to your sanctuary, place any image that you regularly contemplate in the space's northeast corner. If you can avoid it, do not pray or meditate facing south, southwest, or west until you're certain that you can "digest" the energies of those directions.

Room Remedies

Your space tells your story—try to tell that story well! To do this, you might provide some of the rooms in your home or office with a theme that invokes a planetary/elemental/doshic pattern that agrees with you and that space's Vāstu floor plan. When feasible, assign each room of your house to the quadrant where you determine that it would be best situated; when you don't have the flexibility to do this, do what you can to create a healthy relationship between the chief qualities of the quadrant in which the room appears and the qualities that the room ought to possess. Where a room falls only a bit short of the ideal, your options for remedying it are manifold and easily implemented; where there is strong negative confluence, you may need to pull out all the stops, and invest substantial time and effort in bringing about détente between your purpose and that space's propensities, two energies that cooperate but reluctantly.

Remember the variety of alternatives from which you can choose when you need to resolve a situation. Suppose you are a vāta person for whom there is no practical alternative to a northwest bedroom. If you find the room disturbing even after you properly place your bed, arrange your possessions, and paint it a vāta-pacifying color, you may still be able to use diet and exercise, meditation and yoga, Ayurvedic herbs, or more esoteric methods to achieve a state of confluent alignment. Should none of these solutions resolve your plight, only then should you consider the more drastic step of exchanging that space for another by ripping out the plumbing and converting your bathroom into your bedroom.

This applies to whole houses as well as their constituent rooms: attempt all reasonable remedies before abandoning ship and abandoning that dwelling. Suppose, for example, that you live in an apartment, or a row house, and you share a wall with some disreputable neighbors. You can attempt to remediate this situation by estimating which of the Three Doṣas is most out of alignment in your fellow citizens next door, then painting your side of that wall an appropriate doṣa-reducing color (one that won't disturb your own doṣas). Then, every time you look at that wall, the influence of its color will encourage you to broadcast a "balancing" energy toward those neighbors. You could also create a small altar at that wall, and shepherd harmony into that region of your space. An astrological remedy may also help, if you can determine the planetary pattern that has become adversely activated. Above all, repeatedly express your intention that this "challenged" space be rendered peaceful.

Offerings to the Elements

The Five Elements should be honored in the regions that they rule, whether the context be a room, house, estate, or city. When a room appears in a portion of a house in which it does not naturally belong, this homage to the Elements becomes particularly utilitarian, since it can be a means by which you achieve greater sukha in that space. In selecting your offering, pay close attention to the principle of confluence: If the Element you wish to honor is weak in every room of your home, and also in your horoscope, you may (generally speaking) strengthen it with abandon. But if the Element that is weak in your room (or home) is in other rooms (or in the remainder of your dwelling, and/or in your horoscope) strong, then honor it without enhancing it by making a small, "token" offering to it. Never use a floodlight when a candle will suffice.

Earth: A handsome crystal, rock, mosaic, terra cotta object, or other solid, heavy item that speaks of stability is generally welcome in the southwest corner of a room or building, particularly when the southern or western directions are in some way perceptibly activated in that space. Such an object will then act to "nail down" the energy in the space. A boulder, tall tree, or other large item will perform a similar role for a garden or a large property. The size of the object can be determined by the extent to which the southwestern energy is already activated in that area.

Aromas are a good medium for honoring the Earth Element, since Earth rules the sense of smell, the sense that is more directly and deeply wired into the brain than any of the others. A potentially hazardous variety of aromatherapy arises from using harsh chemicals, such as cleansers formulated with chlorine or ammonia, and from the formaldehyde that outgases from plywood. Beneficial results follow from using natural scents; essential oils, perfumed candles, potpourris, incense, and fresh flowers (which also create a deep resonance with Space) all contribute to stability, well-being, and other Earth-associated benefits.

Choose specific fragrances according to your Ayurvedic constitution or condition, the quadrant in which a room appears, and the purpose to which a room is devoted. Mild, cooling fragrances like rose, vetiver, and lavender pacify pitta and relieve Fire; being calming, they are particularly useful in rooms like the bedroom where tranquility is desired. Cedar, frankincense, and bergamot are examples of hot aromas; they reduce kapha and vāta, balance Earth, Water, and Air, and stimulate activity in rooms—like a living room—that are dedicated to entertaining guests.

Water: The northeast section of any room will usually benefit from a small fountain; this is particularly true of a meditation room that does not occupy the northeastern corner of your home. Fountains or fish tanks or even an elegant carafe of water can work well in the northwest corners of rooms, in the office or elsewhere, that are dedicated to strategizing. A pond or flowing water can do the same for the northeast of a garden or an estate, as can a temple or shrine. Water can also be respected simply by leaving a space's northeast corner empty.

The sense of taste is associated with Water. Good food consumed with thanks, well-digested, assimilated, and appreciated, is a fine offering to the Water Element.

Fire: One good method of respecting Fire is to admit plenty of sunlight into your home; when sunlight is in short supply, full-spectrum bulbs can help to compensate for the lack of solar irradiation. When posited in the southeast, a candle, oil lamp, or copper fire pot acts to focus Fire's energy inside a building; a stone lantern or fire pit works similarly in the southeast of a garden or parkland.

Fire rules sight and form, which makes artwork a valuable offering to the Fire Element, particularly art objects that provide a sense of spiritual uplift (a quality associated with Jupiter) or of refined sensuality (Venus). Joyous representations of ecstatic experiences of life further the development of good space, sukha, within your home. Dark, menacing images of conflict, misery, danger, distress, dread, disaster, or poverty activate the power of malefic planets like Saturn and Mars, and encourage misfortune to come your way.

Generally speaking, the images you least want in your home are those of the phantasmagoric ilk (involving demons, sorcery, necromancy), and those related to death. Ritual objects that were used to conjure up the spirits of dead ancestors are particularly unwelcome, no matter how striking they may be. A friend of mine recently made a dramatic ritual disposal of a "compelling wood carving" that had been used in New Guinea as a spirit repository, an artifact that houses a departed person's spirit during the period immediately after death. A continuous stream of difficulties (and some tragedies) began to afflict her and her family shortly after she brought the reliquary home; after bidding the object goodbye, her life went promptly back to normal. Coincidence perhaps, but one in line with Vāstu's expectations. Restricting yourself to benign art forms is the better option, just in case.

Air: A house that admits breezes without becoming too windy indoors, that ensures ample inner space within which air and its accompanying prāṇa can circulate, offers ongoing respect to Air. Wind chimes and prayer flags in the northwest are appropriate offerings for the Air Element, as are sticks of incense.

The Air Element rules the sense of touch, and rich textures are also apt offerings for it. To enjoy a relaxing massage with oil is to show consideration for the Air in your body, by reducing and balancing your vāta.

Music, which is technically ruled by the Space Element, is also a good offering for Air when that music acts to simultaneously center and uplift one's mind and consciousness. Sanskrit mantras, Gregorian or Tibetan chants, recitations of the Koran or other sacred books, sacred music from around the world, folk music from most traditional cultures, sounds of the savanna or rainforest, the murmuring and crash of ocean waves, orchestras of cricket fiddles—all may serve your purpose. Indian classical music assigns different modes (*rāgas*) to different times of day, to help listeners and musicians alike align themselves with movements of energy diurnal and nocturnal.

Remember that, as with the other senses, what you listen to will help determine what you become. If you listen endlessly to the blues, in a blue room, and make it a habit to wear navy blue or black, don't be surprised if you, too, turn blue. Nurse a series of beers while listening to too many country-music tales of tears, and you too may descend into melancholy. Indulge in speed metal, industrial techno, and gangsta rap without a consciousness-raising purpose, and you will evolve in those directions: garbage in, garbage out. Choose life-affirming resonance instead, and find your prāṇa enhanced.

Space: Leaving the center of a space empty, except for the occasional flower offered there, is a fine way to show reverence for Space. You also respect Space when you strive to develop well-balanced, thoughtfully practical responses to the questions of how full your spaces should be, and what items should fill them. An excess of furniture produces clutter, which breeds energy stagnation, which promotes stagnation of prāṇa in the bodies and minds of a residence's inhabitants, which can aggravate vāta. An insufficient amount of furniture permits the Air Element to become too active, too rajasic, which can also aggravate vāta. A judiciously filled space encourages prāṇa to flow freely, thus nourishing sukha in those who live there.

Color

Color can be used to reinforce traits that are weak, or weaken attributes that are too strong. When a room's qualities are too "cold" (for example, a "Watery" room like a bathroom that inhabits a "cool" part of the house, like the northwest), warm tones will heat it up. Cooling colors, like light blues and greens, are good choices for the walls of a "hot" room, like a kitchen, that is located in the southeast. Red or yellow may help strengthen the fire for a kitchen in a home's northwest, which the Air in that quadrant may have an inclination to "blow out." Obsessed with food and eating? Dining in a blue room will help suppress your appetite. Lost your taste for food? A bright red dining room or area can help that appetite to return.

Bright colors have a generally expansive effect on a room's space, while dark colors tighten a room, circumscribe it, reduce its expanse. Muted colors calm; brighter, more intense colors stimulate. Intend to use the living room for entertaining? Swathe it in yellow. Prefer it as a haven? Swaddle it in mauve. If passion is one of your passions, then adorn your bedroom in red; if you'd rather devote your time there to shut-eye, opt for a calmer color.

Be wary of decorating any room with a single hue, taking a lesson from how the color pink is used in certain contexts. To wit: Some jail cells are painted entirely pink, and some mental hospitals have pink rooms, both used for temporary detention of agitated inmates. It's difficult to become intensely angry in a wholly pink room, for pink—in the particular shade known as Baker-Miller pink—prevents the body's rage hormones from being released. Remain too long in that space, however, and you may end up unbalancing your hormones.

Marie's daughter, Sarah, has long wanted to repaint her bedroom, which has been pink ever since she dropped anchor in those quarters. Now that she's a pre-teen, she's becoming more insistent that the room needs a new shade. Even without knowing precisely why, she knows intuitively that she is no longer willing to feel "held down" by pink; instead, she craves the freedom that a different hue can offer. While her decision might be perceived as a relinquishing of the trappings of childhood, it may also relate to a desire (conscious or not) to shift from being the meek, cowed girl she once was into the more assertive (if sometimes annoying) adolescent. We hope that the change is not being motivated by an unconscious wish to become more indulgent of her anger.

While other shades may not produce effects as dramatic as those that pink can exert, each of them inescapably wields its impact on both the house and its inhabitants.

Earth Tones: In the tints of browns, tan, russet, terra cotta, et al, earth tones enhance the power of the Earth Element, and the stability and sustenance that Earth offers.

White: Ruled by the Moon (milky white) or Venus (radiant white, blue white), a luscious white can promote refinement of perception and discernment, and contribute to a tranquil nature in the person exposed to the hue. In excess, this type of white can aggravate kapha, and eventually vāta, promoting sappiness, schmaltz, emotional instability or hyper-sensitivity, and capriciousness.

Bright, titanium dioxide white is a colder, drier color than is ivory or cream. In India, this tone of white, the color of bleached bones, is the color of death. Widows in India have traditionally worn white, not black; brides there still predominantly wear red, the color of life-giving blood; they never wear white.

Red: Ruled by the Sun (deep, dark red), or by Mars and Ketu (bright red), red in appropriate proportion energizes, promotes appetite and digestion, and activates drive and determination. In excess, red aggravates pitta, which can amplify egotism, self-centeredness, irritability, impulsiveness, and obsession.

Orange: Ruled by the Sun, orange and its variants (like saffron, peach, and coral) aid awareness, aptitude, and vivacity. In excess, orange aggravates pitta, and encourages arrogance, pretentiousness, and vanity.

Yellow: Ruled by Jupiter, yellow facilitates digestion, lifts the spirits, and promotes a philosophical frame of mind. In excess, yellow (which has been said to be the color most favored by the insane) aggravates pitta and kapha, and magnifies overconfidence, lavishness, self-indulgence, and acquisitiveness.

Green: Ruled by Mercury, green calms and reassures, vitalizes, heals, and facilitates a youthful attitude. In excess, green can aggravate kapha and pitta (when in the form of yellow-greens) or kapha and vāta (blue-greens), weaken the nerves, and muddle one's discriminative powers.

Blue: Ruled by Saturn, light blue offers the generally benevolent face of the Saturnian attributes: practicality, constancy, consistency, a calm disposition. In excess, blue aggravates vāta, constricting channels of circulation, depressing the appetite, depleting the tissues of vitality.

Indigo, Violet, and Black: Ruled by Saturn, indigo and violet stimulate subtlety of cogitation, enhance the powers of contemplation and introspection, and facilitate spiritual inspiration. Black boosts a sense of detachment, and stimulates a stark realism that can easily mutate into unprincipled expediency. Excess of any of these hues (black in particular) can attract tamas, feed trepidation, augment negativity, foment melancholy, lead to isolation, and generally facilitate the outward expression of one's inner Shadow—that difficult-to-access portion of the personality that promotes selfishness and resists transformation.

Painting specific rooms the colors of their ruling planets will activate the corresponding indications of those planets, so it's wise to establish a selection of hues in line with your individual perception of your planetary affinity. You might choose a palette according to the directional position that the rooms have in the home (red for southern spaces, green for those in the north, radiant white in the southeast, indigo in the west, etc.) or according to their purpose (red for the kitchen, green for the study and home financial center, radiant white for the entertainment area, indigo for a bedroom).

If you're feeling particularly powerful, you may even choose to decorate your entire house in a single base shade, one that reflects the planet you most want to activate. The potential advantages of this course of action are great, especially if you have a competent astrologer of Jyotiṣa who can advise you as to which planet you can most safely laud in this manner. The danger is that, even if said planet and its indications agree with you to a significant degree, you may not be able to "digest" such a substantial activation of its energies; that planetary wave may "swamp" you, rather than take you for a ride.

You can try decorating your meditation room with the color and other correspondences of a planet that you are trying to propitiate, and then meditate there while facing in the appropriate direction, testing your breathing and monitoring your prāṇa to discover how well you've aligned with any particular day's planetary pattern.

You may choose to do something similar in the room where you daily spend the most time. Such customized décor will, by activating the appropriate planet and its indications, make your life more exciting. It will not, however, resolve all the issues in your life for you; it may even aggravate a few, but such provocation will be your signal that you need to address such themes with greater innovation and alacrity.

You can even let your adulation for nature, and for life itself, spill into the outdoors by planting flowers of appropriate colors in the appropriate direction within a small patch of your garden (being a Vāstu adept, your garden would of course have its flower beds arrayed around a central Brahma Sthāna). You can similarly assign to each direction the plant types that resonate with their associated planets:

Sun: large-trunked, tall-growing, strong trees; red flowers
Moon: oily or sap-filled trees; white flowers
Mars: thorny trees; red flowers
Mercury: fruitless trees; green leaves
Jupiter: fruit-bearing trees; yellow flowers
Venus: blossoming trees; white and very fragrant flowers
Saturn: gnarled, unattractive trees; blue and violet flowers
Rāhu and Ketu: same as for Saturn and Mars, respectively*

*Southwest is a good corner to let go wild, to reflect the Nodes' unruliness; alternatively, one can place there a large boulder, or some other heavy thing that is similarly Earthy.

9 Vāstu in the Garden

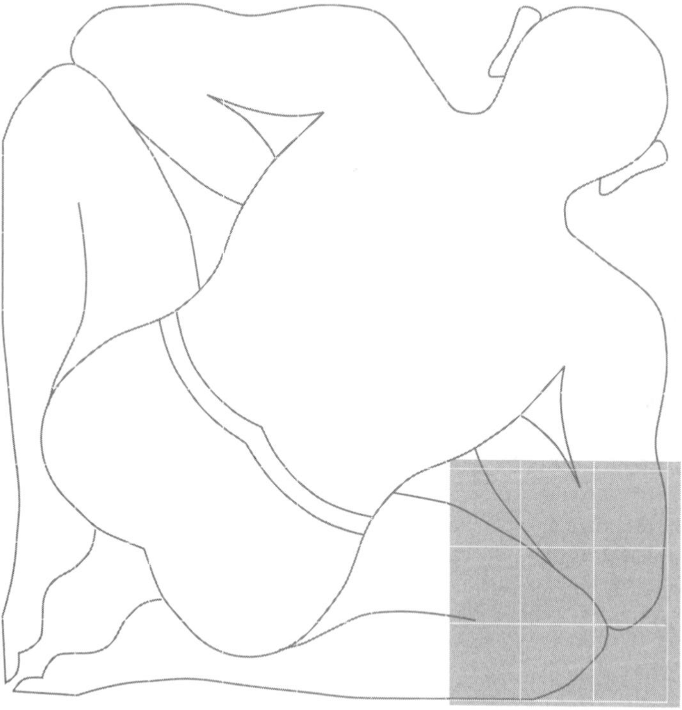

A Walled Paradise

The English word "paradise" comes from a Persian word that means "enclosed park" or "walled garden." A garden should be a paradise, a haven, a refuge from the speed and raucousness of modern life—a space of delight. As Creator of your own potential Eden, you're in charge of determining how best to make this paradise idyllic for you. Do you want a haven that will maintain itself, or a heaven that you will be called on to labor in daily?

What message do you want your garden to send to the cosmos? Do you want your cultivated space to shout "Success!" or to murmur "Beauty"? Is sensuousness your aim, or sanctification? Do you seek the drama of triumph over adversity, the sumptuousness of opulence, or the serenity of contemplation? Will your creation display mystery and complexity, or directness and simplicity? Your horticultural statement should reveal a sense of the balance of dualities—fire and water, brightness and shade, sparsity and luxuriance—within you. If you incarnate in your Elysium some flavor of this desired harmony, nature will match and enhance it.

Gardening is one of the few spheres of today's transient, capricious society that offers constancy; consistency with plants, in the activity of caring for and nurturing them, can foster stability in life. The garden can serve as your present-day link between your past and your future, between everything that you are connected to at this moment and everything that you most want to be connected to in the next. The vegetable kingdom's very immovability endows it with a style and degree of stability far beyond anything the perpetually animated animal kingdom can imagine, a relative permanence against which we can measure ourselves and our achievements as we traverse life's transitions. Gardens express, in verdure, the personal narratives of their growers, a summing up of all the gardens in which these artisans have ever played a part. Just so, Hassan Fathy's later buildings reveal the level of subtlety and elegance he had achieved through all his previous architectural projects. Your yard's spring countenance recapitulates the aggregate of your life's springs; the "mellow fruitfulness" of its summer epitomizes your every hot season past. Though some of what appears in your plot will be defined by factors seemingly outside of your control (including rain, cloud cover, pests, and the like), these factors can, in fact, be affected for the better or the worse by your overall state of well- or ill-being.

Your garden speaks the truth of your soul: the awareness of what's working right within you, of what is wrong and must be changed, and whence that change might arise. Before you lay out your garden, review your connections with the flora with which you feel a strong camaraderie. Include in your garden, if you're able, vegetation (trees, in particular) that you recall fondly from your childhood, flowers and leaves whose fragrances evoke sweet emotions, favorite colors that brighten your days. Array in this oasis plants that attract the birds and insects whose voices speak to you of fecundity, the butterflies and reptiles whose hues and presence enthuse and reassure you.

I spent my early summers in the little Texas town where both my parents were raised, and where both sets of grandparents then lived. Each summer's sultriness was made less severe by the omnipresence of cicada thrum, a friendly sound made by an affable insect. Now, when I return there in season, or when I visit some other region that cicadas frequent, like Eastern Australia, or the South of France, I find in their boisterous noise a sort of nourishing mnemonic encouragement, a return to the sweetness of a grandmother's cornbread, or the reassurance of a grandfather's guiding hand. That memory envelops me for some moments in a cocoon of loving security, a continuity of present with past that breathes into me new confidence for the future.

Dedicate yourself to a plant, and it may surprise you grandly. Some years ago, friends in Brattleboro, Vermont, made professions of faith to the night-blooming cereus, inviting it into their lives by ensconcing cuttings in wide earthen pots behind sunny windows, safe from the bitterness of New England's winters. These tropical specimens have responded with exuberant growth, and with periodic buds that, though they commonly come but one at a time—and last but a night—fill the room with a divinely heady bouquet.

Refuse to give up on a plant, and the plant may respond when you least expect it. Plant wizard Luther Burbank is said to have developed cacti without spines solely by reassuring his specimens that they had nothing to fear in his vicinity, and so could put down their defenses. I once met a man who cared for a cactus devotedly, carrying it with him each time he moved. After two decades, it finally elected to flower.

Civilization vs. Wilderness

To grow a plant is to make a covenant with nature, which can remind us how crucial it is for each of us to relate to the natural world in a healthy way, that we may help to protect and defend it against mindless human onslaught. The vast majority of our species has, when offered the choice, chosen civilization over wilderness, a choice which perhaps was defensible when we were less numerous than we are now. The conventional Vāstu view holds that the garden, as an embodiment of order and righteousness, should be kept clean and tidy, free of weeds and decay, a tamed microcosm that reflects an image of what Vāstu envisions the macrocosm could become. Here, however, we must part company with Vāstu orthodoxy, which too often permits the urge to impose neatness to supersede more natural, organic forms of cultivation that might appear "wild" to the human eye.

Long ago, when less of India's unbridled wilds had fallen to the developer's axe, the ancient nomadic Vedic seers hymned the great rivers and mountains, the sanctuaries of solitude to which they retreated for inspiration. But the descendants of those seers, when they became town-dwellers, looked back on the untamed landscapes that had sheltered their ancestors and found them primitively chaotic. Culture in that later era was considered to spread outwards from the center of human activity, from the temple and palace, with kingdoms recapitulating the ancient cosmology of creation in a process of "sanctification through settlement." At the city's center, squatting on its Brahma Sthāna, nominally the purest, most sanctified space in the city—seemingly the most orderly space in the realm—would sit a grand temple, an abode of the gods. *Naraka* ("hell") was located just beyond the developed territory's borders, where "civilization" had not yet reached; "civilized" people dumped their rubbish there.

This process of settlement, perpetuated for centuries, resulted in multiple centers of civilization expanding amoeba-like into ever-dwindling pockets of rough country. Today a substantial proportion of educated Indians believe that their nation has a moral imperative to "civilize" much of what little natural areas they have left, by building dams, factories, and similar "temples to progress."

Honest students of Vāstu, though, cannot afford to sneer at a swath of wilderness as an inconvenience to be clear-cut, in the same way that they would be ill-advised to think of a building site as a mere tract of dirt. If our buildings are to come to life, they will first need to feel the life of the land. Our feeling for prāṇa's natural pulse as it streams through our Vāstu spaces becomes enlivened only after we learn to blend and assimilate direct experience of the "great indoors" of the interior body and mind landscape with direct experience (however minimal) of the great outdoors. As your awareness of prāṇa's movements within and without mounts, so increases the extent of your alignment with your spaces.

Even the strictest and smallest of backyards requires some representation of nature in its more primal, uncultivated form, some reminder of the vigor of nature that humankind has not yet shackled. Lawns are not enough; a lawn is "nature under totalitarian rule," as Michael Pollan observes in *Second Nature: A Gardener's Education.*

Gardens are infinitely superior to lawns as boundaries between humans and nature. A garden is a stage on which nature can pirouette and swoop, a laboratory for experiment, a crucible of omens. Gardens are translators, go-betweens, facilitators of micro-macro communion, midspaces between unbridled nature and the sterility of the "parking lot," the "green desert" that is a lawn. "We seek [in a garden]," writes Pollan, "a way to use nature without damaging it."

A garden is a meeting place where humans and nature can dialogue about the selection and arrangement of plants that further the health of garden "society," about the extent to which individual plants should be supported at the expense of the "greater good" of that space's biodiversity, the degree to which the gardener should intervene, and the extent to which he ought instead to rely on "masterly inactivity" to achieve his ends. These many issues reduce down to two: "How natural do I want my property to remain? How cultivated—and thus, how human—do I want it to become?"

Ask these questions fully aware that your every action will further constrain nature's unfettered freedom; and answer according to the dictates of your surroundings. A garden that grows wild will clearly be a better fit for a sparsely populated county than for an area that has been swallowed by conurbation.

We clothe ourselves in so many layers of human-scale skins that we oft neglect to include in our environments some representation, however small, of the wild chaos that is Nature Untamed, unbeholden to Man. Let your garden go wholly native, and the waiting forest, prairie, or desert will quickly recapture it, but even that region of nature thus unbridled remains a human construction, defined as it is by its context and the manmade constraints placed on its freedom: an Amazonian tribesman in a suit and tie, the Aborigine sitting quietly at the bar.

Human construction and cultivation are no doubt the foundations of modern civilization, but our chief concern as Vāstu students should be to generate microcosmic paeans to the full spectrum of the macrocosmic scheme of things. Few of us can recreate the forest primeval in our backyards, but each of us can invest some time and energy to nourish what little wilderness around us still clings to life. Protecting worthy environments, particularly those shielded by fortuity (and property lines) from the developer's insatiable bulldozer, provides us with a meaningful reminder of who we are and whence we came—which is Vāstu well applied.

A garden gives us the opportunity to generate layers of surrounds that exemplify the gamut from chiefly wild to chiefly cultivated. Gardens are not stable; they achieve stability in dynamism alone. A garden is a delicately balanced ecosystem that requires constant attention from its creator, lest it disintegrate; for it to thrive, the gardener must contribute some of his own toil, sweat, prāṇa, and attention.

The outer skin of our natural environment should be as feral as is feasible, as little tainted by the relentlessly human drive to tame. Denizens of the outback or the tundra may find wilderness incessantly pressing upon them, but the majority of us who dwell in urbs, suburbs, and exurbs have to consciously pursue wildness if we are to enter into some form of dialogue with her. No matter who you are or where you live, nature is waiting for you, as close as the flower box in your apartment window, or the little patch of backwoods near your back door.

The Garden as Transition

The path that takes you from your home into your garden leads you from the relative civilization of your house into the relative wildness of your yard. A gentle transition from residence to residue—the latter being, in this case, the garden—promotes gentility in life; an abrupt transition fosters brusqueness, and consequent vāta disturbance and disharmony.

You can design for Vāta-reducing continuity as you construct your transitional space and your garden by using some of the same materials that play a part in your house. Examples of such amiable transitions include a partially enclosed "garden room" that is part garden and part house; a trellised walk that connects house with garden; and an attached conservatory or greenhouse. Another option is to invite the greenery to embrace the dwelling, for "A building finally becomes part of its surroundings when the plants grow over parts of it as freely as they grow along the ground."*

There are many theories that address the question of where the garden should sit vis-à-vis the house. The most generally accepted of them directs that there should be more open space around a house in the north and the east than in the south and the west. The presence of flowing water is good, especially in the northeast, particularly when it flows west to east or south to north. Pools are also welcome in the northeast, provided that they are not so large as to take the limelight away from the house. Water behind the house can destabilize the energy of the entire property; the degree of destabilization will depend on the incidence of confluent factors (the pool being located in the southwest; the pool being elsewhere but the land falling away toward the southwest; lack of trees, walls, or other barriers behind the pool; etc.). Stagnant water anywhere fosters stagnant prāṇa.

The garden's ground should be lower on the north and east sides than on the south and west (as should be the case for the parcel as a whole). Tall trees are welcome on the south and west, near enough to keep the house cool by blocking the afternoon sun, but not so near that their roots could grow to endanger its foundations. The natural rise of the property should be in the southwest; if it's not, a mound could be constructed there, or raised beds could be added. The southwest is also the area that should be left freest to grow wild.

For those who entertain in the garden, the grill should preferably be located in the southeast. Better in the southeast than a grill, though, is an open fire pit, a space around which the solitary individual can sit to contemplate and envision the future, a focal point where people can congregate for chat or deliberation, to ponder and plan, as humans have done ever since we harnessed fire. Even when nothing is aflame in it, the fire pit can serve as a meaningful focus of attention; if it can be seen from inside the house, so much the better.

Gardens do well when structural clarity of external form—a recognizable

* Christopher Alexander, Sara Ishikawa & Murray Silverstein, *A Pattern Language*, p. 1136

landscape with edges, pathways, thresholds, and a decipherable core—is coupled with its creator's internal passion. Gardens ought ordinarily to have square or rectangular borders, with internal lines that may be straight or curved depending on the statement its steward means to make. Formal French or Mughal gardens are precise in the angularity of their paths; Chinese garden paths wind, following the routes that chi seems to favor most in that terrain. There is much to be said for a wall around the garden, to keep out noise, to punctuate the boundary between what is garden and what is not, and to provide privacy.

The most private area in the garden is often the ideal corner for a "garden seat," a quiet, cozy spot where one or two people can sit quietly and commune with nature. Vegetation at this site should be thick enough to enclose it partially, that sitters can enjoy concentrated solitude. A private nook for meditation and the performance of auspicious rituals should also find a place somewhere in the garden, preferably in the northeast.

However the garden is laid out, its southwest area should shelter its largest trees and bushes; shrubs, grasses, and medicinal or sacred plants should be assigned to the northeast; culinary herbs do well in the northwest. The inner Brahma Sthāna, the garden's heart, the crucible of its intentions, the sacred space where the gardener's aspiration manifests and spreads outward, should be left mainly empty. It may, however, display at its central point (*bindu*) a globular mirror, a sundial, or (in climates that permit it) a small planter that hosts a jasmine plant, or a shoot of the ever-popular, eternally auspicious holy basil (*Ocimum sanctum*, which is known in Sanskrit as *tulasī*). Such a planter also does well in a courtyard, should your home possess one. Tulasī's role may be taken, in a cooler climate, by an herb or blossom that similarly epitomizes for you the sanctity and purity of nature: a rose bush, a sage plant, a saffron crocus. Grape, pomegranate, and fig are among the other plants that are said to benefit a house when they're near to it.

Trees

Trees have served as focal points for human activity, both sacred and secular, since very ancient days. Artisans sit and work beneath the shelter of their boughs, yogis and monks meditate under them, children enlist them in their games, lovers carve their initials into them. Hug a tree with openness and affection, and, in most cases, you'll find that tree offering you relaxation, renewed vigor, and friendship in return.

We also need trees to "frame" our civilization for us, to structure our lots and neighborhoods, to shade our streets, to house our birds and beasts. The trees that we domesticate deserve in return our attention and affection. Vāstu texts provide long lists of the trees that are regarded as worthy of appearing in the garden and those that should be shunned. Most varieties of *Ficus* are regarded as holy, and specific species are assigned to specific directions,* but other trees with milky sap (a notable *Ficus* feature) are generally frowned upon. Thorny plants are not popular in Vāstu, nor are stunted plants, whether naturally underdeveloped or tortuously pruned into bizarre shapes. As always, Vāstu offers remedies for inauspicious situations: For instance, when a forbidden tree appears near a house—and for some reason the specimen cannot be cut down—a homeowner can plant an auspicious tree between the house and the proscribed tree to ward off the predicted untoward effect.

Vāstu expects you to select sacred trees for at least some corner of your property, and since few of Vāstu's holy trees thrive in temperate climes, you should turn to the varieties that your local culture has deemed sacred. The English, for example, have long revered the oak, the ash, and the birch, among many others. Growing a tree that is native to your locale and that is generally regarded as sacred there is a fine way of expressing your reverence for nature, particularly if you select a tree whose qualities activate a benevolent planetary pattern.

After creating a shortlist of arboreal prospects that are sufficiently sacred, use practical factors to determine which tree will be most auspicious for you: Consider how big it will grow (and how much space you have for it to grow in); whether you wish to make your botanical statement in flowers or fruit, in shade, or in the type of foliage; how much leaf litter you're willing to contend with; whether or not you're sensitive to the tree's pollen; what uses (medicinal or otherwise) you can make of it; and so on.

The Mystic Garden

As you permit unbridled nature to enter your garden, in whatever

---

*Plakṣa (*Ficus lacor*) is said to give good results in the north, Vaṭa (*Ficus benghalensis*) in the east, Uḍumbara (*Ficus racemosa*) in the south, and Aśvattha (*Ficus religiosa*) in the west; on the other hand, Plakṣa is inauspicious in the south, Vaṭa in the west, Uḍumbara in the north, and Aśvattha in the east.

form, you transform that space into one where divinity can come and jounce up against you, nuzzle you, fancy you. The wilder you let the garden grow, the greater the prospect for divine encounter. From the earliest moments of humankind's self-awareness, divinity has summoned us to sacred mountains and rivers, caves and springs, arbors and groves. When people abandoned rural life for urban existences, they took their sacred spaces with them in the form of gardens. Like the "paradisiacal" Persian walled garden, the many abbeys, cloisters, monasteries, and sanctuaries of the Western spiritual traditions have each sheltered a garden.

Even today, English churchyards sport gardens dedicated to the comfort of God and visitor alike. On visiting Upper Clatford, in the Hampshire area of the British countryside, I was pleased to take in the surrounds of its lovely 12th-century church, which has grounds so remarkable in their pleasing union of tree, shrubbery, and greensward that they had been entered in the All-England Churchyard Beautification Competition. Just up the road is the church at Abbott's Ann, whose perimeter wall is lined with giant chestnut trees that are centuries old.

A mere half-hour from this bucolic beauty is the cathedral city of Winchester, whose noble minster boasts its own greenery. Winchester Castle hosts a charming example of a medieval palace garden, a quiet nook created for a queen's meditations. Built to a more human scale than later royal landscaping efforts, the garden is so elegantly textured as to encourage even the idle tourist to fall into an agreeable reverie.

To the north of Hampshire is the university city of Oxford, with its botanical garden; also nearby is Waterperry Gardens, specifically designed as a setting for meditation. Quite dissimilar on the surface, both gardens fit well into their respective milieus, one an urban environment, the other a more pastoral setting. Both properties entice callers to contemplative walks; both promote awareness of the unique beauty of individual plants and the relationships that can be created between them. Both are cases in point of how humans and flora can fashion a blissful, tranquil idyll together.

The enthusiasm that the Divine Presence has for garden spaces has led Vāstu adepts to suggest that auspicious rituals be regularly performed in the garden. Such ceremonies invite deities, nature's spirits, and other such lively presences into your garden, and thus into your life. At the very least, these visitors can "fertilize" and teach you how to nurture your plants, as they've done in places like Scotland's Findhorn, in a vegetable garden where, despite inhospitable soils, three botanical devotees followed the guidance of the plants' guardian angels to reap a rich and plentiful harvest. Just so, these deities will help you render your yard lush and lively, an oasis bursting with prāṇa and enthusiasm that will flood into your home and saturate you and your family with its vitality.

Sprites, elves, "devas," and similar beings had long been made welcome in Western gardens, but have more recently been discouraged. Garden gnomes, those harmless figures of amusement, are often all that remain of the divine personalities that were once beckoned into the garden. If appealing to the deities does not suit your disposition, then consider orienting yourself in relation to energy and the directions. You could, for example, emulate Feng Shui, and plant your idyll in a portion of your land that will improve indications in some important sphere of your life. Northeast is for Feng Shui the direction of knowledge and learning. Plant your garden in the northeast, and your own knowledge and learning will flourish (provided, of course, that your garden flourishes). Plant it instead in the east, and it will benefit your health; to the north, your career; and so on, according to the Feng Shui scheme of things.

Structure your garden according to the Vāstu scheme of things instead, and you will strengthen the planet, Doṣa, Element, and Great Trait that each particular direction represents. Alternatively, you can use your garden as a means of divining how your life is going. One way to develop such "divination by shrubbery" would be to create a Vāstu Puruṣa Maṇḍala for your garden, plant separate beds for the four cardinal and four intermediate directions, perform auspicious rituals to "activate" your "apparatus," then keep a close watch on which portions burgeon and which dwindle. A bed that refuses to do well despite repeated, focused attention may well indicate some impediment in the area of life corresponding to that direction.

For its cultivator, a properly tended garden can become a vital, cordial co-creation with Mother Nature, making this portion of your land—which you don't actually live on—potentially the most important part of your dwelling. You can best take advantage of the prāṇa, beauty, and encouragement that your garden offers you by cooperating with nature, aligning your creation respectfully with hers.

10 Building from the Ground Up

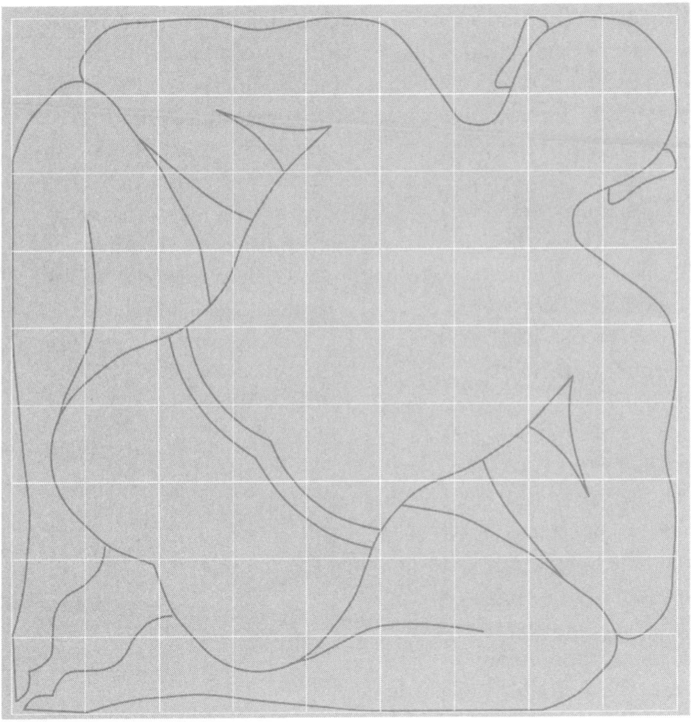

Dharma and Rūpa, Bhāva and Rasa

Mother Nature becomes co-creator of your garden, or of your dream home or office, when your hand and eye are guided by the principles of *dharma*, *rūpa*, and *bhāva*. Your *dharma* is "what you are born to do," your ideal path through life. Your building's dharma is its function, the task it's created to perform. *Rūpa* means "form," indicating the shapes and modes of spatial arrangement that best incarnate your home's mission. Vāstu concurs here with the well-known modern architectural dictum: "Form follows function."

Form flows from function; *bhāva* flows from form. *Bhāva* means "state, condition, circumstance"—both the home's atmosphere, which arises as a result of its function and form, and your "internal atmosphere," the state of awareness that arises in you when you inhabit that residence. From bhāva is generated *rasa* (essence, sentiment, aesthetic experience), your life's flavor. *Rasa* in Sanskrit means "juice," in all senses of that word; the world's rasas (which chiefly include water, lymph, blood plasma, semen, the sap in plants, fruit and vegetable juices, alchemically prepared metals, tastes, and emotions) are the "fluid realities" of our lives. The flavors of the juices that make up our realities combine to create our personal emotional rasas, the subjective perceptions that water our souls.

Delicious rasas make for a delectable life, a life of sukha. A truly satisfying life is *rasātmaka,* filled to the brim with pure, refreshing emotions that permeate down to our very cores. Healthy rasa begins to ooze into our lives when our bhāvas, our normal states of being, get "well cooked." The home is one cauldron in which we stew our bhāvas into rasas. Harmonious forms create cordial bhāvas, which facilitate the production of ever-healthier rasas, and ever-deeper sukha; unhealthy bhāvas do the opposite.

Life contains nine basic rasas:

śṛṅgāra, the richness and beauty of romance
hāsya, the gaiety of mirth
karuṇa, the compassion born of melancholy
raudra, the ferocity of fury
vīra, the nobility and prowess of heroism
bhayānaka, the oppression of fear
adbhuta, the amazement of awe
bībhatsa, the repulsion of disgust
śānta, the peaceful, meditative state

We search for rasa in each substance and action that we encounter, drawing from each encounter the rasas we crave. Our many rasas, internally created and externally derived, blend to form the most prominent rasa of the moment. Ideally, each rasa that your home produces will eventually resolve itself into a harmonious state of peace, the ground on which all the other rasas should play. Peace of mind produces tranquility, eliminates cravings for the pleasures of the senses, and promotes repose in the knowledge of the Absolute Reality. Subjective experience (rasa) and objective condition (bhāva) interact continually in an everlasting tango of potential and attainment.

Favorable life circumstances do not always promote contentment; an unusually high percentage of lottery winners commit suicide as a result of being unable to "digest" their sudden bounty. The wise among us make a virtue of adversity; given lemons, we make lemonade. A few innately "lucky" people have bhāvas and rasas that slide easily into alignment; the rest of us have to work for our sukha. The most accomplished among us strive to turn our very lives into juicy works of art:

"We are drawn to call something beautiful whenever we detect that it contains in a concentrated form those qualities in which we personally, or our societies generally, are deficient. We respect a style which can move us away from what we fear and towards what we crave: a style which carries the correct dose of our missing virtues. That we need art in the first place is a sign that we stand in almost perpetual danger of imbalance, of failing to regulate our extremes, of losing our grip on the golden mean between life's great opposites: boredom and excitement, reason and imagination, simplicity and complexity, safety and danger, austerity and luxury."*

The rasa you co-create with your home produces the message you send to the world. Let the Vāstu Vidyā work through you as you build and decorate your home, and she will concoct the details of your life into a pattern of rasas that will be optimal for you. Those rasas will then bear you on waves of juicy bliss into a state of peaceful contemplation.

---

*de Botton, op. cit. p. 156

Assisting Space to Find Itself

Rudyard Kipling once wrote a story, aptly titled *The Ship that Found Herself*, about a new ship on her maiden voyage. The vessel gains character and identity, and eventually coalesces into an individual, when all her various systems and parts come into harmonious alignment with one another. A room, a building, or a garden that has been properly constructed and filled with "cooperative" objects can similarly coalesce into harmony. Remedying the Vāstu defects in your current spaces can do much to improve your life, but your Vāstu arrangement will best agree with you—and your home or office will "find itself" more easily—if you get the opportunity to create it from the ground up.

For planning and preparing our building, we proceed step-by-step from the instant that a longing to build first arises in an individual's mind until the moment that the happy owner enters the newly-constructed edifice. The steps are:

Establishing the need for a building
Selecting an architect
Investigating and selecting the land
Fixing plot boundaries, buildable area, location, and orientation
Selecting materials, designing the building and its ancillary structures, and setting their prime dimensions
Groundbreaking and first entrance

Establishing the need for a building

The first step in constructing anything is to ask how necessary it is to build a structure at all. You should have a definitive need for a house or office (or casino)—not just a capricious craving that demands to be satisfied. There is nobility in constructing useful structures, particularly those like rest houses, temples, wells, and pools that benefit others as well as oneself. To build a building on a whim, or because you want to keep up with (or surpass) the Joneses (or the Chiangs or the Patels), or merely because you have the resources to build one, will not promote real sukha.

Once you've determined that you require a building, you should have a sincere desire to do the job right, lest you later be tempted to cut corners and produce a less-than-satisfying end result after the excitement of the initial process has waned.

Even if your desire to do the job right is sincere, your plan should fit realistically within your budget, without depending optimistically on revenue that might or might not eventually come your way.

Though you may have the financial resources to erect the structure you require (or desire), you cannot merely follow your own architectural muse: The building's facade will need to fit in agreeably with its surroundings, and sit well with your neighbors.

Selecting an Architect

Once you're certain that you need a building, you'll need to find an architect. First preference should go to a practitioner who is both fluent in Vāstu language and proficient in Vāstu's sister vidyās; this designer should enjoy an intuitive feel for the interplay of edifice with environment, residence with residue.

If no Vāstu builder is to be had, then select an architect who plans for utility, stability, and beauty. "Utility" includes practicality in all its forms (like a spacious, well-lit kitchen, and a well-ventilated laundry room that is easily accessible), but the greatest utility is to have a space in which your soul has room to grow. Your home or workplace is your temple, your spirit's sanctuary, your personal sacred space, and it should feel that way. Your structures are your personal statements; make sure that they convey what you want them to convey.

Buildings that Speak

From Alain de Botton's book The Architecture of Happiness*:*

John Ruskin proposed that we seek two things of our buildings. We want them to shelter us. And we want them to speak to us—to speak to us of whatever we find important and need to be reminded of. (p. 62)

In essence, what works of design and architecture talks to us about is the kind of life that would most appropriately unfold within and around them. They tell us of certain moods that they seek to encourage and sustain in their inhabitants. While keeping us warm and helping us in mechanical ways, they simultaneously hold out an invitation for us to be specific sorts of people. They speak of visions of happiness.

To describe a building as beautiful therefore suggests more than a mere aesthetic fondness; it implies an attraction to the particular way of life this structure is promoting through its roof, door handles, window frames, staircase and furnishings. A feeling of beauty is a sign that we have come upon a material articulation of certain of our ideas of a good life.

Similarly, buildings will strike us as offensive not because they violate a private and mysterious visual preference but because they conflict with our understanding of the rightful sense of existence—which helps to explain the seriousness and viciousness with which disputes about fitting architecture tend to unfold. (p. 72)

The notion of buildings that speak helps us to place at the very center of our architectural conundrums the question of the values we want to live by—rather than merely of how we want things to look. (p. 73)

Many architects are so wedded to their theories that they try to bully their clients into building what they as architects want built, not what their client requires and prefers. Before you select an architect, do yourself a favor and study Tom Wolfe's book *From Bauhaus to Our House*, which will show you what you're up against, and will at least make clear to you who to avoid. In the words of Frank Lloyd Wright, a good architect works by:

Exalting the simple laws of common sense—or of supersense if you prefer—determining form by way of the nature of materials, the nature of purpose so well understood that a bank will not look like a Greek temple, a university will not look like a cathedral, nor a fire-engine house resemble a French château, or what have you. Form follows function? Yes, but more important now, form and function are one. *

* Preble, *Artforms*, 5th edition, 1994, p. 246

Before you meet with your chosen architect, you should ponder the question, "What can materialize in this space, and how might it do so?" by considering your chief life goal (*puruṣārtha*), your individual nature (*varṇa*), and your stage of life (*āśrama*). Whether consciously aware of them or not, each of us has four goals in life: *dharma*, *artha*, *kāma,* and *mokṣa*. *Dharma* means "doing what you are born to do," following your ideal path through life; artha is the drive to achieve material prosperity; kāma is the goal of satisfying legitimate desires; and mokṣa is the goal of realizing that there is more to life than duty, wealth, and gratification. To accommodate puruṣārtha, in the Vāstu context, you'd ask whether fulfilling your desire of building a new house would be the right use of your wealth as you travel along your life path.

If so, then you would want to build that house in a neighborhood that best agrees with your varṇa. *Varṇa* ("color, delineating characteristic") is your pattern of activity in the world. Knowing your varṇa lets you select a vocation that fits you well. Marriage with someone of the same metaphysical "hue" is more likely to be satisfying than marriage with someone whose outlook, preferences, and attitudes are substantially different from your own.

There are four basic varṇas, describing specific types of people: *brāhmaṇas*, who live for knowledge, *kṣatriyas,* who are natural managers and fighters, *vaiśyas*, who are instinctive traders and merchants; and *śūdras,* people who are close to the earth, who enjoy physical labor. Each varṇa has its own Vāstu palette. The Vāstu for a brāhmaṇa house, where learning, studying, worshipping, and chanting fill the air, will differ from that fit for an active kṣatriya household, a busy vaiśya family, or a hardworking śūdra clan.

This division forms the basis for India's caste system, which classifies people by birth, since a couple who share a varṇa are likely to produce children of the same "hue" (in this sense, varṇa resembles pedigree). Varṇa was not originally rigid; people in India were once free to do whatever they liked with their lives, for in their original sense, the four varṇa*s* speak to innate nature, not the nature you're assumed to have as a function of birth. Unfortunately, ever since the priestly and princely classes conspired to make caste rules inflexible dependent on birth, the varṇa concept has been too often used in India to shackle society, not to facilitate its development.

Nowadays, one person or another in every household will display traits from each of these categories: Senior citizens may go back to school to get advanced degrees, while the young may elect to "drop out" of society. Everyone exercises (we hope), and numerous people of many different backgrounds work with their hands. Today, you can think of your varṇa according to which of the four main categories best characterizes you and your brood overall, and build the necessary structure accordingly. Do you and the majority of your family members spend most of the time reading and studying? If so, you'll need ready access to sources of information, plenty of lighting, lots of shelf space for books, and comfortable accommodations for reading. Will you dedicate most of your time to buying and selling? Then you'll want to surround yourself with the trappings of commerce. You may even want to dedicate one room of your house to a small home office, even if you conduct your principal business from another location. Your home workplace can act as a "proving ground" for concepts, or even products, that you can then scale up in your main trade.

Whatever your natural "tint" may be, wherever your innate talent lies, you'll want to work to develop it to its greatest possible fruition, phase by phase. You'll find that it will express itself distinctively over the course of your life, according to your *āśrama*, your "stage of life." Each āśrama produces a different life focus, and requires a different Vāstu methodology.

The four basic life stages begin with *brahmacarya*, which extends from birth through the end of adolescence; the second stage is *gṛhastha*, the period between adolescence and menopause (or the male equivalent thereof); *vanaprastha* happens when you retire into semi-retreat; *sannyāsa* is life's terminal phase. Brahmacarya is the period during which you should learn whatever you need to fulfill your dharma, according to your varṇa. During gṛhastha you create a household: marry, have children, work. Vanaprastha is when you devote increasing attention to your spiritual health while you play with your grandchildren and continue to offer advice to your children. Sannyāsa is the stage during which you prepare for your final journey by spending progressively more time in quiet meditation and contemplative seclusion.

You should try, when planning your house, to address the questions of which life stage you, your spouse, and your children occupy at the time the house is built, and where all of you are headed in the future—insofar as you can tell. Study your individual natures, select appropriate goals, extrapolate their implications through the stages of your life, then look for an architect who can incorporate your requirements into a blueprint that blends in durability and charm—this builder must be one who can give you a clear, workable plan for answering the question, "What can materialize in this space, and how might it do so?" Only after you've found such an individual will you be suitably prepared to structure your land into a space where you can materialize your plan.

Investigating and selecting the land

Your land should be in every way secure: in an area not prone to earthquakes, tornadoes, hurricanes, or other violent acts of nature; not too close to a river, ocean, or other body of water that might rise and inundate you; far from any war zone, rural or urban; unlikely to be chemically or biologically polluted by cattle pens or feed lots, nearby industries, waste dumps, or radiation sources; and insulated from noise pollution. Living too close to public institutions like theaters, government buildings, tourist attractions, temples, churches, police stations and the like is also unwise; there is far too much traffic at such places, which promotes in them a strong energy of rajas. You should also make sure that you're not setting down roots next to rogues, charlatans, rascals, scalawags, or other mischief-makers. Choosing your neighbors carefully is good Vāstu.

Natural beauty in a site is, from the Vāstu point of view, desirable but not essential. Vāstu evaluates beauty from the inside out, not the outside in; from the center to the periphery, from the subtle to the densely material. Loveliness is less about the site's "skin," its external appearance, and more about its prāṇa and soul. Bring this "interior" perspective to your eyes (outer and inner) when you go out to look for land, and you'll find it easier to "see" clearly when you ask yourself the question, "What can materialize in this space, and how might it do so?"

If you have a personal *jyotiṣi* (Jyotiṣa astrologer), ask him or her even before you begin your property search whether your horoscope promises land and a house in your future, and if so, when. Better to let the right moment arrive and then proceed from that point, instead of embarking on a course of action at a time that promises little chance of success. When the right moment does arrive, the astrologer can augment an analysis of your birth chart with *praśna* (horary astrology) to shed light on questions that come up as you proceed through the processes of property acquisition and construction.

If you don't have a personal astrologer, find another adviser whom you trust to give you good counsel as you contemplate your situation and possibilities. Advice becomes particularly essential once you find a piece of land that you like. You'll need to evaluate the overall prevalence of benevolent and malevolent influences in the property, and the strength of each, before you can declare the space to be "good" or "bad." Even a "good" space, moreover, may not be right for you (even if you are a "good" manager of space) if your capabilities can't address its advantages and challenges. Our talents, however advanced, may not be suited for certain situations: You wouldn't call an electrician when plumbing is required.

Should you become captivated by a particular property, you may forcibly—if wrongly—convince yourself that it is unmistakably right for you. Without an observer and guide to audit your conclusions, you can easily enter into a relationship with a site that, even if the location is objectively advantageous, may make you miserable, weaken you, or even destroy you.

When both a property and its landowner enjoy apposite attributes, and both align cooperatively, results that trend toward sukha become likely. When the space shows promise but the owner does not, the latter individual may not be able to develop that space to its full potential. When the space is inauspicious but the person controlling it is talented, whichever of the two (the space or its possessor) is stronger will probably prevail (though the ultimate result in a closely-matched contest may only become evident after the building and the person have existed together for some time).

And when the space and its proprietor are both substantially deficient, and are ill-suited to one another, their confluence presages an inhospitable residence; any good results that may occasionally occur through the intervention of some unusually munificent fate are not likely to be sustainable for long.

If you're looking for undeveloped land where you can build your dwelling from the ground up, you'll have to decide between a site that is surrounded by nature and one that sits within a village, town, or city. This decision will narrow down your potential answers to the question, "What can materialize in this space, and how?" You could no more build a farmhouse in Manhattan than you would erect a brownstone tenement in rural Arizona; neither residence (Vāstu) would agree with its surroundings, its "residue" (*vastu*).*

*The term *vastu* (short "a") refers to the raw material used for construction and the surroundings remaining after the structure is finished. *Vāstu* (long "a") refers to the philosophy itself as well as the completed structure.

Rural or urban, an ideal site for human habitation should be situated in a moderate climate with an accessible water supply, and the location should have an even topography with a gentle slope. The soil should be fertile enough to support animals and the growth of useful plants, and dense enough to support structures well.

What climate is "moderate" for you will depend on your Ayurvedic constitution and condition. For instance, residents of the United States who have a pitta-predominant nature should think twice about putting down roots in the tropics, or in the Deep South (Mars, a pitta planet, rules south). Vāta people generally don't do too well in desert or semi-arid areas, especially in the windy mountain West (Saturn, a Vāta planet, rules west). Someone in whom kapha preponderates may want to avoid the humid northeast and northwest (ruled by the kapha graha Jupiter and kapha-vāta graha Moon, respectively).

Topography

Śastauṣadhi-druma-latā madhurā sugandhā
snigdhā samā na suṣirā ca mahī narāṇāṁ |
Apy adhvani śrama-vinodam upāgatānāṁ
dhatte śrīyaṁ kim uta śāśvata-mandireṣu ||

Ground that is soft, even, of sweet smell and taste, abounding in excellent herbs, trees and creepers, and not hollow underneath confers all-round prosperity even on those people who take rest on it to relieve themselves of the fatigue of travel; how much more will it do for those who build a permanent home on it and live therein?

Bṛhat Saṁhitā 53:88, p. 484

An ideal plot of land is generally smooth and flat, with a minimum of mounds and dips (natural or man-made), neither having a central depression nor a raised midsection. Gentle contours promote gentle movement of prāṇa; an uneven landscape agitates prāṇa, requiring more effort to make it tranquil.

For good drainage, and to encourage prāṇa to flow serenely, the site's ground should slope gently. The type of land that Vāstu likes best, in the northern hemisphere, is characterized by a natural slope from south (high) to north (low), from west (high) to east (low), or from southwest (high) to northeast (low). The southwest portion of the plot is thus ideally its highest point, and the northeast, its lowest part. Downward slopes from southeast or northwest toward northeast are permissible; authorities disagree on whether or not land that slopes from southwest toward southeast or northwest is acceptable.

As with your plot, so with your view: boulders, knolls, hills, mountains, tall trees, high walls, giant buildings, or other elevated points that "back you up" on the south, southwest, or west sides of the property are good, and are far less welcome on the north, northeast, or east sides. A valley or other natural depression, or a body of water, is less welcome on the south, southwest, or west than on the north, northeast, or east.

On your land and in your building, the southwest quadrant is the ideal location for an elevated counterpoint to a northeast low. This arrangement permits sattvic light and fresh, enthusiastic prāṇa to stream into your space through your northeast portal, flow up in a "high tide" against the "mountain" of tamas in the southwest, then lap agreeably at the shores of the other quadrants.*

Practically speaking, though, a gentle grade in a downward slope generally takes precedence over the slope's direction. Steeply plunging inclines encourage erosion that can endanger the structure's foundation. A sheer drop behind a building also encourages the prāṇa of the house and its surroundings to cascade downwards and to be lost. If you can't arrange for southwest to be your high point, at least keep your land's highest elevation to your structure's back. If prāṇa, air, light, and water circulate well on your property, you'll somehow find the energy to cope with whatever extra rajas or tamas might arise due to poor directionality. Lose all your prāṇa, though, and even abundant sattva will avail you little.

When I visit Hawaii's Big Island, I usually stay with friends who live on the Kona Coast, the western, drier side of the isle. This is a good choice from the climatic point of view, though less beneficial from the perspective of

*One alternate to this "southwest high, northeast low" approach is the archaic drainage-based theory of the *Bṛhat Saṁhitā*, which was inspired by the caste system, and dates from an era when each caste would have had its own quarter in a town or city. This theory, which espouses a different slope for each class, says that laborers (śūdras) should have land whose declivity is toward the west. Traders (vaiśyas) should have southward-sloping land. Executives, political leaders, and armed personnel (kṣatriyas) should obtain sites that fall away to the east. Land for academics, intellectuals, teachers, scientists, and clerics (brāhmaṇas) should decline toward the north.

directionality, since the house faces west. The topography of the residence, like that of most of the island's homes, slopes inexorably downward rather steeply. The loveliest time of day there is dusk, when whoever is home sits out on lawn chairs near (not under) the coconut palms to watch the blood-red sun sink grandly into the ocean. Beauty and utility here trump theory, and demand that the building's back be nestled into the hillside, which it is. The incline behind the house may prevent the sattvic light of morning from cascading into the building at sunrise, but it provides for spectacular sunset vistas, and multiplies the gorgeousness of the full moon when she comes over the mountain after nightfall, or sets plumply in the early morning.

Soil Conditions

Rich soil on your plot of land promotes the fruitfulness of all endeavors there, even if you're not planning an extensive garden. You can get useful hints about the site's fecundity from the type and abundance of vegetation that already occupy the land, and in the same way you can garner clues from the species of birds and animals that frequent the location. Gentle birds and mild animals, flowering plants, useful and fragrant herbs, and fruit-bearing trees all attest to the fertility of soil, the presence of adequate water, the effects of a congenial climate, and the land's moderate "personality." Land that is covered with rocks, anthills, or termite mounds, an area infested with flying or biting insects, or a property where thorny and poisonous plants thrive, has a "harsher" personality, and is—generally speaking—best avoided. Land that has been reclaimed from water is also better left alone.

The soil's color and feel should be soft but rich, its odor and taste sweet. Even the sound that it makes when struck by spade, pickaxe, or boot should be resonant. Another test: Put cows, calves, and bulls on the proposed property, and let them graze. If the bulls get spirited, and start to pursue the cows, attempting to mount them, the land is likely to promote the same kind of virile fertility in those who dwell on it.

Traditionally, one would examine a site's fertility and ability to sustain vegetation by testing it carefully with a variety of annuals over an entire growing season. A simpler investigation involves sowing grain on the site and seeing how long it takes to germinate. Sprouts appearing within three days suggest good soil fertility; five days is middling; anything longer brands the spot as inferior.

Vāstu also offers simple, effective methods for ascertaining the ground's compaction and load-bearing capacity. One involves digging a pit 2 to 2 ½ feet square, and 2 to 2 ½ feet deep, at the center of the site, then refilling the pit with the excavated earth. If some dirt is left over even after the pit is completely refilled, the soil is of good quality. The bigger the pile of earth that remains after refilling the excavation, the denser the ground is, and the better it will support a building. If the pit gets refilled with precisely the amount of dirt that it originally held, the ground is acceptable. That ground is undesirable where the excavated dirt is insufficient to refill the hole.

You can also fill a similar hole with water, walk 100 paces away from it, and return. If the water level has not dropped in that time, the ground is good; if it has dropped slightly, it's okay; if the water is gone or nearly so, forget it.

Excavation can also give you an idea of the kind of "energy" you'll be inheriting from previous inhabitants. Ashes, bones, or other buried debris suggests the presence of a lingering energy that you are unlikely to digest easily. A small amount of such remnants can be removed and discarded, but where human refuse is pervasive, the top six feet of soil should be replaced with fresh, pure earth from elsewhere.

Site Shape

Vāstu ever prefers the symmetry of square or rectangular sites—though it's important to note that small square or rectangular plots sandwiched between bigger lots are often unsuitable.* Triangular, circular, semicircular, pentagonal, hexagonal, drum-shaped, and L-shaped sites are generally disapproved of, even if symmetrical, though some sources do approve of the apsidal shape (*gajapṛṣṭa*), a combination of square and semicircle. Some authorities also conclude that a circular plot is acceptable if a circular house is built on it (acceptable, perhaps, but probably not conducive to relaxing).

Triangular structures may likewise occasionally work on triangular plots of land, as at the junction of two river valleys, or within the delta where two roads meet or diverge. The Indian city of Allahabad, which guards the junction of the mighty rivers Ganga and Yamuna, shelters a fort at the point of their convergence. The stronghold's general

*Ancient zoning restrictions proposed square lots for brāhmaṇas, and rectangles of increasing width-to-length ratios for kṣatriyas, vaiśyas, and śūdras.

Flatiron Building, New York City

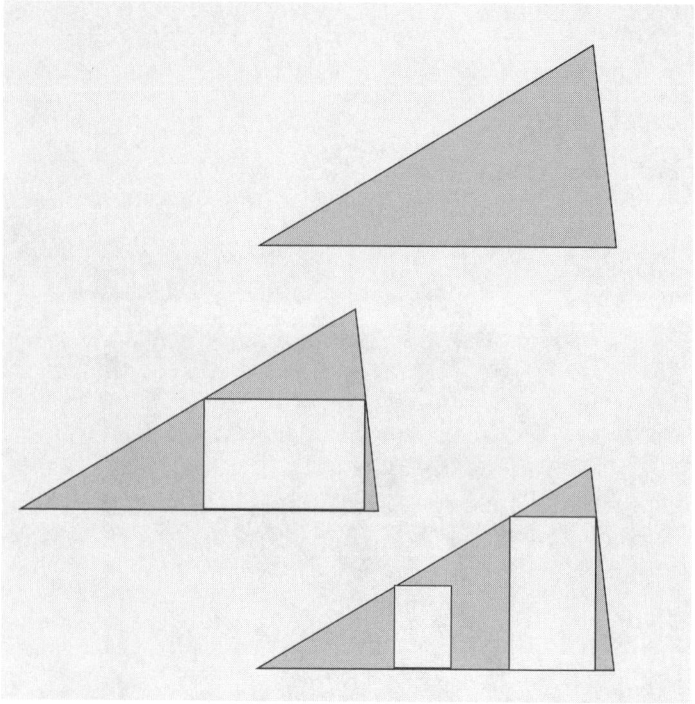

triangularity fittingly reflects its martial function (triangles symbolizing the fiery warrior planet Mars).

New York's famous Flatiron Building is stationed within the triangle where Broadway crosses Fifth Avenue at 23rd Street. This Big Apple icon, generally regarded as the first true skyscraper, wears its age well. We must wonder, though, how stable this site has been for its tenants, particularly those on the ground floor at the triangle's apex, with traffic and its associated wave of energy headed in their direction from both Fifth Avenue and Broadway, the wave "breaking" on the building's point as a bow wave breaks over a ship's prow. The situation would have been substantially different had the traffic flows and their associated energy proceeded north instead, leaving the Flatiron occupants in the wake of the traffic wave. Even then, some triangular instability would remain, particularly in the structure's many triangular rooms, whose energy is as fiery as that of the larger edifice that contains them. The building's very name

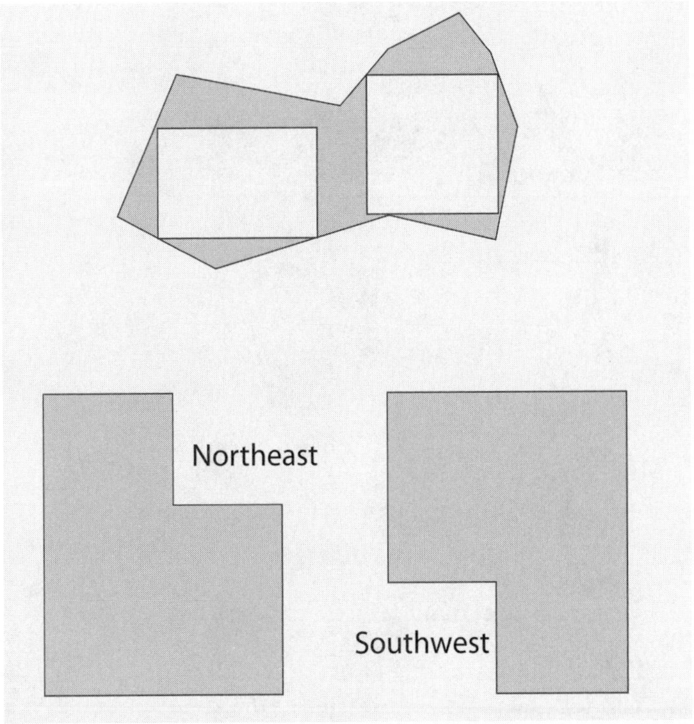

reflects a fiery nature, one that "irons flat," pressing and steaming all who plunge beneath its prow.

Often the wisest plan for a triangular piece of land is to turn it into a square or rectangle, bartering apices for stability. Those who insist on building on or within a triangle will usually find that its energies center at its focus, and that the energy at that spot can often become too intense to efficiently digest.

Irregular plots of land are as little favored in Vāstu as are irregularly shaped rooms. Jagged boundaries generate irregularities in the movement of prāṇa, reducing the benefic resonance that we intend to create. A large plot can have squares or rectangles demarcated within it, by means of fences, walls, hedges, or lines of trees. The small "scraps" of land left over can be converted into flower beds, rock gardens, groves, small orchards, garden ponds, and the like.

Sites that are square or rectangular with a symmetrical extension to the north or east sides of their northeast corners are generally

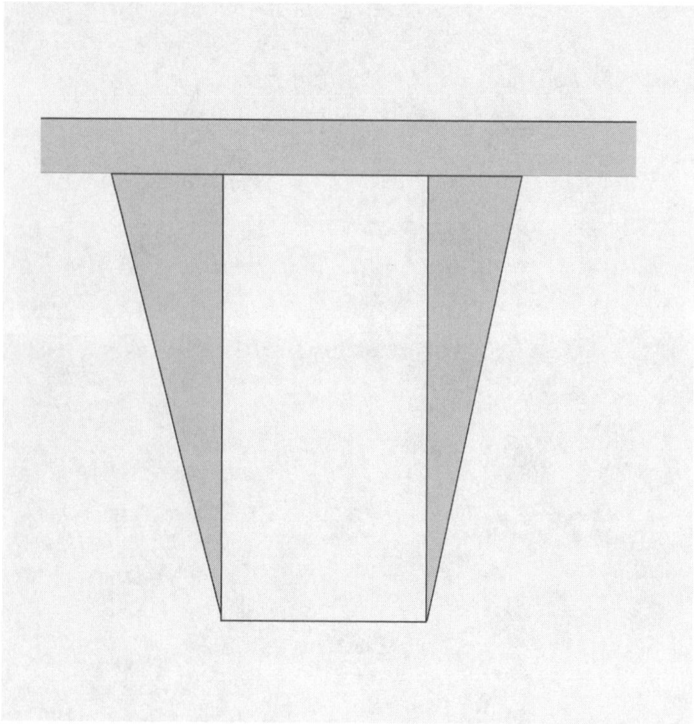

regarded as auspicious. Some authorities suggest that an extension from a square into the southeast direction will be good for female inhabitants. (These soi-disant, modern "authorities" sometimes quote an ancient text or tradition, and while their opinions are often worth acknowledging, I prefer not to give them credence by mentioning their names.) A northwest extension is regarded by some as being good for social activities, business ventures, or other pursuits involving groups of people. No one likes extensions into the southwest.

One way to contend with a southwest extension is to convert the plot into a square or rectangle by adding more land alongside the extension, if possible. A simpler solution is to truncate the "extensions" and turn the remainders thus produced to some constructive purpose. If the remnants are themselves squares or rectangles, structures can be built on them. Plots with missing corners can usually also be remedied by addition or truncation.

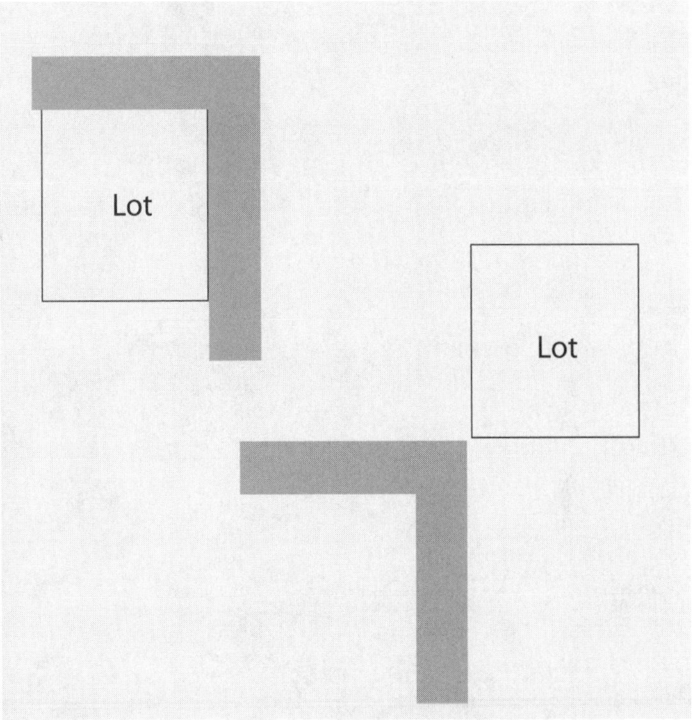

Vāstu authorities often prescribe the "trimming" remedy for a "Tiger-mouthed" property (one whose front is significantly wider than its back) where a residence will be built. "Trimming" is also often the best choice when a symmetrical plot is wrongly aligned with the cardinal directions. The benefits to be gained by good alignment will usually outweigh the land sacrificed to achieve the realignment.

Roads

The average building site requires good road access. When the plot lies along only one road, or when only one thoroughfare is the main road, the structure's longest outside wall should usually run parallel to the main boulevard, except when that road lies to the south of the property, since south is such an undesirable direction in Vāstu. This is also the case when the only thoroughfare near the property is a lane or alley. Plenty of exceptions to this rule exist,

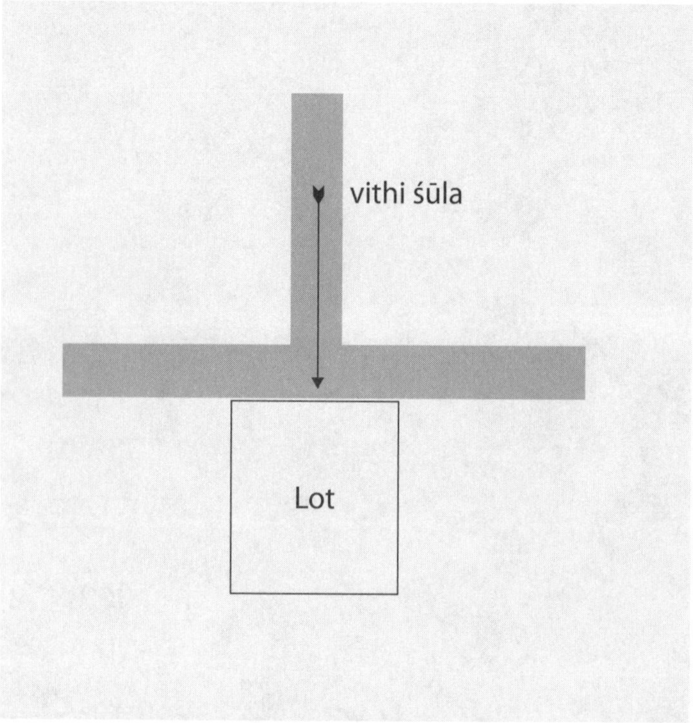

however, and sometimes depend on a site's "gender." In Vāstu, this is determined by the comparative length of a plot's sides: A property whose north-south length is greater than its east-west length is female; male sites are longer east-west than north-south. So when the main road along a property is to its south, aligning the structure with south is permissible (though alignment with east is preferable) provided that the site is female. When, however, such a property is male, buildings on it do better having their entryways and longest walls facing the rising sun.

If more than one main road defines your plot, first preference should always be given to east as the direction to which the front door should face. If that is not possible, then the direction of choice, in descending order of preference, should be: north, then west, and finally south. Many Vāstu commentators observe that the best site is one that has roads on both its north and east sides (at least in the northern hemisphere). Such a plot dictates that the proposed

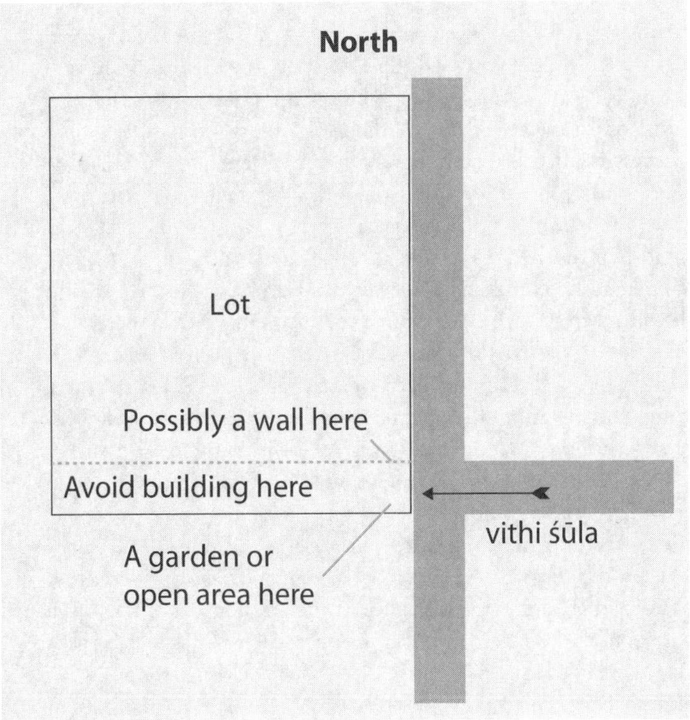

building would face either east or north and would incorporate the open space that Vāstu desires to have in those directions (provided that the roads are lower than the property). A road to the west is acceptable; if possible, avoid plots whose only thoroughfare is on the southern side.

Tracts of land with roads on all four sides are typically reported to be generally good, though some authorities say they are suitable only for public buildings (temples, churches, government offices, clubs, libraries, schools, or hospitals), or for multi-family dwellings. Buyers are cautioned to avoid busy intersections, both for obvious reasons (dangerous traffic, pollution) and on more subtle grounds. Crossroads energy is so potently transient that it overexcites the quality of mobility in the prāṇa that flows through nearby houses and their inhabitants. This will generate an excess of vāta, which will destabilize everything and everyone who lives in such a residence.

Corner lots are good, particularly when located on the northeast corner of an intersection. Even better is to have a "bound angle" corner lot (shown above), the two roads that front it acting as energy "moats" for the house—in effect, keeping the energy contained within the plot. An "open angle" lot (where the lot is directly opposite a bend in its access road) will require both substantial fencing, to demarcate it carefully, and some protection from attack by the bend of the road, which acts as a *vīthi śūla,* a "road spear" (here *vīthi* = "road").

A road that dead-ends at a site also becomes a vīthi śūla. The very active energy of the road will "skewer" any land that lies in its path, which will act to disturb the happiness of anyone who lives there.

Properties at the end of dead-end streets put their dwellers, not surprisingly, in a location where prāṇa stagnates. Potential there generally remains unfulfilled, because there is no ongoing movement of prāṇa to inspire the residents, though there is plenty of vāta energy that pools in the residence. The resultant "unstable energy with no outlet" will actively promote disharmony.

A T-intersection abutting a site has plenty of prāṇa movement available in the form of the T's crossbar, but most of the time, that energy merely enhances the influence of the T's stem, which acts as a spear pointed at the site's heart. For an "open angle" lot, the two roads forming the angle create a "spear point" that acts like a T-stem.

"Spears" that point at your property from the north or east sides of northeast, the south side of southeast, or the west side of northwest are said to be acceptable, provided that the spear does not point at the heart of the building you erect there. Vāstu experts have varying opinions about roads that terminate on the east side of southeast, the north side of northwest, and the west or south sides of southwest. Some say these are all unfavorable, while others state that they are all barely acceptable.

Unfavorable spears are said to be remediable by means of cordoning off or selling off the land that's being speared. Care must be taken to eliminate sufficient property so that no unfavorable extension remains after the operation. Suppose, for example, that a vīthi śūla is attacking the property from the east side of southeast. If you sever a slice of land that covers only half the width of the property, you'll leave behind an irregularly shaped polygon that has an extension to the southwest, which is highly undesirable. In this case, your excision must include a slice at least as wide as is the offending road, one that extends to the full thickness of the property. Should you decide to keep the land, you will do well to use it for a neutral purpose such as some sort of garden.

Even permissible "spears" become impermissible with multiplicity. In other words, vīthi śūlas that exist on the south side of southeast and the west side of northwest are individually okay, but become unfavorable if both appear together, in negative confluence. One exception: Roads can come in from both the north and east sides of the northeast corner. A property that is surrounded by roads on three or four of its four sides and is being stuck by "spears" on three or four of those sides is too afflicted, and should be rejected. A lot surrounded by four roads, all of which have T-instersections, is particularly afflicted.

A real-world example of vīthi śūla difficulties is evident at the residence next door to where some friends live in Albuquerque, New Mexico. The neighboring house has a road T-ing in front of it, which might in itself be remediable, particularly since the house faces east. But the land on the property falls away to the west, and the easterly direction, which should be low and open, is wholly obstructed by a view of the bulk of the Sandia Mountains. Add to that the existing asymmetries of house and plot, and a front door that appears to fall within the Saturn or Rāhu portions of the front wall, and what might be merely a painful "spear" has most likely been transmogrified into a deadly one. Indeed, the owner of that house is reported to have suffered through one misfortune after another ever since purchasing it.

Patterns and Energies

Vīthi śūla is a good example of the subtle criteria that you must evaluate in a site. Another subtle criterion is the pattern of the site's surroundings, which will guide what will "fit" there. As the authors observe in *A Pattern Language*:

> "... no pattern is an isolated entity. Each pattern can exist in the world, only to the extent that it is supported by other patterns: the larger patterns in which it is embedded, the patterns of the same size that surround it, and the smaller patterns which are embedded in it."*

Settling on a site means settling on a meta-pattern, a "pattern of patterns." A site's every feature, natural and artificial, spatial and

* Alexander et alia, op. cit. xiii

terrestrial, contributes to its meta-pattern. Your mind's-eye image of your desired structure will need to fit comfortably into the patterns that are to surround it, if you and that structure are together to generate good space, and a good narrative.

An illuminating example of this principle in reverse sits in Winchester, England, where just outside the Great Hall, a majestic building nearly ten centuries old, sits a Law Courts Building that is barely 30 years old. Save for some echoes of the "flint in wall" decoration of its distinguished neighbor, the newer structure's modern lines, concrete construction, and contemporary fittings are wholly, jarringly out of place in the square that the Great Hall dominates. The location for the newer project was ideal, but its conception and execution were fatally flawed.

When you find a lot that speaks to you, one that displays many of the traits that would benefit you, you'll thus want to keep your ego well in check as you envision what it might become. No good will emerge, in the long run, if you insist on chopping down a number of handsome, healthy trees just to erect an overblown mansion that blocks your neighbor's view. Let compassion for trees and respect for your neighbors temper your creative vision, and the ultimate result will be far more satisfying.

The writer John Ralston Saul uses the phrase "balanced individualism" to describe the attitude of the person who graciously accepts the need for individuals to fit amicably into their environs. He offers this example as one worthy of emulation:

"On the edge of a river in a deep mountain valley [in Korea] a great Confucian teacher, Yi On-chock, built himself a retirement house when he left government service in 1516. The five Confucian qualities with which until then he had governed other men were … the arts of peace; of goodness; of superior behavior, which is the opposite of the petty and mean; of propriety or grace; and finally, of the just use of power.

"… The house he built is an expression of those qualities. When I came upon it I was immobilized without being able to identify the cause. At first, I had not even consciously seen the house. It wasn't so much a matter of its modesty and integration into the place, although it had both. There was no hint of the man's ego. No sense of his having built as opposed to having found a way to be part of the place. But the longer I looked, the more I could see something which expressed itself as harmony. Grace, yes, but harmony above all in its own terms and in those of nature. The materials, the lines of the myriad of free-standing walls, the roof lines, all swam into the surrounding land, the rocks, the river bed. … As I walked through the passageways it was as if the human flowed from one to the other in a discrete sonnet."*

How wonderful to have the "thesis" of materials juxtapose against the antithesis of environs to resolve into a sweet synthesis, a "discrete sonnet" of concinnity. If this appeals to you, then take the advice of Alexander Pope, and "consult the Genius of the Place." Each place has its "genius," an intelligence that guides its development. To the extent that the genius incarnates topographically, you'll have to work with the land's every idiosyncrasy, its prevailing winds and rainfall, slopes and hollows, knolls and bogs, gravel beds and thickets, wringing their best from them, enhancing them when they embellish your verse, reproving them when they threaten to monopolize your poem.

Sometimes the land's spirit may appear in the flesh, muse-like, in the form of some custodian of the space, someone who serves as a medium in the structural séance of courtyard and flagstone walk, garden seat and basement shelf. Occasionally this "sagacity of the terrain" will embody itself via a succession of owners and managers, each succeeding or failing to the extent that he or she heeds the genius' call, each handing down a more "knowledgeable" piece of ground (sometimes newly invigorated and more confident, sometimes sadder but wiser) to the land's next steward.

You must familiarize yourself with a site before you'll be able to consult its genius, or even discover if that genius is awake or asleep, friendly or hostile, responsive or wounded. If this spirit is in a bad mood, how much effort will be required to bring it around? If awake and alert, how accommodating does it seem? Answers to such questions being often hard to assess, you will at least want to get a feel for whether the land that you like also likes you: whether it's inclined to cooperate with you or is more likely to obstruct you at every turn.

You can learn from land you're considering by spending some time on it sitting quietly, receptively, letting your thoughts flow through your mind without trying to hold onto them. As you succeed, however

*John Ralston Saul, *Unconscious Civilization*, pp 192-193

briefly, in letting go of your attachment to your own perspective on the world, you'll start to perceive patterns from the land's perspective. Perhaps your Vāstu eyes will suddenly catch a glimpse of some defining feature of the property. Maybe you'll see or hear an omen, an event that offers a clue as to whether the world approves or disapproves of your proposed action. You might just get a gut feeling as to whether the plot is good for you or not. If you let it, the site will spill its secrets, someway or other; you need only to be able to discern what's being said.

While you wait for the site to confirm or reject your plan for it, you should evaluate it in more mundane fashion. Begin with what you know about orientation to align yourself with east, north, west, and south, and see what you can see. Look for welcoming or foreboding patterns in the rocks and trees, in surroundings close and distant, in nearby houses and buildings; get a feel for which direction is most "right" for a structure to be placed on that space.

Living beneath or in close proximity to power lines, microwave relay towers, or other radiation sources is unwise, but subtler energies can also mar the prospects of a piece of land. Terrestrial *nāḍīs* (ethereal vessels in which prāṇa moves) create earth *marmas* (critical energy points) where they intersect. Structures or heavy objects that sit on the marma points of a room or structure "damage" those marmas, and the prāṇa that flows through them. Similarly, building on a land nāḍī, or worse, at a land marma, where the land nāḍīs intersect, destabilizes the energy of both the nāḍīs and the structure that obstructs them. If you can't locate an expert who can assist you in locating the nāḍīs on your land, you can do it yourself by using your breath, your instinctive gut feeling, or some similar method.

A site's "energy" can also be permanently influenced by an event of marked intensity, positive or negative, that happens atop it. Land that used to be occupied by a temple or church is powerfully oriented to the other world, and so may be less able to support your sukha in this one. Land that has been scoured by an inferno or struck repeatedly by lightning, where a pregnant woman has died in childbirth or after a miscarriage, or where a newborn has died must also be eschewed. The same goes for locations that have been the site of a murder, that are in close proximity to a graveyard, or are otherwise "polluted."

If you fall in love with a site whose subtle energy is "off," you may discover remedies to set it right, either by "exorcising" such otherworldly negatives, or by transforming them. The Tibetans, for example, sometimes use Buddhist *stūpas* as "pins" or "nails" (*kīla*) to "nail down" unstable components in a space; one of the most famous examples of this remedy was the one that "tied together" two slopes not far from the Potala Palace in Lhasa. But even such corrective processes offer no guarantee of success, and an individual is usually better off forswearing energetically troubled sites in favor of others that are less inauspicious.

The Last Word

The ideal plot is hard to come by; in the words of the Roman poet Horace, "Nothing is beautiful from every point of view." As noted earlier, Varahamihira, the ancient author of the *Bṛhat Saṁhitā*, provides the last word on the subject of property selection:

Tat tasya bhavati śubhadaṁ yasya ca yasmin mano ramate |

Any site becomes auspicious for a person, provided that it gladdens his heart.

Bṛhat Saṁhitā 53:95

If you are diligent, and able to cope with adversity, you can be confident that you will, eventually, find some way to coexist with a site that appeals to you so strongly that you can't let it go.

Potala Palace in Lhasa

1 Ordering Your Space

After selecting a piece of land that gladdens your heart, a property with which you can create a good relationship, ask your second Vāstu question: "How full should this space be, and how empty?" For that space to meet its full potential, how natural ought it to remain, and how consciously cultivated ought it to become? How much should it be structured in relation to its "residue," and how independent should it grow to be?

Once you find tentative answers to these questions, you can begin to parcel and structure your land.

Fixing plot boundaries, buildable area, location, and orientation

Orient the Site

Determine first the cardinal directions, using a gnomon (a post whose shadow can be used to calculate true east geometrically) or a magnetic compass (adding, in the northern hemisphere, 2 ½ degrees toward the southeast from magnetic east to yield a close approximation of true east). You can also determine the cardinal directions through nocturnal signposts, e.g. when you face toward Polaris, the Pole Star, you are facing north. To check your work, or to determine east if all else fails, match prominent features in the nearby landscape against a detailed topographical map.

Orient your building to the cardinal directions, never to the intermediate directions (not even the well-beloved northeast). All else being equal, an east-facing front wall and door work best. Some commentators aver that this means true east, while the Vāstu text *Mānasāra* opines that, while true east is good for liberation (*mokṣa*), orienting a home to *eṣa prāci*, which is slightly northeast of true east, better supports the pursuit of duty, affluence, and gratification (dharma, artha, kāma). Precise knowledge of true east is essential for this principle, since *Mānasāra* entirely rejects orientation to *āgneya prāci* (a slight deviation southeast from true east).

Another opinion: East or north is good for worldly prosperity, west or south for retreat from worldly affairs. Yet another perspective: Orient the building to face prominent natural features (mountains, rivers, lakes, etc.). Today, in most places, lots are small, and orientation is defined by road. In the ideal arrangement, your building will simultaneously face both its access road and the center of the square site you draw out on

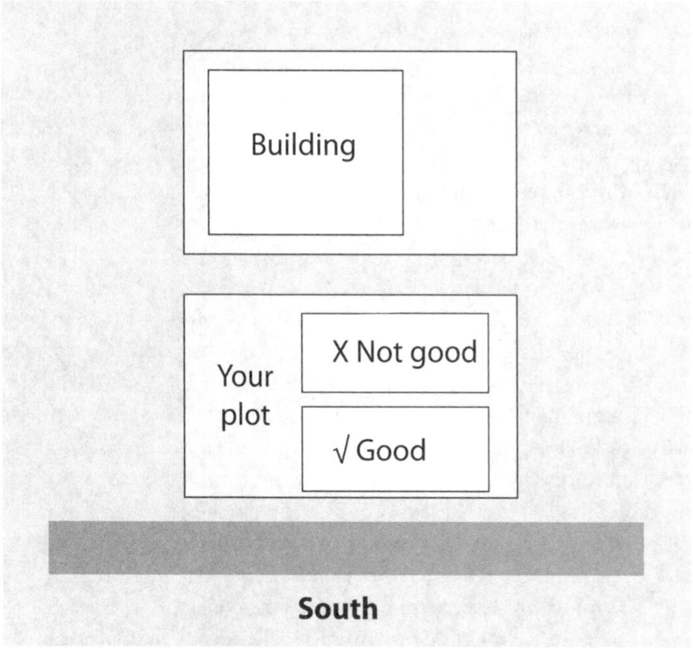

your plot of land. Even if the road sits to the inauspicious south of your plot, this school of thought suggests that your structure should face the road, particularly if another building sits to the north of your site (since opening your front door directly onto that northerly building will put you at the mercy of its energy).

Since we well know south's innate inauspiciousness, owners of south-facing plots will want carefully to consider potential remedies for its overly Martian oomph. One possibility: Circle the house with a high, strong wall, putting the main gate in an auspicious segment of the south side (such as in the fourth, fifth, or sixth of the nine equal divisions of that side, as counted from east to west), then have the actual entrance to the house on a better side, like east. Vimalananda, my mentor, proposed something comparable to a friend of mine who had a plot with an access road that lay to the site's south. He advised my friend to extend a long driveway along her property's eastern periphery, so that the de facto entrance of her residence would be from the northeast instead.

Lay Out the Boundaries of the Buildable Space

Once you've determined how to orient the structure itself, decide how much land you want to leave unoccupied, and how much you want to use for your construction. Remember that roughly half of your land should remain as unbuilt "residue," and that there should always be some space reserved for wild nature (nature that is as wild as possible for that location).

Regardless of how the land is shaped, you need to draw a square within it, to demarcate the area that you intend to develop. When your land is sufficiently large, create your square to occupy half or less of the total area, the rest remaining open (the smaller, set-aside square will itself ideally contain 50 percent or more of undeveloped land). It's best to orient this square within your parcel so that there's more open space to its east and north than to its west and south; some say at least 50 percent more should be set aside for the east and north directions (e.g., a ten-foot wide band of open space on the west and south should be matched by at least fifteen feet of open space on the east and north).

If the size of your demarcated square is between 5000 square feet (a little more than .11 acres, roughly 71 feet on a side) and approximately 90,000 square feet (roughly equivalent to two acres, about 300 feet on a side), then divide it into quarters by adding a north-south line through the midpoint of the northern and southern sides, and an east-west line through the midpoint of the eastern and western sides. The northeastern and southwestern quadrants of such a square have equal preference as locations for the main structure, the northeast being the best of the directions, and because it leaves to the southwest the majority of the land that can be kept "wild" (undeveloped), and the southwest because it leaves to the northeast, the area that most needs to be left open, the majority of land that can be cleared. The northwest quadrant of a plot gets third preference in this site-selection regard, and southeast is least favored for this purpose. Your edifice should face both your access road and the center of your inscribed square, which means that your building should occupy the southwestern quadrant of the square if it is to face north or east, and should sit in the northeastern quadrant if it is to face south or west (the exact positioning being determined by the location of the property's access road).

When you have a very sizable plot—larger than two acres—

subdivide it again, until you have a square that is roughly two acres, and build on the northeast subdivision of the southwest quadrant, or the southwest subdivision of the northeast quadrant. For a small plot (less than 75 feet wide), superimpose on the site the largest square possible, create the quadrants, then slightly offset toward northeast or southwest the central point of the building from the center of the squared site on which the structure will sit. The central points of a site and its building should coincide only rarely for public buildings (temples, commercial structures), and never for private residences—this spatial concurrence makes the prāṇa of the structure too "active" to be easily assimilated.

Even on a site that is tiny—on which your main house occupies practically the entire square—you should surround your main building with sufficient space so that one person can freely circumambulate it. When orienting your foundation plan within your square, again try to have the majority of its open space to the east and north (50 percent more in these segments than those in the west and south).

Once you have your square (and, if need be, your quadrants), generate a large Vāstu Puruṣa Maṇḍala for your chief structure, and smaller Vāstu Puruṣa Maṇḍalas for your garden, guest house, and other sections and structures. Orient each of these to the cardinal directions!

Determine the size of the Brahma Sthāna for each room in each structure based on the number of modules in your Vāstu Puruṣa Maṇḍala (usually 8 x 8 or 9 x 9 for a residence), then decide how you wish to preserve these Brahma Sthānas inviolate. Where the climate allows, turn the center space of your structures into a courtyard; otherwise, make it the center of your living or working space in the form of an indoor courtyard, atrium, fountain, or pool, preferably with a sizable skylight above it.

Selecting materials, designing the building and its ancillary structures, and setting the prime dimensions

Selecting materials

Vāstu is agnostic on the subject of materials; it advocates the use of whatever materials are most appropriate for the local climate, particularly those that are available nearby and are abundant, renewable, and resistant to attack (by the elements, vermin, etc.). Good building

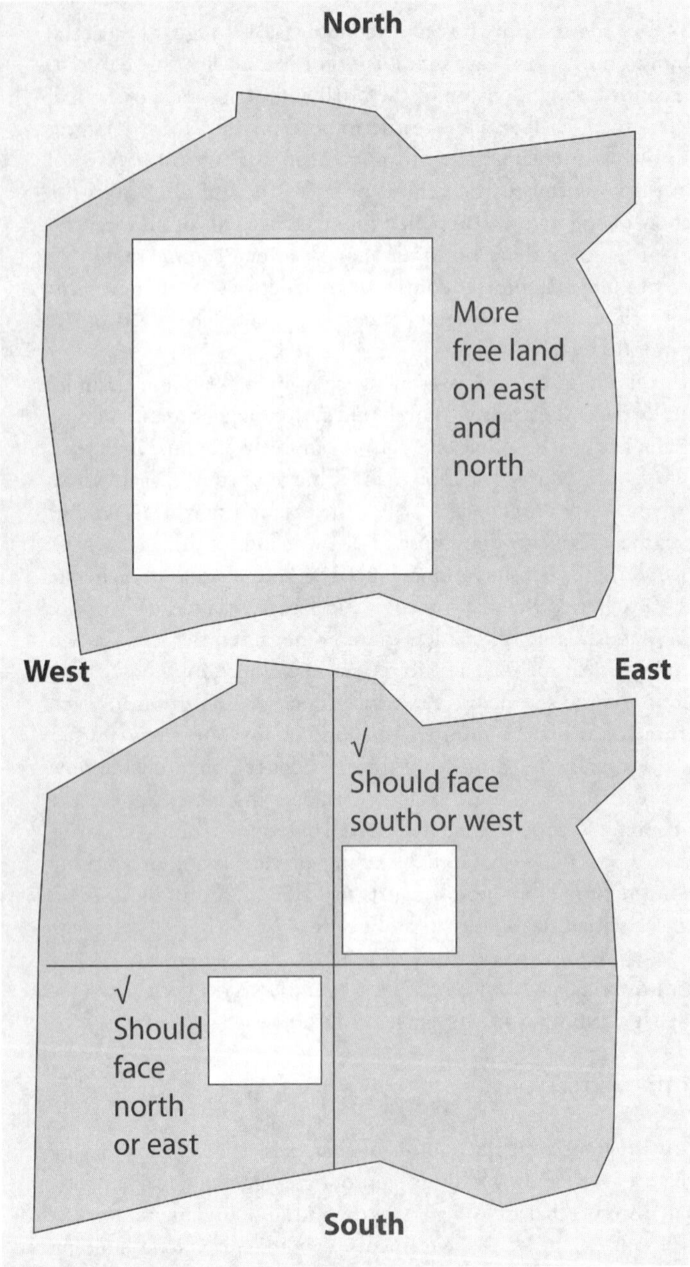
North
More
free land
on east
and
north
West
East
√
Should face
south or west
√
Should
face
north
or east
South

materials provide effective protection from whichever affect of the Five Elements is most excessive in the environment—light, heat, cold, wind, water, sound. Adobe, for example, is quite appropriate for the desert, in New Mexico or Arizona as well as in Mali or Egypt, because it is durable and can maintain comfortable temperatures within a range of a few degrees during day and night. One estimate suggests that about one-third of the world's people live in earthen houses; some adobe structures in Egypt are more than 3,000 years old.

Other earthy materials, including brick and stone, are also good. One theory suggests that water-derived rock like sandstone and limestone is better than igneous rock such as granite or basalt, on the premise that Water, as embodied in the stones it shaped, is a more soothing energy to have surrounding you than is Fire. Wood is also good, and cob and straw-bale structures can similarly work well in some localities. All-metal buildings and reinforced concrete structures are held to be generally less desirable, as these materials interrupt the circulation of prāṇa.

Climate

Climate will help determine both your materials of choice and your structure's qualities. This influence is amply evident in England, a country so greenly prolific that you can be well hidden from people using no more than a hedge, and so wet and cold that there is great incentive to spend as much time as possible indoors. This turned an Englishman's home into his castle, gardening into a national passion (plants being easy to grow), and shop-keeping into the national livelihood (each shop offering a welcome respite, however brief, from the rain and chill).

The desert's hostility likewise shaped Arab architecture. Heat, glare, and sandstorms forced desert dwellers to "turn their backs to the outside" by huddling their homes together on narrow streets and then building inner courtyards to open themselves to the sky instead of the landscape. To build, in an arid region, a South Seas-style home, which hospitably entertains every passing breeze, would be as "wrong" as to build a Middle Eastern house in Hawaii or Tahiti.

Traditional desert architecture in the Old World uses the inner courtyard, which traps cool night air and releases it gradually during the day, as an air-conditioning system. The compass termites of Western Australia use analogous structural technology to air-condition their hives, maintaining the temperature inside their nests to within one degree of 31°C (88°F), day and night, summer and winter, even as the external temperature varies between 3°C (37°F) and 42°C (108°F). The termites build towers, which always point north (the direction of greatest sunlight, and so heat, in the southern hemisphere), which they regulate climatically by controlling the flow of air through the towers. When wind blows across the tops of the towers, air is sucked through the nest, creating what is known as a "stack effect." The termites control airflow by blocking and opening the nest's channels in which the air moves, and the result is comfort.

When even insects can find effective, low-energy-cost solutions to their climatic challenges, what keeps us supposedly more intelligent animals from following suit? Why do we instead forsake tried and true building materials for concrete, and continue to sacrifice land to suburban sprawl? How long will we affluent of today be able to afford our prodigiously wasteful high-energy, high-consumption lives? Vāstu requests us instead to search for sustainable answers to the puzzles of our lives by creating homes and offices, towns and cities of more manageably human dimensions. Accept limitation willingly, and the world will cooperate with you; demand more from the world than it can healthily offer, and you set the stage for ultimate environmental ruin.

Fix the Proportions and Dimensions

Before you set your dwelling in the direction of a McMansion, take a moment to investigate the Small House Movement, and begin your house's design phase by settling on the minimum reasonable size that will work for you and yours. Once you have an order of magnitude in mind, decide on a square or rectangular layout. For a rectangle, fix the ratio of the sides at 1:1¼, 1:1½, 1:1¾, or 1:2. *Mayamata* permits 1:2½ or 1:3 for monasteries and hermitages (and, by extension, for dormitories and such). Some Vāstu texts direct that your building's east-west dimension should be longer than its north-south dimension; others suggest just the opposite. Make your decision according to your local climate and the surrounding natural features.

Bṛhat Saṁhitā suggests fixing the building's height as a proportion of its width, suggested proportions being 1:1, 1:1¼, 1:½, 1:1¾, or 1:2; other writers suggest 1:2⅛ or 1:2¼ as well. Yet another school proposes fixing the building's height so it's a full multiple of one side of the "module," one module being the smallest square of the chosen Vāstu Puruṣa Maṇḍala. Creating this proportion ensures that the inside of the house will be filled with full cubic modular spaces. For example, a square 9 x 9 Maṇḍala that is 63 feet on a side has a 7 foot module (63 feet divided into 9 equal portions = 7 feet), which thus permits the building's height (or, for a multistory structure, the height of each upper floor) to be 7 feet, or even 14 feet. A square 8 x 8 Maṇḍala that is 28 feet on a side has a 3.5 foot module (28 feet divided by 8 = 3.5 feet); the height of a building on this Maṇḍala could thus reasonably be set at two full modules (7 feet), three full modules (10.5 feet), or four full modules (14 feet).

If your floor plan has a (more common) rectangular module, use its width (its shorter side) to fix your structure's height. "Height" here may be basement top to roof top (if the roof is flat); ceiling to floor; ceiling to middle of foundation slab; or ceiling to bottom of slab.

If you lack access to a Vāstu advisor when faced with this and similar options related to building height and proportions, the nature of the site and its surroundings will characteristically winnow your choices down to two or three; then the final decision can usually be made with the help of a "gut" feeling, on the basis of which option feels most likely to "cooperate" with its environs.

A home's absolute dimensions are commonly determined by means of the *Ayadi* calculations, which calibrate the building's dimensions with the position of the moon in the horoscope of one or more of its owners; the calculations also attune the spatial measurements to the structure's *yoni*, its orientation with the directions. A Vāstu house is designed to be a living organism, one that ought to resonate with its inhabitants. The house's master or mistress (or both) actually get "wedded" to it by Ayadi means.

Where possible, the house's rooms should possess dimensions that are multiples of the house's module. Square rooms, which are best in metaphysically-oriented buildings like temples, are appropriate in a private dwelling for the shrine room, study room, and other similar spaces that focus chiefly on the reality of the non-physical (including even the kitchen, where the energy of the divine is invoked into food).

As you consider which room to place where, keep asking yourself the question, "What can materialize in this space, and how might it do so?" Determine a room's position based on its purpose, on the sun, and on the prevailing winds (in a dwelling that permits outside air to circulate within it, this natural air flow should not be permitted to blow odors and smoke from the kitchen or aromas from the bathroom into the house). Other essential considerations include how freely prāṇa can circulate through the arrangement of rooms, and the overall "statement" that you want the house to make.

Another climate-centric decision relates to windows and doors that face one another. Feng Shui warns against such configurations, to guard against loss of prāṇa; Vāstu advocates for such arrangements, to enhance cross-ventilation. Whichever system you choose to follow, windows should by and large be square or rectangular, and should open upward or outward.

When generating a sketch of how you want your residence to appear, remember the residue, which in this case is the building's "negative space." "Positive space" is the space occupied by the structure you build; "negative space" is the space that surrounds your construction. A home's "negative space" helps to define it, by creating an area that helps to protect the building while nurturing its prāṇa and purpose.

Be sure to carefully choose the house's "spokesroom," its epitome, the focus around which the rest of the house organizes itself; the attention demanded by that room's prominence of position, decoration, and orientation will channel the overall flow of the house's prāṇa.

As you plan, remember that the intersection points of the longer diagonals and the exact middle points of the geometrical room plans should be taken to be vulnerable points (*marma*), and you shouldn't build on these. Likewise, keep the center of each room, and the center of the house as a whole, as open as possible.

Balance openness with concealment by creating small, private spaces for you and yours. Make some of these areas kid-sized, for children love to hide in tiny, cave-like places; make other niches secure, for valuables, archives, and other secrets. Sprinkle your large open spaces with areas like alcoves that people can use to remove themselves temporarily from the main current of home life. Ensure that you have plenty of storage room; adequate closet space keeps corridors free for prāṇa circulation, and fosters a healthy sense of individuality in the communality of a family living situation.

Fire

Live flame has been a critical element of human existence for a million years or more, and there is still no worthy substitute for a home fire. Choose the spot for your fireplace carefully. In the tropics or subtropics, the fire pit is best placed in the open central courtyard; in temperate and subarctic zones, where central courtyards are usually eschewed, a fire will do you more good in the kitchen, den, or living area. Establishing a fire in a common space permits people to use it as a focus for "talk, dreams, and thought"; be sure to make that space central enough so that glimpses of the flames can be sighted from other rooms. It's helpful to put near the fire another visually striking object or scene (e.g., a compelling painting or photo, a sculpture, a window that opens onto a vista), to preserve that dynamic of focused attention for times when the fire is out.

At a primordial level, the sun is our source of fire, and of food. In general, as we noted before, there should be more open space in the northerly and easterly directions than to the south and west; east and north should also have more windows and doors, and more balconies and verandas. The ground should slope lower toward the north and east, areas that should not harbor the tall structures or obstacles that are permissible on the south and west. In warm climes, this situation takes advantage of the morning sun, which offers more light and less heat than the afternoon sun, whose intensity gets blocked by the trees and other shade producers situated on the south and west.

Water

Wells, cisterns, underground water tanks, and the like should in general occupy the property's north or east portions, but quality of water takes precedence over location. A swimming pool is best located within the northeastern triangle (the half of the property that sits to the east and north of the diagonal that bisects the land from northwest to southeast).

Bath tubs are good on all walls except the northeast; shower stalls on the north or east wall are permissible. Wash basins may appear on the north, northeast, east, or west walls, but not in the northeast corner; toilets likewise should not occupy the bathroom's northeast corner, as waste water is not welcome there.

Upper Rooms, Lower Levels

Basements and cellars should be dug under the whole area of the house, or under the northeast corner; they are also suitable under the north or the east sides, or both. Entry should preferably be from the northeast, on either the east or north side. Basements are good for parking areas, storerooms, and temporary offices, but not for permanent residences.

An upper floor should cover the same area as the lower floor; if less, the upper story should be built on the south or west side, or on both the south and west sides, with one room on the northeast side of the northwest-southeast line. Another option is to build a U-shaped top floor, leaving the east or north side—the open part of the *U*—as an open terrace. If you want but one room on the top floor, put it in the southwest corner. Avoid making your attic your primary storage space, lest clutter there obstruct the circulation of air and prāṇa in the home.

Stairs

Stairs (and elevators) are good in the southeast and northwest, and acceptable in the southwest, but should always be avoided in the northeast, and should never appear in the center of the house or opposite the main entrance. Stairs that spiral should ordinarily proceed in a clockwise direction from bottom to top, and should be wide and gently curving.

Front Door

The front door, the chief portal through which the public and private worlds connect, is of paramount importance to home or office. Just as the mouth is the human body's largest orifice, the door, the house's main orifice, is its "mouth." The front door's threshold should be at ground level or raised slightly above it, but never below. *Mānasāra* says the front door's height should be at least twice its width; other authorities suggest a multiple of three.

A house's portal should simultaneously provide protection for residents and make guests feel welcome. In older Indian buildings, doors were built short and set low, to force visitors to bow in reverence to the home and its occupants, and to prevent sudden external assault, by bandits, evil winds, or untoward energies. An alternative approach, widely favored in ancient forts, is to construct twisting, turning entrance passages that end at large, strong doors.

Temples and other public buildings may have their main door in the center of their principal wall, but a residence should not, for such a door would be directly in line with the Brahma Sthāna. This would, says *Bṛhat Saṁhitā*, act as a *śūla* and "wound" the Brahma Sthāna by "piercing" it. It's better either to locate the door in one of the portions that flank the wall's center, or in a portion that supports an agreeable planet, one whose indications are consistent with the intentions of the house's owner and other family members (see the section "The Jyotishical Door" in Chapter Seven). Such entrances attract good fortune into the home.

Another theory, presented in *Some Glimpses of Science and Technology of Vāstu Śāstra*: "An eastern door gives happiness, a western door gives material prosperity (*puṣṭi-vardhanam*), a northern door gives wealth, and a southern door gives *mokṣa* (freedom from "earthly bonds and tensions")."* For this purpose, the main door should be in the northeast quadrant for an east- or north-facing building, in the southeast for a building that faces south, and in the northwest for a building that is west-facing.** Vāstu prefers that you fix your structure's front wall according to its *yoni*, its orientation with the directions. You can then, by careful calculation, create a yoni that will support the front door that you prefer.

Some say that a house's front and back doors should be aligned directly opposite one another in space (allowing, of course, for intervening walls); as with windows, this enables the free movement of energy in and out. In this view, offsetting the doors from one another obstructs direct movement of air and prāṇa between them, which aggravates vāta. Some commentators take this quest for symmetry to apply to doors in upper stories, which they say must correspond in number and position to the doors in the floor below. Others argue that no two doors should be absolutely opposite each other. Yet other specialists support the two-

---

*Sthapati, op. cit. p. 147

**Yet another approach follows the *nāma rāśi*, the constellation that corresponds to the phonetic value of the first name of the home's owner. According to this theory, those born with nāma rāśis in the *Guru Varga* (Aries, Cancer, Leo, Scorpio, Sagittarius, and Pisces) should have east-facing homes and south-facing shops, and those with nāma rāśis in the *Śani Varga* (Taurus, Gemini, Virgo, Libra, Capricorn, and Aquarius) should have west-facing homes and north-facing shops.

doors-in-one-line policy, since two doors that are in the same line are said to be one door, and a single door is said to bring victory, peace, and liveliness. Some say that it is inauspicious for the total number of doors in a house to be an odd number (3, 5, 7, 9, etc.), but that a house with an even number of doors (2, 4, 6, 8) will bring its occupants respect, progeny, and wealth. Here again, let your gut be your guide. Regardless of the number and placement of doors you have, they should refrain from unbidden movement, for a door that swings on its own betokens uneven prāṇa, and incipient misery.

Front doors, which are best made of hardwood, should make pleasing sounds when they are moved. You should highlight your portal by painting it, or by carving it decoratively with noble birds or beasts, benevolent, benign images of deities, and the like. Many Indians define the entrance of their homes by placing a small platform for a jasmine or basil plant within a small courtyard that leads to a festooned entry porch.

Transitions

Vāstu much prefers that staircases, bathrooms, and toilets are outside the core of the residence, within the inside-outside transition zone that the veranda, porch, or terrace defines. Open verandas are said to be best on the northeast. One-sided verandas are most suitable on the north or the east; two-sided ones on north and east, south and east, or north and west; and three-sided ones on either the west, north, and east; or the north, east, and south; but never in the south, west, and north; or the east, south, and west. A four-sided veranda is said to be appropriate only for a religious building.

Confluence (and common sense) apply to transitional zones as well, which is why we must take several grains of salt when a "Vāstu specialist" makes a statement like, "A portico built in the southwest end of either the south side or the west side will cause the death of a child, untimely death, disputes, and loss of wealth."

When you house a tenant on your property, the portion of your structure that the tenant occupies becomes part of your encircling "residue." If you intend to rent out a portion of your home's principal structure to a tenant, you'll be best off occupying the south and west portions of your building yourself, and renting out the north and east sides, ideally with separate northeast entries for each section. In a two-

An opulent portal

story house, it's better to have the owner on the first floor and the tenant on the ground floor. If only one room is to be rented out, that should preferably be a northwest or southeast room, not one in the northeast or southwest.

If instead you intend to rent out a cottage or other dwelling that is separate from your main structure, the best placement for such an "outbuilding" is in the southeast or northwest of your property. Where space permits, garages are better built separate from the houses they serve. A garage usually works well on the southwest side of your property's southwest-northeast line, and is unwelcome in the northeast. Typically, no secondary structure should appear to the east of the line that joins the northeast corner of your house with the northeast corner of your fence or boundary wall.

Boundary Walls

There is a profusion of opinion on the question of where to place a gate in your boundary wall or fence. *Bṛhat Saṁhitā* prefers that the house always sits to the right as one enters into the property through the gate, which means that a south-facing house should have an eastern gate, a southerly gate ought to open onto a west-facing house, and so on. Another school of thought insists that the main gate should always be on the northeast, with another small gate opposite the main door of the house on the east side. Most agree that the gates should appear in the fourth of the nine portions of the wall (as counted from east or north). Again, follow your heart and instinct in your decision, as variations on this theme are numerous. No one, it should be noted, proposes gates in the southwest.

There is general agreement that a wall that encircles your property is better if it's higher and thicker in the south and west than in the north and east. Solid brick, stone, and cement walls are good in the south and west, particularly if a vīthi *śūla* (spear-like road) or some other sort of "spear" is pointed toward the house. "Segment fences," either vertically spaced pickets or staves, or horizontally spaced slats or rails, are optimal on the north and east sides.

Any structure surrounded by a wall should be set back at least one-ninth the length of the squared plot from the wall (the width of the Paiśāca Vīthi of the Vāstu Puruṣa Maṇḍala for your squared plot).

Vāstu at Work

At work as in the home, the usual Vāstu principles apply: Orient the structure appropriately, allocate rooms and other constructions according to the directions, and decorate according to the statement you wish to make to the world.

The process begins by selecting the right site for your type of business (retail shops in busy locations, think tanks in quieter locales), which should face in the direction whose description and associated planet most fits your needs (e.g., north for a business like accounting that involves large numbers of numbers). Create a square building plot on the ground you have available to you, then design your space according to your requirements.

A factory should in its general organization follow the pattern elucidated by the image of the Vāstu Puruṣa: control systems (the head) in the northeast, electrical substation (right arm) in the southeast, general administration services (the feet) in the south or the west, which are also good directions in which to position the heaviest machinery. Manufacturing lines should (like the abdominal organs) proceed in a generally clockwise, north-to-south and east-to-west direction, with waste cleared through the southwest and the shipping dock (left arm) in the northwest.

Floor plans, of factory and office building alike, should have just the right degree of open air and space. When the dividing walls of individual cubicles are too high, they can inhibit the free circulation of light, air, and prāṇa in the area; too low, and vāta can become generally deranged in the space, fomented by the resultant lack of privacy and the oversocializing that ensues. Within the cubicle, care should be taken that, whatever direction the desk may face, the employee's back is not left unprotected by being exposed to an open doorway.

Northeast is a good corner for the reception area; bookkeeping and accounts do well in the north. Southwest can be a good quadrant in which to place the offices of those company staffers who have the most responsibility. Within individual offices, follow the usual drill: Safes and valuables in the north, heavy items of furniture in the south and west, communication equipment and computers in the southeast or northwest. Keep the northeast section of each office, as well as its Brahma Sthāna, as empty as possible. Even your desktop can benefit from arranging it according to the Vāstu Puruṣa Maṇḍala.

Decorate your office with the same care that you would decorate your home, preferring the warmth of wood to the cold of metal, with sturdy, functional desks and chairs, and plenty of natural light. Curtail your temptation to possess the latest gizmo, and settle instead for reliable, tried and true technology. Select colors and styles according to the planet that is most closely associated with the type of business you have: dark and conservative for Saturn, bright and bold for the Sun, experimental and quirky for Rāhu, rich and variegated for Venus.

Keep all Five Elements happy by utilizing space efficiently, and piping in calming but intelligent music; ensuring good air quality; maximizing natural lighting; hiring good cooks for the cafeteria; promoting "good taste" in ornamentation; and using fragrance cleverly but sparingly. Do not insult the Five Elements with weird angles, bizarre noise, off-gassing chemicals (from poor quality plywood, paint, carpet, or other building materials), garish artificial lighting, junk food, idiosyncratic furnishings, or extreme smells.

All this holds particularly true for the reception area, the "face" that your company shows to the world. Your reception space summarizes your company; make that summary a good one! Give yourself a firm advantage over the competition by decorating the reception area with the best that the Five Elements have to offer, including natural light, the sight and sound of a fountain, and a well-considered palette of colors. Then add a receptionist to the mix, one well-matched to the environs and whose every action expresses the tone that your establishment is striving to set.

Groundbreaking and first entrance

Vāstu tradition calls for the performance of worship rituals at critical junctures during construction, in particular at the moments of groundbreaking and the laying of the foundation, as well as when the main door is erected and when you enter the new structure for the first time. You lay the energetic foundation for actually achieving your creative goal when you keep that goal in plain view, which rituals can help you to do. Rituals symbolically transform a small site into your own personal universe, keeping the site's "residue" in balance as you erect a residence there, assisting you to progressively "take possession" of your space as it progressively permeates your awareness.

When you signed on the dotted line to purchase your plot (a moment that we hope your astrological advisor selected as being particularly auspicious), you stated clearly your intention to act as steward of your chosen site. Rituals restate and reinforce this intention, symbolically replacing what is chaotic and "uncivilized"—the residual energy of previous residents, the property's own natural imbalances—with active respect for selected elements of the external environment. Your gratitude to the constituents that make up your personal cosmos invites them to participate in your life in positive, sukha-promoting ways, particularly when you express that gratitude at astrologically opportune moments (see Appendix Three).

Of the many crucial construction-related, ritual-worthy events that Vāstu describes, the two most momentous at the beginning of the process are breaking ground and establishing the foundation; the first entrance into the new edifice, occurring at the end of construction, is similarly weighty. You can perform the rites by yourself, or you can hire a specialist in rituals to perform them for you. Such rituals should ordinarily be performed when facing north, northeast, or east, to harness the naturally sattvic, charitable, growth-promoting energies that reside in those directions.

Groundbreaking

The foundation ritual, which is usually known as *Vāstu Pūjā* or *Bhūmi Pūjā*, should be held in the site's northeast quadrant, at its center, or at a spot on the lot that is particularly alluring, markedly powerful, or otherwise exceptional. This rite's purpose is to:

- "awaken" the Five Great Elements that make up the site.
- accentuate the positive indications and diminish the negative tendencies of the Ten Directions, by reiterating and reinforcing their natural alignments.
- reduce or eliminate any undesirable subtle energies, particularly those deposited there by previous residents or users of that space.

The procedures for performing this worship are numerous. In your capacity as creator of the structure, your task is to induce the nonsectarian Ten Directions and Five Great Elements to cooperate with you, in whatever way you see fit. If you like, you can follow a procedure from Vāstu tradition, or you can create your own ceremony according to the tenets of your religious affiliation, making the process as complicated or as simple as you please. If you relate well to archetypal personalities, then you can involve your guru or mentor, your personal deity or family deities, local deities, the Nine Planets, the Ten Directions, the Vāstu Puruṣa, your ancestors, and the Five Great Elements. At a minimum, you could perform a simple ritual for the Five Elements.

The ritual that you choose will likely include words, some of which may be mantras. The Sanskrit word *nāmarūpa* means "name and form," which implies that your every utterance influences the manifested ("formed") reality around you. Vāstu is nāmarūpa; the system teaches the right words that allow you to create healthy space, and offers methods to create spaces that will be fit to host the words. Ordinary words create commonplace spaces; words of power contribute power to their surroundings. Judiciously chosen and properly pronounced mantras can contribute materially to assisting your building to take form.

In addition to your general veneration of the Five Elements and other universal building blocks, each ceremony should somehow, in whatever way you choose, explicitly express your purpose in performing it. When establishing the foundation, for example, you will want to express appreciation for the qualities of stability and support that are the purview of Mother Earth. You can do this with methods Native American, if you so desire, or by means Chinese, Japanese, or African. If you prefer the East Indian idiom, you might include appreciation for *Śeṣa* (aka. *Ananta*), the thousand-headed serpent who supports the earth on his thousand hoods, embodying the residue that becomes a residence once it is bound down. Ritualists usually bind Śeṣa down by determining a spot where Śeṣa can be regarded to be present, then driving a wooden or metal peg into the ground there to fix that position as the center of the microcosm that is the structure-to-be.

First Entrance

Your initial entry into a new building (*gṛha praveśa*) symbolizes the arrival of prāṇa there. A newly completed structure is like a baby about to be born, with windows for its eyes, ears, and nostrils, and the front door for its mouth. Your first step into your new residence is like an infant's first breath, the beginning of an ongoing stream of inhalations and exhalations that will last the life of the dwelling. That first step deserves the same sort of celebration that a birth deserves.

Your gṛha praveśa ritual can contain any element of solemnity that you may deem appropriate, including such procedures as *garbha nyāsa*, in which, one evening or night, a casket or coffer that contains precious metals and gems—offerings to the Nine Planets—is buried on your property. Even if your own gṛha praveśa is less elaborate, you should at the least host a rich feast for your many relatives, friends, and neighbors. Feeding people on such an occasion elicits from them blessings for the success of the endeavor (particularly if the food is good!).

You may decorate your home completely before you formally enter it to stay, answering as you do the questions, "What items should fill this space, and how should they be arranged?" and "What qualities should these items possess, to achieve the results desired?" Or, you may enter first, and decorate after. An essential part of your decorating involves the careful placement of sacred objects in appropriate places. Some of these may be sacred only to you; some, like deity images, may be more widely revered.

Deity Images

Rūpa-saubhāgyād dhyāna-bhāvo jāyate |

By a harmonious form, a meditative mood is induced.

Vāstusūtra Upaniṣad, II:23

Vāstu has long held that the stationing of a deity image near your front door can act as a sort of general safeguard for your entire home. Any image that you respect, a *yantra*, a geometrical form, or an anthropomorphic image can serve this purpose, provided that you have sincere faith in it, and that you treat it with the same respect that you would treat a valued family member. The deity's image acts as a gateway to the actual cosmic force that the deity embodies, which effectively makes insults to that image equivalent to insults to the Universe—with the potentially catastrophic repercussions that such offenses imply.

Popular in many Indian homes are images of Sarasvatī, the goddess of learning; Lakṣmī, the goddess of wealth; Viṣṇu, the Preserver; and Śiva, the Lord of Death and Transformation. Probably the most popular image of all is that of Gaṇeśa, the generally gentle, elephant-headed Remover of Obstacles. Lord of learning and wisdom, granter of the wishes of his devotees, Gaṇeśa is beloved of all.

Gaṇeśa is worshipped at the beginning of any auspicious act. As lord of the Earth Element, he is the essence of firmness; to laud Gaṇeśa is to make both yourself and your actions more deliberate, more likely to succeed.

As the son of Śiva (the embodiment of *puruṣa*) and Pārvatī (the personification of *prakṛti*), Gaṇeśa embodies the supremely transcendent power of intelligent discernment (*mahat*). This intense sagacity is what makes Gaṇeśa the *gaṇa īśa*, the "lord of the *gaṇas*." The term *gaṇa* encompasses a wide variety of realities, including the sense organs, all types of classifications and classified things, and disembodied intelligences. In his role as Gaṇa Lord, Gaṇeśa helps us to eliminate any gaṇas that impede our perception of reality, be they unruly senses, inaccurate classifications, or disturbing apparitions of any kind (specters, phantoms, ghosts, ghouls, mind viruses, or merely evil thoughts).

As a small eight-year-old boy with the head of a large elephant (it's a long story), Gaṇeśa facilitates the union of microcosm with macrocosm. And as lord of the *Mūlādhāra* Cakra at the base of the human spine, Gaṇeśa presides over *Kuṇḍalinī*, the transformative energy that sleeps within us. What a concentrated parcel of correspondences is this little part-pachyderm, part-person!

All too often, otherwise well-meaning people treat the image of this powerful deity as if it were nothing more than an ornamental statue. Some years back when teaching at a large yoga center—one that espouses many of the tenets of India's traditional cûlture—I entered its dining hall to find an effigy of Gaṇeśa sitting atop the milk dispenser. Perhaps he was presiding symbolically over the room from that spot, but he was also being neglected; though food was everywhere, none was being offered to him. Elephants have elephantine appetites, and Gaṇeśa loves to be fed, particularly with sweets. This is not a situation that Gaṇeśa is likely to find pleasing, and an unhappy Gaṇeśa is more likely to add obstacles to life than to remove them. I'm pleased to report that after I voiced my concerns, he was quickly relocated to more agreeable surroundings (for him).

A deity image is not an essential addition to your home; millions of people have lived happy lives of fulfillment without them. If you do elect to welcome a deity into your home and proceed to ignore or insult it, do not be surprised if things go consistently wrong in your life.

Acknowledge instead that deity's presence by treating it as you would an honored guest, and you will encourage the universe to cooperate with you through it.

Conclusion

Deities, next-door neighbors, or visitors that you invite into your home are witnesses to the story your structure tells, and how well it tells it. Shapes, patterns, colors, textures, perspectives, light: All these parts of "Vāstu speech" are there for you, the "architectural orator," to concoct into unique Vāstu phrases and sentences to convey who you are and how you live. A work of art is incomplete until enjoyed by an art lover; a structure is incomplete until enjoyed by the person who lives or works there. If you complete your Vāstu work of art by enjoying a harmonious, mutually nourishing, reciprocally supportive relationship with it, one that extracts a sweet, juicy rasa from your shared bhāva, then those who interact with you and your creation will share in that rasa. "Make your guest your God," says one Sanskrit phrase; involve God in your life, as you do whenever you host a guest, and those salubrious, satisfying Vāstu juices that you generate will nurture you as well.

Your task in life is to derive good rasa from whatever you do in your space, regardless of how you do it. Begin by studying your own constitution (*prakṛti*) and condition; understand your own "attribute profile," then draw correlations between yourself and the attribute profile of your space. Get your bearings; find your "sweet spots," where sukha seems to pursue you; align your body, your breath, and your brain; remain alert at all times to how you might enhance any conditions of "rightness" that may develop.

Our civilization relies on each of us to preserve organization and create concurrence within its spaces by cultivating accord within ourselves, and our own spaces. The Indian ideal of a well-cultivated space is a temple, which in effect is a person constructed of stone, whose indwelling soul is the Lord. A temple provides meaning and nourishment to all who visit and conveys a sense of connectedness in space and time. A well-constructed and coordinated dwelling provides a similar blessing for its occupants.

Meanings change, of course, for houses and people alike. Sometimes home and homeowner change in tandem; sometimes they do not, as when you find that a house that has been lucky for your ancestors is not particularly lucky for you. If your father and grandfather prospered in your ancestral home and you do not, it may simply be that your inherited wealth has made you lazy. But it may also be that your own "attribute profile," as expressed in your personal constitution, horoscope, genetics, and upbringing ("nature and nurture") in combination with your personal mythology, no longer quite jibes with the attribute profile of your inherited home. In such cases, you can use the principles of Vāstu to assist you to create new concordance between you and the old homestead, transforming your personal narrative into one of success and sukha.

In all circumstances, remember this:

Tat tasya bhavati śubhadaṁ yasya ca yasmin mano ramate |

Any site becomes auspicious for a person, provided that it gladdens his heart.

Like you and your home, the Vāstu Vidyā also evolves constantly, its story always transforming. Wherever she goes, we can be certain that her motto, the prayer she prays for all builders everywhere, will never change:

May all enjoy suhka!
May all be free of illness!
May all perceive auspiciousness!
May no one ever have to suffer misery!

May each of us strive ever to live up to this ideal!